Crossings
in Text and Textile

Katherine
Joslin
and Daneen
Wardrop,
editors

Crossings in Text and Textile

University of New Hampshire Press
DURHAM, NEW HAMPSHIRE

University of New Hampshire Press
An imprint of University Press of New England
www.upne.com
© 2015 University of New Hampshire Press
All rights reserved
Manufactured in the United States of America
Designed by Vicki Kuskowski
Typeset in Requiem Text by Alice W. Bennett

For permission to reproduce any of the material in this book, contact Permissions,
University Press of New England, One Court Street, Suite 250, Lebanon NH 03766;
or visit www.upne.com

Library of Congress Cataloging-in-Publication Data
Crossings in text and textile / Katherine Joslin and Daneen Wardrop, editors.
pages cm.—(Becoming Modern: New Nineteenth-Century Studies)
Includes bibliographical references.
ISBN 978-1-61168-642-5 (cloth : alk. paper)—ISBN 978-1-61168-644-9 (ebook)
1. Clothing and dress in literature. 2. Textile fabrics in literature.
I. Joslin, Katherine, 1947– editor. II. Wardrop, Daneen, 1952– editor.
PN56.C684C76 2014
809'.933564—dc23

2014018113

5 4 3 2 1

 THE COBY FOUNDATION, LTD.

The editors and publisher gratefully acknowledge the support of the Coby Foundation, Ltd.

Becoming Modern:
New Nineteenth-Century Studies

Series Editors

Sarah Way Sherman
Department of English
University of New Hampshire

Rohan McWilliam
Anglia Ruskin University
Cambridge, England

Janet Aikins Yount
Department of English
University of New Hampshire

Janet Polasky
Department of History
University of New Hampshire

This book series maps the complexity of historical change and assesses the formation of ideas, movements, and institutions crucial to our own time by publishing books that examine the emergence of modernity in North America and Europe. Set primarily but not exclusively in the nineteenth century, the series shifts attention from modernity's twentieth-century forms to its earlier moments of uncertain and often disputed construction. Seeking books of interest to scholars on both sides of the Atlantic, it thereby encourages the expansion of nineteenth-century studies and the exploration of more global patterns of development.

For a complete list of books available in this series, see www.upne.com

Katherine Joslin and Daneen Wardrop, editors, *Crossings in Text and Textile*

Sarah Way Sherman, *Sacramental Shopping: Louisa May Alcott, Edith Wharton, and the Spirit of Modern Consumerism*

Kimberly Wahl, *Dressed as in a Painting: Women and British Aestheticism in an Age of Reform*

Hildegard Hoeller, *From Gift to Commodity: Capitalism and Sacrifice in Nineteenth-Century American Fiction*

Beth L. Lueck, Brigitte Bailey, and Lucinda L. Damon-Bach, editors, *Transatlantic Women: Nineteenth-Century American Women Writers and Great Britain*

Michael Millner, *Fever Reading: Affect and Reading Badly in the Early American Public Sphere*

Nancy Siegel, editor, *The Cultured Canvas: New Perspectives on American Landscape Painting*

Reading Dress Series

Series Editors

Katherine Joslin
Department of English
Western Michigan University

Daneen Wardrop
Department of English
Western Michigan University

This series engages questions about clothing, textiles, design, and production in relation to history, culture, and literature in its many forms. Set primarily in the long nineteenth century, it examines the emergence of modernity by exploring the interweaving of material culture with social history and literary texts in ways that resonate with readers and scholars at the turn into the twenty-first century. The editors seek books that offer fresh ways of relating fashion to discourse and of understanding dress in the context of social, cultural, and political history. Such topics might include, for example, analyzing American, British, and/or European notions of style or tracing the influence of developing modes of production. As with the Becoming Modern series generally, the editors especially welcome books with transatlantic focus or that appeal to a transatlantic audience.

Reading Dress is a subseries of Becoming Modern: New Nineteenth–Century Studies, published by University of New Hampshire Press.

Katherine Joslin and Daneen Wardrop, editors, *Crossings in Text and Textile*

Kimberly Wahl, *Dressed as in a Painting: Women and British Aestheticism in an Age of Reform*

Ilya Parkins and Elizabeth M. Sheehan, editors, *Cultures of Femininity in Modern Fashion*

Katherine Joslin, *Edith Wharton and the Making of Fashion*

Daneen Wardrop, *Emily Dickinson and the Labor of Clothing*

Contents

Contents

Color illustrations follow page 138

Introduction

KATHERINE JOSLIN AND DANEEN WARDROP

This is a collection of essays about how we dress, what it costs, and how we read it. Writers look at fabrics and designs from the early nineteenth through the early twentieth century, a period of remarkable change in textiles, production, labor, and fashion, especially in the reform of female dress as a sign of modernity. Readers will delight in the ways that language itself brings actual garments vividly to mind. The "sprigged muslin robe with blue trimmings" that Jane Austen draws for us. The "leather jerkin and breeches" that Nathaniel Hawthorne remembers as he constructs history. The sly turns of phrase that William Thackeray employs to dress the "prettiest little foot in the prettiest little sandal in the finest silk stockings in the world." The struggle of London's *Pall Mall Gazette* in 1868 to depict the bustle, "an infinity of trimming in the form of buttons, bows, barrettes, rosettes, rouleaux, tassels, fringes, flounces, and festoons." The dramatic changes in women's fashion that Jessie Fauset expresses in the modern asymmetry of her heroine's bias-cut gown with its "uneven hem-line reaching in places to her ankle." We've labeled the study *Crossings in Text and Textile* to announce up front the cross-disciplinarity that combines prose writing with clothing style, text with textile. This combination offers a fresh twenty-first-century emphasis on the overlap between verbal workings and material culture.

Fashion is political. It draws attention to class codes, delineates gender identity, and reflects the raw fact that economies of production and consumption can exist in a dynamic of suffering and prosperity. It also marks distinctions between countries and even, increasingly over the decades and centuries, between larger continental regions, especially as world trade patterns emerge with greater prominence. To find our historical footing in a study of clothing is to position ourselves at a point where the energies of national and global patterns of manufacture and purchase intersect. Again, fashion is politics, but it's not politics as usual, because the materiality of clothing reveals the palpable, tactile edge to matters of state, by its very tangibility rendering those matters undeniable.

The essays in this book take seriously fabrics themselves—homespun, linen, muslin, cotton, worsted, silk, and lace. Entire empires have been built on textiles such as silk or cotton, with the attendant routes of commerce formed on the desire for and use of those fabrics. The study of the raw materials needed to produce textiles reveals economic powers even as it charts the turn of a silk sleeve as a woman in one country moves her arm in a gesture that encompasses—or denies—the work of a person in another location many latitudes distant. The study of dress includes some of the richest, most opulent, most aesthetically pleasurable of artistic venues but at the same time some of the most brutal exploits of economically disadvantaged workers in the enterprise of garment making. The examination of clothing as a useful compass for reading social geographies is an approach we advance in this collection.

The essays move dynamically through time, focusing on the politics and cultural clashes surrounding the eighteenth-century revolutions in Europe and America and moving forward to the industrial revolution and global empires based on trade and the preeminence of machine-made fabric over homespun, of prêt-à-porter over hand-crafted garments. They move through the alteration of the female silhouette through the decades, from constricted styles to looser drapings on the body, and consider clothes that a man might select.

Garments hold stories about nations, and seemingly superficial details of dress disclose keys to national identity, signaling ideological differences and struggles within and among countries and regions. The authors in this collection show the business of presenting national and regional attire as seen in France, England, the United States, South Asia, and the Congo. According to these essayists, at different points in history the French seem more openly "artificial" in fashion; the British shun the French and affect a "natural" style of dress; Americans acknowledge and even desire the elegance of European fashion yet favor democratization; and Europeans in Africa cling to the order of strict European dress while Africans sometimes show more versatility in wearing the attire of both continents. Stories of nation also highlight global crossings and interconnectedness, referencing the discrepancies in economic conditions between nations in which the existence of raw materials, the means of production, and the ability to consume the product are in conflict. Examinations of the global economy are undertaken by essayists like Laura George, who delineates the connection between India and England.

The intersection of text and textile locates the relationship between language and dress, as together they structure the fashion scene over the century.

It remains impossible to overestimate the extent to which fashion magazines, such as the nineteenth-century *Harper's New Monthly Magazine*, for instance, shaped popular society in expression and couture. Many of the essayists in this collection examine this intersection, analyzing, for instance, the women's mill magazine *Lowell Offering*; the London magazine *Queen*; the Anthony Trollope—edited *St. Paul's Magazine*; and the Harlem Renaissance magazine *The Crisis*. Writer and fashionista interacted in these publications to express themselves in tropes that readers became expert at discerning, which is to say they absorbed a discourse of attire attendant upon both word and image. Such publications shaped popular society, chronicled the rise of the middle class, and referenced female agency. Furthermore, the similitude of printed paper and printed fabric is looked at by essayist Amber Shaw as a kind of conflation of the represented thing and the thing itself; in other words, with fashion magazines and rag newspapers, the production of the fabric became the very book or magazine, the weave of the page coexistent with the weave of dress fabric, the text with the textile.

Clothing makes a powerful artistic statement that indexes the extent to which a wearer can control the means of production. While couture expresses cultural convictions, confers the advantages of social belonging, and carries with it attendant pressures brought about by marketing, it also allows individual expression sparked by creative agency. Through choices in apparel, spanning both pop and "high" culture, both craft and art, many women and men came to see the creation and development of identity as occurring through the acts of making and assembling a wardrobe. Perhaps no mode better exemplifies this process than the artistry that takes on the performative quality of the "half-world" woman, or demimonde—that is the artist-actress-prostitute who, at the turn of the century, lived a life partially as muse in order to find a vantage as a creative agent herself. Some women turned to the demimonde life of performativity in order to be able occasionally to reverse the gaze and find perspective on social and political inequities so as to make artistic gains where possible. Performance clothing highlighted social issues and illuminated the roles a woman artist could choose for herself.

Artistry certainly forms a strong component in forging one's subjectivity or identity, and fashioning apparel for the body often complements that process of fashioning a self. A person in search of self can start by choosing to "wear" personae suggested by particular attire. Some of the essayists scrutinize the conflicting sides of identity as each side contends with the other through the medium of dress. To the large degree that gender and race are constructed, a person may use apparel to announce solidarity, persuasion, independence, or commitment to a blended or emerging identity. As concerns gender, cross-dressers decide to shape their social reception by making choices in attire, as Abigail Joseph's essay on 1870s transvestitism demonstrates. As concerns race, some mixed-race women may choose to accentuate or embrace racial identity, as Kimberly Lamm shows in her essay on the writer Jessie Fauset, who portrayed characters dressing in response to their own and others' perceptions of ethnicity. Somewhat similarly, Hope Hodgkins suggests that Jean Rhys chose the terms by which she allotted elements of her Creole ancestry from the Dominican Republic to inform her fiction.

These crossings in gender and race inhered for class as well, as we can see when Amy Montz and other essayists note that the perceived line between the middle class and the déclassé proved extraordinarily thin and shifting. The same dress worn by the same woman in a different context could turn what was socially labeled ordinary into what was deemed provocative. In the case of the demimonde, as Margaret Stetz points out, the difficulty of discerning the line between chic and risqué was aggravated further. In the case of a black woman, the distinctions proved more difficult yet, as she had to contend with others' perceptions of the fashionable African-American woman, which could be "flipped with cruel ease into [seeming] evidence of her lasciviousness," as Lamm points out. Virtually all people, female and male, in every period discussed here, determine identity through clothing selections, as in the essay by Babak Elahi, in which men were invested in displaying political affiliations by donning particular menswear. Individuals were endowed with a honed sense of subjectivity as conferred by their choices of apparel.

We trace the side-by-side development of discourse and dress together as they denominated social and economic patterns of the time period. In some ways the crossing between text and textile plays out William Carlos Williams's famous injunction to poets, "No ideas but in things." The "thing-ness" of this inquiry insists upon the inseparability of concept and object. It unfolds in the silk flounce, the cotton collar, and the exacting descriptions of them.

We offer synopses of the essays, arranged in chronological order, with the exception of the first essay, which starts in the middle of things, so to speak, as a way to focus the many cultural and aesthetic crossings at play throughout the period. From there, the timeline of *Crossings in Text and Textile* proceeds from the early eighteenth century through the early decades of the twentieth century, each essay augmenting the historical concerns of dress and discourse, as follows:

Abigail Joseph launches the collection, her essay, "Excesses of Every Kind," mapping out issues that occupy the chronological center of this study, including crossings in gender, and crossings between the making of material things and the making of language. Analyzing male and female styles of dress, Joseph showcases instances of blurred gender identity at an important point in time for gender history and for gay history. She looks at the turn from the cage crinoline of the mid-nineteenth century to the bustle, a seemingly absurd exaggeration of style that was described and lampooned by fashion magazines. *Queen* joked in 1868: "The more flounces, ruches, bows, and pompoms, the more the shirts are looped up in bunches, the better is the wearer's right to consider herself elegant." The essay uses queer theorists, including Jeffrey Weeks, to place the bustle on the backside, not of fashionable women, but of cross-dressing men. Joseph details the trial of Frederick Park and Ernest Boulton, seemingly caught in the act as drag queens or even prostitutes, and peels back the layers in the notorious case to reveal that the ladies of the fashion plates are likewise performing gender through dress. If drag queens could so successfully disguise their bodies, what were the ladies doing? Examining newspapers, letters, trial transcriptions, and fashion magazines, Joseph works at the nexus between style and verbalization of style, arguing that in some cases language and fashion develop together; for instance, during the trial of Park and Boulton, the words "drag" and "camp" both sprang up in relation to garb. In such cases, it is exceedingly difficult to draw the line demarcating the difference between costume that is ordinary and clothing that is dramatic, between high style and promiscuousness, and these matters of discernment complicate the project of reading class and gender through dress.

Babak Elahi in "An Epitome of Times and Fashions" focuses on male attire as Nathaniel Hawthorne imagined it during Puritan times. The conflict in the early days of the nation for men of the middle class led to a shift toward what Richard L. Bushman calls "vernacular gentility," a blend of aristocratic refinements of Europe with the republican virtues of hard work and parsimony, an American mix of swallow-tailed coats and workingman's jerkins. Elahi negotiates several frameworks of time in his study, considering the attire of the seventeenth-century Puritan period, the eighteenth-century American Revolutionary period, and Hawthorne's own early nineteenth-century period to show the values reflected in clothing choices of the emerging nation.

The American republic was not usually fashion forward, often rejecting the aristocratic styles associated with English and French styles, opting to wear the homespun and patchwork better suited to the American ethos of work and democracy. Elahi appraises Hawthorne's *The House of the Seven Gables*, *The Blithedale Romance*, and "Howe's Masquerade," to show characters concerned with an ethos of labor and egalitarianism. So occupied was Hawthorne with presenting such values that in the earliest period, around 1690, even the Puritan ghosts wear clothes, which prove available to political interpretations of American virtues. Through the charting of such historical periods, Elahi demonstrates the existence of an emerging middle-class ideal that values frugality and spending, work and relaxation, usefulness and refinement. His essay elucidates both republican ideals and manufacturing developments in the making and wearing of clothing in the developing nation.

Laura George in "Austen's Muslin" looks closely at the fabric of muslin as well as the female garments it made possible at the turn into the nineteenth century, during the Regency Period. For Jane Austen's women, muslin allowed a "natural" flow of garment against the skin in "pale, matte, columnar gowns." Grounding her ideas in Theodor W. Adorno, especially in his 1935 letter to Walter Benjamin, George analyzes the "expressive significance" of a "changeant" fabric like muslin, one that is inexpensive and relatively fragile, the fabric that calls out the one footnote in Austen's oeuvre. "Changeant" comes from the French and is used to describe cottons, silks, or wools that are interwoven with contrasting colors in warp and weft, a descriptor that George uses both literally and metaphorically. Baldly stated, she shows how muslin can vector the social world of Austen's early nineteenth-century England. Approaching her study of *Northanger Abbey* by way of material culture, George expands upon an early scene in Austen's first novel, in which Henry Tilney and Mrs. Allen engage in a conversation that turns toward the fabric of muslin, Mrs. Allen initiating the conversation in order to prompt Henry to comment on Catherine Morland's beauty. But Henry pursues the conversation in terms of the textile itself, in the course of which he remarks upon its durability in relation to its cost. George uses this critically well-traversed conversation to demonstrate how muslin becomes the grist for a mode of discourse that pins economic and material factors to the social relations in the novel. The discourse resonates throughout the novel in a tangible way; George sees the industrial processes used to make the textile as "inextricable from the fabric's weight, color, and finish." She assesses muslin's importance in terms of its availability due to changes in manufacturing, its alteration of the discourse of polite society as it became fair game for conversation, and its effect on the "materiality of the book itself." Muslin and the empire gown it made possible and accessible to reveal "fabric as a made thing" with the "seams showing," much like the text of the novel *Northanger Abbey* itself and the genre of modern realism.

In her essay "William Makepeace Thackeray's Fashionable Humbugs," Amy Montz presents an astute study of two elements that she sees as typically linked in nineteenth-century texts—nation and fashion. Montz argues that through the two main characters in *Vanity Fair*, Becky Sharp and Amelia Sedley, Thackeray posits French and English standards of dress and consumption, displaying respectively the Francophone propensity toward artifice and self-aware presentation and the Anglophone tendency toward style rooted in the idea of the natural, seemingly devoid of the intent to manipulate the viewer's visual response. The act of constructing a fashionable self is hardly a negligible matter, for it poses serious repercussions for the social status quo, as when Becky, an errant factor in the maintenance of middle-class values, is able to disrupt the existing cultural order. A woman of "low" birth, Becky inserts herself into good company by way of her inimitable style, exemplifying a use of clothing by which a woman can move successfully "within national class ranks." Her skills at self-transformation allow her to maneuver with a power sometimes parallel to that of Victorian men, whose assets include "reading, interpreting, and consuming objects, texts, and, most importantly women," and her choice of dress and adornment also allows her—no small feat—to be able "to enjoy her body." As Montz iterates, "precisely *because* she has constructed a beautiful and pleasing self," the danger she poses to polite English society cuts across both social and national boundaries.

In "Such Hosts of Rags," Amber Shaw identifies a disjunction between the economic roles of the United States and England as they are linked in the cycle of manufacture and consumption. Shaw studies the textile of cotton as a felicitous means to decipher the mid-nineteenth-century interworkings of commerce between the United States and Britain, as those two countries to some extent split the functions of production and purchase. Shaw's argument depends upon a realization of nationality and internationality in her examination of Melville's two stories, the first about wealthy English bachelors and the second about destitute American female mill workers, the twinned pieces used by Melville to prompt readers to assess their own role in a global dynamic of inequality. The hinge between British wealth and American poverty existed in the material fact of the cotton shirts worn by the bachelors in the first story, where the circulation of raw materials and goods from one country to the other shows the shirts to be the "tangible connections between the two halves of the diptych." Bridging the rag paper production of the factory depicted in Melville's "The Tartarus of Maids" and the Lowell textile mills, Shaw also connects the paper production with the rag magazines important to the cultural changes in the United States of the mid-nineteenth century. The interaction of literary production and textile production affected how the magazine, the *Lowell Offering*, written and published by mill "girls," conveyed an optimism undercut by the actual operational policies of mills around the world, and how *Harper's New Monthly Magazine*, the most popular magazine of its day, was used by Melville, when he published his two stories, to disguise his populist critique by setting, without overt comment, the two stories about gross economic disparity next to each other.

Margaret Stetz in "Dressing the Modern Woman" takes us to Woody Allen's *Midnight in Paris* as a route back into history and a means to consider the Aesthetic movement in women's fashion and the "rhetoric of dress." In the movie, Allen's Adriana challenges the expected scenario for women of the period, in that she did not become one of the "'triple M'" women who functioned as "mistress, model, or muse" to a male designer who might position her as object in his art but instead became an artist herself. Cueing from the cinematic woman designer, Stetz seeks actual women designers, asking if there was "in fact, room for women artists in the milieu of the late-nineteenth-century Aesthetic movement, whether these were artists whose medium was cloth, or watercolor, or photography, or the pen?" Stetz includes designers and writers of all sorts who were able finally, though they were women or perhaps because they were women, to comment on fashion because the Aesthetic movement put the comfort and agility of women at the center of attention and readership. Allen's fictional Adriana calls to mind actual women who were working in the couture industry at the turn into the twentieth century, including most famously in France Jeanne Pacquin (1869–1936) and in England Lucy Sutherland (1863–1935), who went by the single name "Lucile." Women dress designers could contribute aesthetic creations but, as Stetz asserts, "could not always control the uses made of their work in masculine representations." Women journalists and authors nonetheless articulated opinions and shaped the popular reception of design and decoration, as for instance in *St. Paul's Magazine*, to which Mary Eliza Haweis contributed. Blurring the line between conservative and progressive thought, Haweis declared in *The Art of Beauty* (1878) that "the fundamental principal of good art" is that "people may do as they like." Aestheticism, the purview of outsiders and Bohemians, included women, and though aesthetic dress was later absorbed into mainstream society, women had entered the discourse and the industry. The crinoline and the bustle gave way in the early years of the twentieth century to "the long, slender skirt."

In "Clothing and Colonialism in Conrad's *Heart of Darkness*," Pouneh Saeedi demonstrates the linkage of attire and oppression in colonial clashes between Europeans and Africans. In one scene, the exploitation of the Congo is foregrounded by the small thread of white worsted, appearing out of place and in surprising contrast on the person of an African. The bit of worsted, a material from the mills of the Western industrialized world, functions in Joseph Conrad's *Heart of Darkness* as a visual and metaphoric crux that registers Europe's manipulation of the continent's people and resources. Saeedi investigates the several ranges of hegemonic codings in clothing, including the attire of an African working for Europeans as a guard who served in a uniform missing one button; the clothing worn by an ineffectual European as he was forced in an emergency to work in pink pajamas; and a Russian whose mixed Asian-European heritage was accentuated by his apparel of colorful patches. Perhaps most striking in Saeedi's analysis is her discussion of the dress worn by the two women in Kurtz's life, his African mistress and his European fiancée, the first wearing clothing at once scant and opulent, including ornamentation from both manufactured and natural sources—most prominently elephant tusks—as a way to suggest simultaneous masquerade and resistance. The second woman, encountered after Kurtz's death, dresses in mourning apparel, the black cloth in sharp contrast to the vivid trimmings and white tusks worn by the first. Saeedi examines metaphors of spinning, stitching, fabric, and clothing, not simply as aesthetic tropes but as metaphors that function crucially in a political register.

Kimberly Lamm in "The Midwife's Clothing: Jessie Faust In and Out of Fashion" delineates the desire of female characters in Jessie Fauset's works of fiction to dress in such a way as "to pass into the American middle class," and as New Negro Women to gain autonomy and credibility. Lamm blends together "language, writing, and fabric" in a consideration of how mixed-race women lived as the "visual emblem of miscegenation," dressing visibly to contend with the assumption that bodies convey a narrative of racialized sex and shame. A carefully selected "dress of green developed in silk and wool, its uneven hem-line reaching places at her ankle" (Fauset *Chinaberry* 35) presents an image of fashionable clothing for a black female who attracts and controls the gaze of those savvy and appreciative of couture fashion. French style connects her to a foreign language, translation, cosmopolitanism, and affluence. Lamm shows the novelist dressing her heroines, and likewise herself, in an emerald gown tempered by a shade of moss. The garment is stylish, fashionable, yet demure, exactly the right inflection to suggest her negotiation between cultural perceptions of race. Further, Fauset uses clothing to reverse the supposition that black women's bodies function as a symbol of exchange in the American cultural marketplace, and to assert instead the value of African-American women's "interartistic" contributions to literature. This crucial component of her work has been undervalued in assessments of the Harlem Renaissance. Because critics have traditionally presumed the subject of fashion to be frivolous, the aspect of Fauset's work that deals in developing artistry through the aesthetics of couture has been overlooked, as has also the power of black women's attire to help in "fashioning selves capable of renouncing the sexual degradation of enslavement and its reverberations." To remedy the relative critic neglect of Fauset's fiction, Lamm turns to the work of Deborah McDowell to show how black women writers used clothing to create characters whose appearance patterned others' assessments of themselves. Surveying two of Fauset's short stories from 1912 and 1920 that appeared in *The Crisis*, the Harlem Renaissance magazine, for which Fauset was an editor, she also shows how the magazine's ads for fashionable attire almost certainly fostered her talent for interlinking word and image. Lamm also looks at Fauset's 1929 novel, *Plum Bun*, to decipher the pattern of African American women's consumption of attire as a means of creating an economically powerful identity capable of deflecting some men's presumption of entitlement in sexual "consumption" of women.

Hope Hodgkins in "Modeling for Men" argues that clothing and language mediate desire between women and men, specifically, in the essay, between Jean Rhys and Ford Maddox Ford. Even as Rhys, born Ella Gwendolen Rees Williams, adopted the hard modern minimalist narrative style, she ornamented her body in the modern mode, "a black dress and hat and very dark grey stockings." Rhys came from the demimonde world of the chorus line and did not discern the line between stardom and the abyss or between innocence and sexual knowledge. It is that line of demarcation that shows the ambiguous nature of her apprenticeship and affair with the famous writer and magazine editor Ford Maddox Ford, who renamed her as the author Jean Rhys. Her work explores the economic tension between the investment in clothing and the gains or losses resulting from the act of seduction, as she wrote later: "When you take money directly from someone you love it becomes not money but a symbol." Hodgkins examines Rhys's first three novels, published between 1928 and 1934, in terms of this economic dynamic, layered with gendered and class perspectives, in which the female protagonist exists as a woman on or over the edge of respectable existence, living as mistress, former chorus girl, mannequin, model, "Gaiety-girl," *flâneuse*, and streetwalker. Her protagonists struggle to differentiate love from domination, class security from male perception of investment, a struggle the protagonists undertake partly through the medium of purchasing and displaying garments. Rhys, part Creole, used primitivist details drawn from her West Indian heritage to add to an avant-garde literary contribution, especially in the 1934 novel, *Voyage in the Dark*, which drew from her memories of childhood in the Dominican Republic. One could say that Rhys was always dressing as she was writing. Hodgkins sees the very style of Rhys's life as emblematic of her writing in its instinctual formlessness that invoked "modernist fascinations with the semiotic."

Crossings in Text and Textile

"Excesses of Every Kind"

Dress and Drag around 1870

Abigail Joseph

"Anything Strange and Out of the Way": The Scandal of Fashion

> "New fashions lead to new crimes. . . . There is no knowing in these days of restless luxury what fashion may not revive."
> —"Odd Fashions," *The Graphic*, April 1870

In March 1870, the *Englishwoman's Domestic Magazine* opened its monthly forecast for "The Fashions" by proclaiming that "instead of laying down general rules on the subject of dress, our task is now to describe toilets which all more or less bear the stamp of fancy costumes": costumes, that is, for a "fancy-dress ball," a masquerade; outfits intended to transfigure their wearer into someone she (or he) is not, to serve as the visual and material apparatus enabling a role to be played, the boundaries of identities to be blurred (figs. 1.1 and 1.2). "The dress of remarkable historical people is imitated with the greatest accuracy," it continues. "If you ask a Parisian couturière to compose a fashionable dress for you, she will begin by asking what style of costume you prefer, and from what historical period she is to seek 'inspiration'; for it is not from one special period only that Fashion borrows ideas—it is from a number of successive but distinct periods, each of which has its own peculiar style." The season's eccentricity, which "has given full scope to the most extravagant fancies in the matter of la toilette," doesn't stop at this sort of schizoid historicism. Capricious "inspiration" also roams geographically—"Every contrast has been tried, every style adopted, and models borrowed from every part of the world, from fur-loving Russia to the poetical and splendid regions of the East"—and it encompasses even choices of fabric, color, and pairing, rendering the most basic building blocks of dress sites of disruptive, enticing surprise: "Anything strange and out of the way is now preferred to what would seem sensible and

FIGURE 1.1 (LEFT): "Ball Toilets." *Englishwoman's Domestic Magazine*, March 1870. *Reproduced by kind permission of the Syndics of Cambridge University Library.*
FIGURE 1.2 (RIGHT): "Evening Toilets." *Englishwoman's Domestic Magazine*, March 1870. *Reproduced by kind permission of the Syndics of Cambridge University Library.*

natural; thus, dark fur on ball dresses, black velvet on gauze or tarlatan are the novelties in vogue, while morning jackets . . . are embroidered and spangled all over with gold and silver. In colours, also, the most extravagant contrasts seem no longer to shock the nicety of Parisian taste . . ." ("The March Fashions," *Englishwoman's Domestic Magazine*, March 1870[1]).

Less than two months after this issue of the magazine proclaimed fashion's manifold breaks with solid standards of "sense" and "nature," Frederick Park and Ernest Boulton—drag queens, actors, best friends, possibly sometimes prostitutes, who had, as *Reynolds's Newspaper* reported juicily, "for some years past . . . been known to go 'in drag' . . . powdered and painted, wearing chignons and false hair, and successfully personating the opposite sex in every external particular . . ." ("The Hermaphrodite Clique," June 5, 1870)—were apprehended by the police, outside of London's Strand Theater, in evening wear that was fancy in a few senses of the word. Stella (Ernest) was in "a fashionable crimson silk, trimmed with white lace. He wore a flaxen wig, with plaited

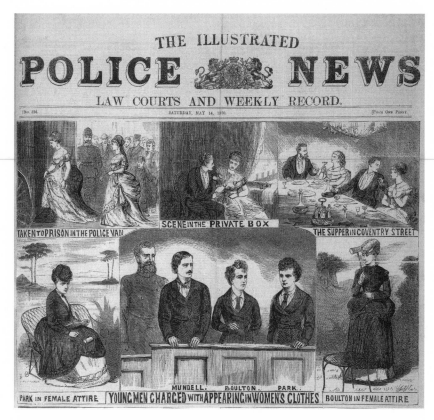

FIGURE 1.3: The arrest of Boulton and Park. *Illustrated Police News*, May 14, 1870. © *The British Library Board, Newspapers Division.*

chignon . . . He had bracelets, and a white lace shawl round his shoulders." Fanny (Frederick) was wearing "a green satin dress, with panier . . . white kid gloves, bracelets, and black lace shawl." Fanny's hair "was the same colour as that of her friend, and dressed in the like fashion, excepting that the back part was done in curls instead of plaits" ("Apprehension," *Reynolds's Newspaper*, May 1, 1870). Like a pair of ladies in a fashion plate, they appeared as a carefully orchestrated duet: their outfits sufficiently similar in form yet different in detail so as to complement, but not copy, one another. As a juxtaposition of near-concurrent media images of their fashions and "The Fashions" suggests with astonishing visual impact, Fanny and Stella's ensembles were of the very latest in cut and color (fig. 1.3).

Booked initially for the misdemeanor of cross-dressing, a charge that was quickly raised to the much more severe one of sodomy, Fanny and Stella were brought into the Bow Street Police Court the next morning, still in their evening wear. Everyone in the courtroom was "astonished" by "the complete case with which they maintained their parts . . . and even [the] most experienced detective officers had to admit that the 'get up' was artistic enough to deceive themselves" ("Capture," *Illustrated Police News*, May 7, 1870). Fanny and Stella, then, were prosecuted for the travesty of their high-style, high-stakes, remarkably successful impersonation of a contemporary—and very controversial—fashionable femininity that was itself all about the audacious flexing of the boundaries around and between modesty and provocation, inspiration and imitation, outrageous novelty and promiscuous citationality.

In this essay my goal is to untangle the strands of overlapping rhetoric, perception, and investment that connect Boulton and Park's radically queer self-fashioning to the contemporary fashion scene that provided much of its material: the physical as well as the figurative "stuff" intrinsic to both its performance and its policing. Looking at the anxieties about gender, dress, and identity that animate both coverage of the drag scandal and fashion/anti-fashion writing contemporaneous to it, I argue that Boulton and Park act as a discomfiting vivification of mid-Victorian fashionability's inherent clash with agendas of heteronormative order: the queer sex scandal reveals fashion's surprisingly endemic leanings into queerness. Correlatively, proposing new interpretations of styles that were compulsively disavowed by their serious-minded contemporaries and have been largely disdained in historical accounts as well, I argue for their constitutive place in the development of gay modes of expression and eroticism. The multivalent extremities operant in the fashions of this mid-Victorian moment—with its increasingly hyperactive routes of circulation, specialized languages of description, outré objects of desire—were, in fact, indispensable to the formation of the gender-bending, extravagantly stylized gay socio-sexual personae that arose, fully clothed, from out of it.

On the night of Boulton and Park's arrest, two search operations were conducted, nearly simultaneously. Detectives raided their apartments and seized their "immense wardrobe of female attire . . . exhibiting the most perfect completeness, even to the minutest details of women's underclothing . . . between thirty and forty silk and other dresses, all of fashionable patterns, and some elaborately trimmed with lace, furs, &c," along with personal photographs and letters ("Capture," *Illustrated Police News*, May 14, 1870). Meanwhile, James Paul, a police doctor, subjected them to genital and anal examinations, searching for physical signs of sexual deviance: he found that Boulton's penis was unusually large, and that "his anus [was] much dilated, and the muscles readily opened.

These appearances and others were undoubtedly caused by the insertion of a foreign body. They were only attributable to the fact of his having had frequent unnatural connexions—one insertion would not cause them . . . The foreign bodies he believed to be those belonging to other men" ("Capture," *Illustrated Police News*, May 14, 1870). On Dr. Paul's suggestion, the charges against the two were ramped up from a cross-dressing misdemeanor to the felony offense of "wickedly and against the order of nature . . . commit[ting] and perpetrat[ing] that detestable and abominable crime of buggery not to be named among Christians" (Cohen 79). A headline-grabbing six-day hearing in May 1870 was followed by a trial—held a full year later—which ultimately resulted in an acquittal.[2]

Critical accounts of these events have, with compelling reason, emphasized their indexical positioning at a crucial moment in the history of (homo)sexuality. "The trial," notes William Cohen, "arose in the midst of the shift . . . from prosecuting specific sexual acts to disciplining the type of person who was likely to commit such acts" (75). Yet the very stakes of that moment—and the exigencies of this case, the not-guilty verdict of which, Neil Bartlett says, still "seems unbelievable" (142)—have placed Boulton and Park, like other queer figures of the pre-Wildean nineteenth century, in a contentious position within accounts of the emergence of "modern" homosexual identity. Bartlett has argued that the drag queens' acquittal represented a quite pointed move on the part of the discomfited jury to suppress the too-threatening fact of homosexual existence in mid-century London: "The evidence of Fanny and Stella's visibility was converted into proof that they didn't exist. . . . Only by silencing, not punishing, the sodomites, could the court breathe a sigh of relief. When Boulton and Park were dismissed, declared improbable if not impossible, the existence of a homosexual culture in London was effectively denied" (Bartlett 142).

Alan Sinfield has tellingly juxtaposed Bartlett's reading of the events with Jeffrey Weeks's earlier claim that the verdict should be taken, rather, as proof of invisibility, or unreadability: that "as late as 1871 concepts of both homosexuality and of male prostitution were extremely undeveloped in the Metropolitan Police and in high medical and legal circles" (117). Sinfield's own, mediatory position is that "probably some people heard same-sex passion loud and clear, whereas others could not conceive of it. It is through that indeterminacy that indirections and evasions—those of the court, and of Fanny and Stella—could flourish." For Sinfield, "the interpretive challenge is to recover the moment of indeterminacy" in which the concept of homosexuality was "emerging around and through instances like Fanny and Stella. . . . To presume the eventual outcome in the blind or hesitant approximations out of which it was partly fashioned is to miss, precisely, the points of most interest" (8).

Sex was not the only sociocultural arena which, in 1870, found itself in the unsettled—and, to many, unsettling—midst of a "moment of indeterminacy." Fashion, too, was headily in flux. For one thing, as much scholarship has shown, it was still reverberating under the phenomenal mid-century expansion of its technologies of production and circulation. Thanks to inventions like the home sewing machine and the paper pattern, as well as technological improvements in the production of fabrics and dyes and in the circulation of media, what had in previous eras been largely the purview of an exclusive upper-class set of consumers spread outward into a vast network of middle-class women; and then, through hand-me-downs and other recycling practices, to servants, to patrons of secondhand shops, and to others whose standing in the fringe spaces of fashion culture was, if not unprecedented, then newly vitalized. Margaret Beetham has argued that what she calls the "exten[sion] of access to fashion down the social scale" was a catalyst for the period's construction of new kinds of femininities, particularly middle-class ones, as well as for the exacerbation of anxieties surrounding those social categories (105).

The hyperactive Victorian fashion business and press, in all of their many outlets, were aimed at an audience construed always and exclusively as female, gendered far more firmly than it was classed. Beetham writes: "The masculine reader might engage with this femininity only as an object of his gaze" (105). And, for the most part, he engaged with feminine fashion only as an object of derision; as Sharon Marcus notes, "the gaze solicited by women's fashionable dress belonged most often to women, for Victorian manliness directed men to admire women's bodies while deriding the fashions that clothed them" (*Between Women*, 117). But the codes of Victorian manliness had margins and defectors; some men would have had different or oppositional reactions toward women's bodies and women's dress. As Christopher Breward writes, "The fact that manufacturers, advertisers, retailers and commentators on clothing directed much of their energy towards engaging the attention of women does not imply in itself that men were excluded from the experience of fashion" (Breward 1999, 2). Breward's work is an important challenge to the long-held view of Victorian men as existing essentially outside the sphere of fashion; he reveals the material and cultural complexities behind the alleged uniformity of men's dress in the nineteenth century. But there has been very little critical rethinking or excavation of the relationship of masculine subjects to women's dress in the period. I want to propose that mid-Victorian women's fashion, so vigorous in its leaps across class lines, might have found its more surreptitious, but no less seminal, ways across lines of gender and (hetero)sexuality as well. It might, that is, have been conducive to the queer vibrations of not only a female homoerotic gaze, as Sharon Marcus has theorized, but a gay male one, too.[3]

Furthermore, at precisely the end of the 1860s, fashionable dress was in transition in a more specifically structural sense as well. The hoopskirt, or "crinoline," silhouette, iconic for its swayingly circular embodiment of Victorian femininity, was giving way to the eccentrically structured, riotously ornamented, anally oriented—and, thus, I will suggest, much queerer—new look of the "bustle" line. To return to Sinfield's language, then: I contend that fashion's "indeterminacy," its imminent upheavals of social and aesthetic certainties, worked alongside the indeterminacy surrounding the concept of "the homosexual," nurturing the atmosphere of simmering anxiety and not-yet-foreclosed possibility in which the "indirections and evasions" surrounding the drag queens' case "could flourish."

INCONGRUOUS SPARKLES: COMPLEXITY, CAMP, AND THE USES OF FASHION CRITICISM

> Why were we so deluded as to predict a lasting austerity of decoration from a momentary spasm of simplicity? Sigh with us, wretched reader . . . There are not only flounces, but flounces on flounces. . . . Would we could say that beads were going also! But no, they are simply transferred from gimp to lace, and remain as sparklingly incongruous as ever . . .
>
> —Scribners, "Trimming," May 15, 1874

"If women's toilettes have partaken of the extravagant at certain epochs in all ages of the world," begins the *Pall Mall Gazette*'s December 1868 dispatch, from Paris, on the state of La Mode—Robes, "certainly at no former period have the garments in which the sex array themselves exhibited a more complex configuration or a greater redundancy of ornamentation than at the present moment." In one sense, this is the sort of myopic hyperbole so ubiquitous in fashion writing that it is practically a convention of the genre. Fashion's cyclical iterations of "newness"—by which it continually re-presents itself as news and perpetually announces, at every "present moment," that whatever is new right now is more so than ever before—are a long-recognized (and oft-lamented) phenomenon that is in fact constitutive, by many accounts, of modern fashion itself. Yet, on the other hand, the *Gazette's* report contains a certain fitful accuracy. Some fashions are newer—are, and remain, bigger news—than others. There are moments when a "New Look" emerges, distinctly and lastingly new enough that it ends up signifying not the mere trends of a season but the defining shape of an era; moments when the silhouette changes. And this was, in fact, one such moment. In or around 1868, as Iris Brooke puts it with expressive bluntness in her 1937 *History of English Costume*, "the crinoline had been consigned to the rubbish heap and the bustle had usurped its 'throne'" (198).

"Crinoline" (more accurately, "cage crinoline") refers to the frame of whalebone or metal hoops connected by fabric tape that arrived on the market around 1856, providing a welcome replacement for the burdensome layers of starched petticoats that had supported women's dresses since the full-skirted silhouette had come back in fashion in the 1830s (fig. 1.4). Over the next decade, in the hands of high-end Parisian designers and their avid ranks of customers, followers, and imitators, the crinoline swelled to its iconic widths; the "breathtaking proportions" that, writes historian and curator Harold Koda, "caught the imagination not only of the fashionable mondaine but also of the caricaturist" (125).

Meanwhile, it was functional and cheaply producible enough that it became, as Penelope Byrde writes, "accessible to virtually every social class, and it was, in effect, the first high-fashion garment to be universally adopted" (58). Thus, despite the near-daily campaign of mockery waged against it in *Punch* and elsewhere, accusing the garment of being not just unwieldy and unattractive but a public health hazard on multiple fronts, the crinoline's fashionability held firm.[4] Serving as the literal base for the distinctive Victorian line—all tiny-waisted, swayingly circular, volatile, gauzy femininity—that it so strikingly articulated, the crinoline had by the middle of the 1860s become an indelible feature of the contemporary visual landscape and had determined the social and discursive ideation of the female body for nearly a generation.

Toward the late middle years of that decade a shift became detectable, as the crinoline's circumference, as well as its universality, gradually deflated. In 1866 the fashion magazines informed their readers of a trend for gored skirts,

FIGURE 1.4: The crinoline silhouette at its height. *Englishwoman's Domestic Magazine,* July 1862. *Picture Collection, The New York Public Library, Astor, Lenox, and Tilden Foundations.* (Plate 1.)

somewhat flattened in the front, with "backward sweeping" fullness that resolved into a train. Fashionable young ladies delighted in the novelty, but these trailing skirts "presented problems out of doors," liable as they were to pick up and spread dirt, to catch underfoot, to trip both wearers and passersby (Ewing 78). "Robes à queue they call these draggling dresses," complained *Punch,* "but it is not at Kew merely that people are tormented by them. Everywhere you walk, your footsteps are impeded by the ladies who, in Pope's phrase, 'drag their slow length along' the pathway just in front of you" ("Ladies," *Punch,* July

FIGURE 1.5: "Promenade Toilets" featuring tournures and bunched skirts. The Queen, September 1869. *Picture Collection, The New York Public Library, Astor, Lenox, and Tilden Foundations.*

29, 1865). Then, in 1868, the criticisms lobbed at both the length of the trains and the breadth of the crinolines before them found their answer. That year, thanks to some zeitgeist-readied combination of the practicalities of dress reform and the fancies of dress design, the skirt's voluminous fabrics were looped up and puffed outward—the dramatic inception of what would later be called the "bustle era" (fig. 1.5).

The cage crinoline itself was traded in for half-crinolines and other undergarments—introduced by the London-based magazine *Queen* in June 1868 as the "bustle, or panier, or tournure (for the bunch at the back goes by a variety of names) just below the waist"[5]—invented to support a fashionable line that fell, in the front, increasingly flat and closer to the body than they had in several decades. Concurrently, on the sides and in the back, it swelled and piled outward in elaborate, profusely decorated constructions variously called "bouffantes," "pouffs," "paniers," etc. Excited by the novelty of these shapes, and drawing upon the wide-ranging repertoire of historical and foreign references noted in the *Englishwoman's Domestic Magazine* column with which I began, designers and dressmakers seemed to come up with increasingly fanciful arrangements of fabric and trim. The new dresses displayed "a medley of materials quite indescribable," as *Queen*'s announcement of the "decrees" of "the fickle goddess," Fashion, continued. "The more flounces, ruches, bows, and pompoms, the more the skirts are looped up in bunches, the better is the wearer's right to consider herself elegant and fashionable."

The *Pall Mall Gazette*'s hand-wringing hyping of the current style's unprecedented "complexity" of "configuration" and "redundancy of ornamentation" makes more sense, then, in the context of its fashion-historical moment. Extending the argument of that opening declaration, it continues:

> The skirt of the robe, which used to be such a simple affair, a long sweep of flowing drapery with nothing beyond its graceful folds to set it off, has now become one of the most complicated productions that can well be devised; and if it is only so difficult to invent as it is to describe, the task of the modiste must be bewildering enough. . . . [There is] an infinity of trimming in the form of buttons, bows, barettes, rosettes, rouleaux, tassels, fringes, flounces, and festoons, almost as complex in their arrangement as a Chinese park. ("La Mode," December 23, 1868)

This is a particularly rich exemplification of several tropes that feature prominently in the discourse around fashions of the late 1860s and early 1870s: the nostalgia for a past moment of simpler "grace," referencing specifically the continuous, visually smooth flow of the just-extinct hoop skirt; the exhaustive listing of variations of that "infinity of trimming," in worked-up tones of simultaneous excitement and disapproval; the recourse, in order to give the drama of these sartorial novelties their full due, to Orientalizing and otherwise exoticizing analogies (here, a "Chinese park") and to a vexed assertion of the impossibility facing those charged with constructing, as well as describing, these "complicated productions."

Similar declarations—of a structural and aesthetic noncohesion so over the top that it produces not only visual confusion but verbal incapacitation—proliferate all over fashion media of this period, and they initiate a line of thought that has been carried into the fashion history of the twentieth and twenty-first centuries. Under the various regimes of tastefulness and functionality that have dominated modern aesthetics, these fashions of the late 1860s and early 1870s have, more so even than other iterations of Victorian dress, fared badly. Characterized as they are by what Elaine Freedgood calls "byzantine design" and a particularly intense overload of the "embarrassing ornament from which various writers—Victorian, modern, and postmodern—take pains to distance themselves" (257), they have been dismissed as absurdities, malignancies even, in histories of both design and gender. Quoting Phillis Cunnington's assertion that "by the 1870s 'the construction of women's dresses was . . . so complicated that it baffled description even by contemporary experts,'" Freedgood notes that this "harsh judgment is a common one" (258). In a 2002 article, for another example, Gina Marlene Dorré writes that "the intricate lexicon of fashionable dress for Western women in the 1870s and 1880s modeled what we now consider to be an outrageous and exorbitant female form. The fashions of the late-Victorians not only scandalized their contemporary audience, but have since haunted costume historians who endeavor to fix them with meaning" (158). But there's a sense in which this idea, supported though it is by theory and history, doesn't hold up. Proffering a misguided notion of "unreadability" that is in fact a failure to read correctly or closely enough, it also fails to account for the perspective of those Victorian subjects for whom fashion's intricate language and opulent objects did contain both appeal and meaning. I want to suggest that these fashions, in their very "outrageousness" and "exorbitance," actually mean a great deal, and that it is worthwhile to enter into—to read, closely, from within—their "intricate lexicon." In recovering that perspective, I also want to expand it to accommodate queer men: those who might have fully identified as transgender, had the category existed; those who, like Ernest/Stella and Frederick/Fanny, went by women's names and female pronouns, yet wore men's clothing with some regularity and seem to hew more closely to the (also anachronistic) category of gay drag queens; and those gay or queer men who did not themselves cross-dress but to whom women's fashion was a site of lively investment and aesthetic excitement.

It is not, I would contend, actually true that Victorian fashion experts were "baffled" by the objects of their attention. Certainly, they liked to say—in characteristically mercurial flits between enthrallment and self-deprecation— that they were: "Formerly trimmings were added to enhance the beauty of the robe," dictates *Le Follet* in August 1869. "Now, on the contrary, the robe is inferior, the additions of trimmings being the subject to be discussed. . . . This state of things cannot last . . . too great a profusion of bouillonnés, ruchings, or plaitings should be avoided." But such disavowals—of interest, of attractiveness, of representational possibility—are almost always belied by what are in fact comprehensive, exacting, and avid designations and descriptions. Complexity doesn't (necessarily) "baffle description": what it does is make description a lot more difficult. For writers and readers, designers and home dressmakers, the stakes of craft and comprehension are raised: to design an outfit, as well as to describe it, to imitate it, or to wear it successfully, requires a heightened flexing of technical and terminological finesse. When fashion media's self-censuring exclamations are reattached to the cataloguing of what has just been warned against or deemed impossible, what emerges is a distinctive tonality: a tonality that partakes of minute distinctions between categories of decorative objects that to an untrained eye look indistinguishable (and, usually, all abject or useless) yet to the expert contain intricate fields of signification; and of a strategically overstated complaint or denial that instantaneously reverses its own performative negation and magnifies, instead, its performatively obscured excitement. It is of a genre reflected in expressions like "I just couldn't!" or "It's too much!"—and, I want to suggest, its appearance in Victorian fashion media bespeaks the emergence, in that media, of a camp sensibility. To reflexively disdain an aesthetic characterized by "coming into excesses of every kind" (as the *Pall Mall Gazette* put it with arch critical interest ["La Mode.-Bonnets," December 17, 1868]) is, therefore, to miss its valences of desire, distinction, and use, and to miss the developmental cadences of this queer pattern of visual and verbal response to that aesthetic. I am positing that a newly appreciative, minutely detailed attention to the textures and languages of Victorian fashion can give us newly acute insight into the language of Victorian queerness, most vividly at sites of their overt conjunction—like the drag scandal.

Remarkably, the words "drag" and "camp" both see their earliest recorded uses in the materials of the Boulton and Park case. In that spring of 1870, while commenters all over the fashion and anti-fashion press are fretting about decoration and display, cosmetics and colors, inspiration and imitation, an editorial in the *London Times* frets that "the most curious part of the story is the influence which these personations had on other young gentlemen of similar tastes . . . 'Drag' might have become quite an institution, and open carriages might have displayed their disguised occupants without suspicion, except to the initiated" (May 31, 1870). And moving from the discourse of paranoia and discipline into that of the "initiated" whose "influence" it fears, Fanny Park, in a November 1868 letter to her "sister" Stella's lover Lord Arthur Clinton (a letter later seized and read aloud in court) is also fretting:

> I cannot echo your wish that I should live to be a hundred, though I should like to live to a green old age. Green, did I say? Oh! Ciel, the amount of paint that will be required to hide that very unbecoming tint. My campish undertakings are not at present meeting with the success they deserve. Whatever I do seems to get me in hot water somewhere; but n'importe, what's the odds as long as you're rappy? ("Men," *London Times*, May 30, 1870).

Discussing this letter, William Cohen notes that "Boulton, Park, and their correspondents draw upon an argot" that is—like the argot of fashion, with which it intersects—"largely unintelligible to those outside their subculture." He adds in a footnote that "at points the interpretive task is a perplexing one for the prosecutor, particularly when faced with translating gay subcultural slang into the Queen's English." The most salient incidence of this perplexity occurs in the transcription of Fanny's letter: "When this letter was entered into the court record, the word campish was misread as 'crawfish' . . . While the court was clearly confused about what 'sodomitical practices' might entail, that it could imagine them somehow to involve crustaceans is startling" (Cohen 116).

The first dictionary to include the word "camp" is James Ware's 1909 *Passing English of the Victorian Era*, where it is defined as "actions and gestures of exaggerated emphasis. Probably from the French. Used chiefly by persons of exceptional want of character" (61). This is usually taken to be an assertion of the French etymology of the word (though its origins have not been satisfactorily decoded). Drawing on Thomas King's argument that camp gesture is "judged as excessive according to the standards of acceptable and conventional bourgeois male deportment" and, simultaneously, the "gestural excess signifies a lack of Self (and thus lack of membership in the social body)," Moe Meyer suggests an alternate reading of Ware's definition: he takes it "not as suggesting that the word 'Camp' is from the French, but that the actual and specific gestures he describes have been imported from France" (65). He continues:

> [If] specific gestures identified simultaneously by exterior excess (Ware's "exaggerated emphasis") and interior lack (Ware's "exceptional want of character") are constitutive markers of homosexual identity, then the first text reference to Camp in 1909 already encodes a homosexual subject. This coding is noticeable both by its definition based on excess/lack and through its attribution of these gestures to the French: the discourse of English Francophobia included the assumption that homosexuality was a French import. (65)

This is convincing; but the historical record of "camp," as Fanny's letter shows us, actually stretches back at least some forty years before Ware's dictionary. Can Meyer's reinterpretation be worked backwards? If by 1909 these "constitutive markers of homosexual identity" were firmly implanted in the cultural lexicon, in 1870 their status therein was much more oblique: that obliqueness—or its degree—is, of course, the locus of the historical and critical debates surrounding the outcome and the meaning of the Boulton and Park trial.

Returning to Alan Sinfield's theoretical mediation, we could assert that for some Victorians—both queer and phobic—this gestural repertoire was beginning by 1870 to be loaded with increasingly specific sexual suspicion, while for others such a correlation was still some distance outside any field of comprehension. For a great many Victorians, however, such a genre of "specific gestures identified simultaneously by exterior excess [and] interior lack"—a genre of acts, objects, and words also imported from France, carrying with them aesthetic promises, erotic enticements, moral threats—was palpably consonant with another category of knowledge and desire fused into something like an identity: fashionability. The "exaggerated emphasis" that Ware's definition attributes to "camp" is, as I've been arguing, an intrinsic feature of mid-Victorian women's fashion, in both its material forms and its discursive manifestations. The association of fashionability with an "exceptional want of character," meanwhile, is hardly an obscure one—with fashion (surface) frequently situated as the opposite of character (depth)—but, as my next sections will explore, it gathers ever-increasing steam in the more anxious and moralistic spheres of Victorian imaginations and media: increasing in both intensity and in a sexual specificity which, though most overtly concerned with female promiscuity, crosses queer paths with male homosexuality and cross-gender identifications.

"Camp," then, perhaps originated—was perhaps, at its origins, understood—as a word that had as much to do with fashion as with queerness. "My campish undertakings are not at present meeting with the success they deserve," wrote Stella in her letter—joking about cosmetics; employing an effeminate vernacular—and the courtroom appears to have been befuddled, if not repelled, by the word (hence the bizarre "crawfish" transcription). What we don't know is how many of those listeners took this befuddlement or repulsion as of a piece with that which they associated with "the female fashions" and their "fal-lals"—the allegedly ludicrous parlance of *Le Follet* and its ilk that, week after week, *Punch* gleefully poached, twisted, and mocked. Fashion's vocabulary, like that of subcultural sexualities, is apt to be mutable and transient, to be little understood in its own moments and largely forgotten afterward: reading the drag scandal requires attention to each and thus may reveal undeciphered affiliations—or spaces for the possibility of affiliations—between them.

FAST GIRLS AND FALSE WOMEN: COSMETIC TECHNOLOGIES, QUEER EMBODIMENT

> "Then do you not think that every girl of the period is a guy?"
> —"Guys in Disguise," *Le Follet*, November 1869

On Wednesday, May 10, 1871, the second day of Boulton and Park's trial, "early in the course of the day's proceedings, two large packages were brought in, containing various articles of wearing apparel taken from the rooms of the defendants in Wakefield-street."[6] First came Inspector Shenton's verbal re-enumeration of his "list of the things which we seized" in the raid: the "sixteen dresses,—satin, rep, and glacé, green cord silk, violet glacé silk trimmed with white lace, black satin trimmed with mauve satin, blue and white satin piped with white satin, mauve rep silk, a blue satin, a gray moiré antique, and a white glacé trimmed with blue satin and lace, and white corded silk," plus a large supply of undergarments and accessories, and "as many as twenty chignons" (Trial 20). Next, the full collection of "articles [was] produced and exhibited amidst much laughter, until the jury said they had had enough." For both sides, the "exhibition" was loaded: the prosecution, which orchestrated it, sought to assert that the size, quality, completeness, style, and cost of the wardrobe proved that Fanny and Stella's cross-dressing was not (as the defense argued) a "lark," or theatrical play, but rather "the business of their lives"—and thus indicative of sexual deviance. Meanwhile, to counter that argument—and to render misleading, gratuitous, and even unseemly the display of the dresses—Boulton and Park's lawyers seek to decimate their value: "But what had they seen?" asks Serjeant Parry, Park's lawyer, with performative disdain. "A theatrical wardrobe, and nothing more . . . £.170. worth of dresses, silks and satins, chignons, boots, shoes, paints, and powder—all these were theatrical . . ." (Trial 37). The theory here was that the verification of the dresses as theatrical costumes, authorized by professional necessity and rendered comfortingly artificial, would obviate the prosecution's implication that their quantity and value indicated an incriminating level of personal investment and permanency.

Reporting the next morning upon what it calls the "chief incident of the day . . . the exhibition of the defendants' costumes 'in drag,'" the *Daily Telegraph* leads with some vigorous editorializing: "Yesterday . . . for the first time in its annals, the Court of Queen's Bench was turned into an old clothes shop," like those found in "the streets around and about Leicester-Square":

> In their windows you see displayed the ghosts of rich silks . . . In the glare of gaslight you might fancy that at such places as these you could attire yourself—supposing you to be the purchasers of female attire—in the height of fashion and elegance . . . But if you are a philosopher of the streets, and peer into the windows of which we speak in the broad glare of daylight, there are few more melancholy spectacles than these repositories of finery which has lived its day. It seemed yesterday as if the whole of one of these Monmouth-street establishments had been scattered over the Court of Queen's Bench . . . Silk petticoats, braided bodices, embroidered skirts, muslin wrappers, bonnets, parasols, boots, and all the paraphernalia of the "girl of the period" dress were turned out ruthlessly upon

the floor. Whether the articles thus displayed were "quite a lady's" costume may be doubted. ("Boulton," May 11, 1871)

This remarkable moment forces into striking juxtaposition the exhibitionary venues of the dress shop and the courtroom. Each of these is a space where items of "ladies' wearing apparel" are put on display, put up for evaluative consideration, for judgment, in ways that are obviously different yet perhaps disarmingly close—hence the shock intoned in the *Daily Telegraph*'s pique and by the jury's laughter. The repeated exposition, verbal and later visual, of the sheer size, as well as the particularly pungent detail, of Boulton and Park's wardrobe suggests a culturally situated erotics of lurid fascination with the materials of fashionability. The case of the transvestite gives amplification and license to an already present urge to deconstruct, with disciplinary and/or voyeuristic intent, the objects that simultaneously conceal and construct the female body.

Just prior to this live exhibition of the wardrobe seized from Boulton and Park's apartment, Martha Stacey, the daughter of the landlady at 13 Wakefield Street, was called to the stand.[7] She was interrogated about the length of her acquaintance with the defendants, about their reliability as tenants, and about their typical behavior and manners (they were, she insisted, unfailingly polite), about their unorthodox patterns of use of the apartment, about the suspect layout of the space itself. It became clear that their occupation of the rented rooms was at striking odds with Victorian conventions of domestic space: they stayed intermittently for two or three days at a time; they came home hours after the building's other inhabitants had gone to bed; they shared an apartment with only one bedroom; their immense stores of dresses and jewels overflowed conventional storage space and often seemed to be the primary inhabitants of the rooms. Interrogation then turned to the contents of the collections. Boulton's attorney asked Martha whether the pieces lodged in the apartments-cum-closets under her care "[were] dresses that would suit for theatricals"; Martha replied that they were indeed: "Just the same." When, next, however, the Lord Chief Justice interposed a follow-up to that question—"Would they have suited them to walk about in if they were ladies?"—Martha said yes, that too: "they were ordinary ladies dresses." If this was already an oddly self-contradictory set of responses to what seems a straightforward-enough line of questioning, things proceed to get only further ambiguated, even as the prosecutor presses, upon reexamination of the witness, for a more clarifying statement: "Did you observe *the kind of women's dress they wore* when they went out," he says, to which she repeats: "They were similar to ordinary ladies' walking dresses" ("Boulton," *Daily Telegraph*, May 11, 1871; emphasis added).

Then:

> *The Lord Chief Justice:* Was there anything unduly gay or flaunting about them? I daresay you know what I mean.
> —Well, my lord, they were very extreme. (A laugh.)
> *A Juror:* Did you observe whether the dresses were high or low?
> —Sometimes they were higher than others. They were mostly high dresses.
> Never low?
> —I do not say never; but mostly they were high.
> *The Attorney-General:* Did they wear bonnets or hats?
> —Sometimes hats, sometimes bonnets.
> ("Boulton," *Daily Telegraph*, May 11, 1871)

This is, as Neil Bartlett has forcefully argued, a crucial moment for the proceedings, as well as for our understanding of them. The "medical evidence" on which the sodomy charge was grounded had failed to provide certainty, with the results of Dr. Paul's examinations contradicted by those of doctors called by the defense to assert that there was nothing abnormal about the anuses of the accused. So when the interrogation turned to the wardrobes—culminating in this moment when, in Bartlett's terms, Fanny and Stella's "precious hoards of . . . frocks and jewels were displayed in court, as if they could give up the secret which the actual bodies had refused to betray" (Bartlett 136)—the case was far from settled. The task that faced each side, the Crown and the defense, was to produce and to secure an incontestable content for the inherently insecure, contested space of the secret. "There was no question that they were frocks," Bartlett paraphrases, and that the defendants had worn them; "the question was, what did the frocks signify? . . . If it could be proved that the dresses had been worn to seduce men, if that was their meaning, then the defendants were definitely guilty . . . The defense retaliated with the argument that their style of dress was indeed the sign of an occupation; it was the professional dress of actresses" (136–37).

Bartlett's reading points up the import of the interrogation of Martha Stacey, among other witnesses, about the specific genres, forms, and implications of Boulton and Park's outfits. If Martha's answer to the question of "kind" could have come down firmly on one side or the other, if the dresses could have been more firmly situated with a resolved bracket of cost or class—as "theatrical" or "ordinary"; "gay and flaunting" or staid, unremarkable; high-necked or low-cut rather than usually high but "not never" low (and sometimes very low)—then the case itself, as Bartlett rightly suggests, would have been easier to make for one side or the other. A conviction might have been achieved, or, on the other hand, the charges might have been dropped: as the attorney general himself suggested in his opening statement, "It appeared that Boulton and Park had frequently acted in private theatricals, and assumed female characters, and, of course, naturally assumed female attire. And if that had been all there would have been nothing to render them amenable to such a charge as this" ("Court," *London Times*, May 10, 1871).

But the legalistic framework, on both sides, had overestimated the straightforward readability of female attire. It failed to take account of the fact that, as we've seen, fashion itself—as system, as scene, and as silhouette, in the broadest terms of the production and distribution of clothing down to the very tiniest ones of its cut and construction—was, right then, in a state that might aptly be termed "very extreme," and the question of "what kind of women's dresses they wore when they went out" was not an easy one to answer. It could be, quite literally, really hard to tell. "Fashions never were in such a vague state as they are now," declares the *Englishwoman's Domestic Magazine* in January 1869, typifying a chronically voiced sentiment in the fashion journalism of these years. The column is here ventriloquizing a "couturière en vogue" whose take on "the probable toilets of next month" has been solicited by the magazine:

> Each lady comes to ask me, not what is worn, but what has not yet ever been seen or worn. The toilet each desires is the inconnue. Their dream is to possess something more beautiful and more strange than was ever seen before. . . . In fact, any lady, whether in Paris or the most remote province or foreign land, may dress herself in the latest fashion by studying and exactly copying a full ball dress of one of the grandes dames of the court of Louis XIV or XV. . . . Formerly such historical costumes were thought suitable only for masquerades, now they are worn as modern toilets by the élite of our fashionable world. ("The Fashions," January 1869)

And not, again, only by the elite. As the quotation indicates, with its gesture toward the "most remote" readerly locations, the demographic reaches of fashion were just now more capacious and fluid than they had ever been before—producing great occasions for the cultivation of both desires and paranoias. "Instead of providing a sophisticated code for distinguishing between ladies, fashion had collapsed that most fundamental divide," writes Margaret Beetham of the elaborately designed styles exported from the louche domains of Second Empire Parisian society. "Extravagant dress and the presentation of the self as spectacle had become the signifiers of both the lady and the prostitute" (105).

Bartlett argues that "Martha concluded that the dresses indicated that Fanny and Stella were regularly and frequently employed as theatricals. She could not let herself imagine that they meant anything else" (137). But in light of fashion's tumultuous states of social and aesthetic rearrangement, we can see that there are a few other ways in which Martha might have understood the questions and meant her oddly self-contradictory testimony. When she finally allowed that the dresses were, after all, "very extreme," she may have meant that they were outside of fashion's social norms: that they looked to her, as Bartlett hypothesizes, like the over-stagey getups of "amateur actors," burlesque performers; or, on the other hand, that they bordered on the garishly oversexed uniforms of prostitutes or, more sumptuously and subtly so, of demimondaines. All of these are categories of "extreme dress" that display a tenacious and, in this period, an especially literal overlap; and all of them already bring to bear their own conflictive implications upon the trial's proceedings. Yet on still another hand, Martha might have meant that the dresses were extremely fashionable: that these "gay and flaunting" gowns looked, indeed, precisely like the very latest in "ordinary walking dresses." In this regard, Martha might have meant that the men who wore the dresses looked like the "ordinary," typical—which is to say typically extraordinary—"fashionable woman" of the moment: like "the girl of the period" cited by the *Daily Telegraph*, describing the degrading spectacle of "all the paraphernalia" of her costumes "strewn across the floor" of the courtroom.

This "girl of the period," as scathingly limned in Eliza Lynn Linton's 1868 polemic of that title, which thrust the phrase with "astonishing impact" into public discourse (Rinehart 4), was "a creature who dyes her hair and paints her face . . . whose sole idea of life is fun; whose sole aim is unbounded luxury; and whose dress is the chief object of such thought and intellect as she possesses. . . . Her main endeavour is to outvie her neighbours in the extravagance of fashion. . . . Nothing is too extraordinary and nothing too exaggerated for her vitiated taste" (Linton, *Girl*, 2). Linton verbalizes and intensifies anxieties, barely hinted at in the breezy rhetoric of the fashion magazine, about fashion's visually disorienting, socially disruptive, and sexually suspect imitative fluidity. "It can hardly be denied that at the present moment [women's dress] offends grievously in three particulars," writes Linton in another 1868 column:

> It is inadequate for decency; it lacks that truthfulness which . . . should be, the base of all that is attractive and beautiful; and its symbolism is in the highest degree objectionable, for it not only aims at what is unreal and false, but it simulates that which is positively hateful and meretricious, so that it is difficult now for even a practiced eye to distinguish the high-born maiden or matron of Belgravia from the Anonymas who haunt the drive and fill our streets. (*Modern Women*)

In terms of unstinting rancor, Linton accuses the girls and women of the period of behavior not so distant from that of which Fanny and Stella stand accused: recklessly dressing up, in "extreme" fashions, as something "unreal" and "false," with the goal of making social waves and attracting male attention—and with the result of betraying dearly held ideals of gender, of national character, of heterosexual domesticity, of procreation itself: no longer "tender, loving, retiring, or domestic," this new kind of English girl looks to marry, if at all, only for money, and "if children come, they find by a step-mother's cold welcome from her" (*Girl*, 29). This new kind of girl has "nothing in common" with "the fair young English girl of the past," Linton writes, "save ancestry and their mother-tongue; and even of this last the modern version makes almost a new language, through the copious additions it has received from the current slang of the day." She looks not to stalwart national heritage but to racy foreign trends for an ideal of desirable femininity: "What the demi-monde does in its frantic efforts to excite attention, she also does in imitation. . . . The Girl of the Period envies the queens of the demi-monde far more than she abhors them. . . . It is this envy of the pleasures, and indifference to the sins, of these women . . . which is doing such infinite mischief to the modern girl" (30). Linton is careful to stop short of accusing her prototypical girl of actual sexual immorality—at issue are "aims and feelings," not "actual deeds"—but "unfortunately, she has already paid too much—all that once gave her distinctive national character." The alleged sodomites are also accused, in the rhetoric of both prosecutors and the media, of "inflicting a stain on the national character" (Trial 55). I want to suggest that the overlap between the vocabularies of female fashionability and its effeminate appropriation hints at the queer leanings that infuse Victorian fashion and reveals that the paranoias surrounding it traverse territory more complex than that of the policing of gender boundaries.

Thanks to the cosmetic novelties embraced by trend-addled girls—and found in Boulton and Park's apartment—the lines of classification that the questioning of Martha Stacey attempts draw around the drag queens' "kind" of dress are, Linton affirms, impossible these days to draw at all: "Thus, with diaphanous tinted face, large painted eyes, and stereotyped smile, the lady goes forth looking much more as if she had stepped out of the green-room of a theatre, or from a Haymarket saloon, than from an English home" (*Modern Women*, 333). And it doesn't stop with the face paints, gold dust, and dyed or false hair whose use became increasingly widespread in this period.[8] Linton goes on to attack—and, therein, to describe—such increasingly bizarre accouterments as false breasts, artificial ears, and even prosthetic stomachs. Undeterred by such denouncements, these "adventitious aids," as she calls them archly, kept crowding the marketplace and imperiling the ideologically imperative boundaries between virtue and falsehood, nature and artifice, bodies and things—and sending askew not only the most sacrosanct stipulations of gender but the most basic truths of the sexed body:

> It comes to be a grave matter of doubt, when a man marries, how much is real of the woman who has become his wife, or how much of her is her own only in the sense that she has bought, and possibly may have paid for it. Of the wife elect, her bones, her debts, and her caprices may be the only realities which she can bestow on her husband. All the rest—hair, teeth, complexion, ears, bosom, figure . . .—are alike an imposition and a falsehood. (*Modern Women*, 336–37)

Here Linton eventually arrives at the point to which her argument is inevitably heading: a questioning not only of which kind of woman one is, but of whether one is really a woman at all.

Given what we know about the convulsive energies and anxieties that sur-rounded Victorian formulations of commodities and femininities, it is appar-ent why all of this should have been so electric in its provocations; why there should be such working-ups of private and public feeling surrounding newly popular modes and means of revealing, modifying, disguising, and amplify-ing the body. Reading the same material from an opposing stance, though, I would also contend that the glamours of these widely available yet reliably scandalizing techniques of fashionability—glamours almost inevitably en-coded in the vocabulary of this genre of anti–fashion writing—could have, for many readers, bubbled up over the top of their intended lines of attack. Pieces like Linton's did, in fact, become unintentional instigators of new trends: "The predecessors of modern T-shirt manufacturers launched 'Girl of the Period' parasols and articles of clothing," writes Nana Rinehart. "It appears that the satirical thrust of the original article was ignored by the commercial exploiters since the products using Linton's title as a label were presumably aimed at the same fashionable young women whom Linton had attacked" (4). And in a variety of (mis)use less directly connected to capitalistic enterprise, the attacks might well have ended up readable for some—both those within and outside of the target young female population—as giddily and covertly instructive illuminators of the hypertrophied style they overtly condemn: as style guides, as slang dictionaries, as flirtation manuals, as drag manuals.

For mid-Victorian cross-dressers like Fanny and Stella, both fashion's promotional media and its antagonist counterparts would have functioned as useful, not to mention entertaining, sources of information not only on styles of dress but on styles of gender presentation—and on the objects, Lin-ton's "adventitious aids," currently available to build up female bodily features where they are lacking or, in this case, absent. At Wakefield Street, along with the dresses, hats, boots, and petticoats, the detectives had discovered "curl-ing-irons, sun-shades, six pairs of stays . . . chemisettes, garters, drawers, five boxes of violet powder, one of bloom of roses (rouge), silk stockings, eight pairs of gloves, one bottle of cholorform, artificial flowers, and a great quantity of wadding, used apparently for padding" ("Young Men," *London Times*, May 16, 1870). All of these might be described not only as objects of fashion but as technologies for the structuring and decoration of the fashionable body. The last is especially notable, and it comes up repeatedly in the testimony: Peter Roberts, subwarder at the House of Detention, mentions "a quantity of wadding which I took from the breast" in his inventory of items stripped from the defendants. (He also says, thanks probably to a confusion of parts and their names, that Stella had on "two bustles," which provoked laughter ["Men," *Daily Telegraph*, May 23, 1870].) Linton's own inventory takes aghast stock of a more advanced contrivance for the same purpose:

> Women to whom nature has been niggardly in the matter of round-ness of form . . . need not despair; if they cannot show their own busts, they can show something nearly as good, since we read the following, which we forbear to translate:—"Autre excentricité. C'est l'invention des poitrines adherents à l'usage des dames trop éthérées. Il s'agit d'un système en caoutchouc rose, qui s'adapte à la place vide . . . et qui suit les mouvements de la respiration avec une precision mathématique et parfaite." (*Modern Women*, 334)

Whether or not Fanny and Stella owned these pink rubber cups, their availability—their advertisement, in the French notice that Linton quotes as well as in, despite itself, Linton's invective—illuminates the tremendous fertility of contemporary fashion, from the "excess of ornamentation" ("La Mode," *Pall Mall Gazette*, April 28, 1869) apparent on its surface all the way down to the artificial supports required at its base, for the project of fabricat-ing femininity—in particular the kind of exaggerated, stylized femininity that has been, from these origin moments, the purview of drag. When the *Daily Telegraph* posits, regarding the "silk petticoats, braided bodices, embroidered skirts, muslin wrappers, bonnets, parasols, boots, and all the paraphernalia of the 'girl of the period' dress" spread out in the courtroom, that "whether the articles thus displayed were 'quite a lady's' costume may be doubted," the line holds a few shades of meaning. On the surface, there is the asser-tion that, when seen up close and in the light of day, the defendants' dresses, which "when new must have looked handsome in saloons and theatres," reveal themselves as shoddy imitations of real fashionable dress. Beneath that, the suggestion that anyone dressed in so flagrant a style—whether a "girl of the period" or a female impersonator—hardly qualifies as a "lady," in the sense of a category of manners and class. And, beneath that, the destabilizing in-sinuation that, just possibly, the prototypical "girl of the period," the persona formulated by means of all this "paraphernalia," might not be a lady—in the sense of a category of gender—at all.

Pointing to a number of sanctimonious editorials that proclaimed the details of the Boulton and Park trial unfit for public consumption, William

Cohen argues that "the spectacular drama" of the case "is directed at a public audience most powerfully incarnated in female form. . . . [W]hen the public is threatened by reports of gender transgression, it comes to be imagined as female" (103). The delicate sensibilities of a feminine public need shielding from the scandalous material at hand, insufficiently signaled by the headlines: "Most cases of this sort bear their character marked on their foreheads," complained the *Pall Mall Gazette*. "No woman can be in any danger of reading about them unless she does so intentionally. But the heading 'Men in Women's Clothes' need not in the first instance have served as an adequate warning of what was to follow and a lady may have been left to make out the underlying filth for herself, or have had to be warned of its existence by some male relative" (31 May 1871). This reflects, of course, the crux of the whole matter: what looks like a woman is actually a man; what looks like innocent cross-dressing is actually sodomy; what looks, perhaps, like a quaint story of mistaken identity—a fashion story, even, aimed at women—is actually quasi-pornographic testimony.

As Cohen points out, a number of media outlets expressed the greatest distress and indignation over the incident, on the night of the arrest, of the "entrance of Park into the retiring room, which is set apart for ladies at the Strand Theatre." The interloper then, as an 1870 pamphlet describes it with chagrin,

> had the unblushing impudence to apply to the female attendant to fasten up the gathers of his skirt, which he alleged had come unfastened . . . This act, simple as it appears on paper, is sufficient in itself to arouse the just indignation of every true Englishman. We can now ask, and with a just cause too, what protection have those who are dearest to our hearts and hearths . . . Is it right, moral, or just that their most sacred privacy should thus be ruthlessly violated? (Quoted in Cohen 104)

There is a hint of sexual violation here: the fear/fantasy (not uncommon in Victorian pornography[9]) that a man dressed in women's clothes might seduce an unsuspecting woman into sisterly bonding that could quickly heat up into something else. The more resonant dangers, as Cohen argues, are "that gullible men will find themselves entrapped by perverts; and . . . that the rights and privileges of genuine femininity will be grotesquely intruded upon"—thus upsetting "the whole basis for difference" on which the gendered social and erotic worlds are founded. "If gender is contingent and mutable," as Cohen phrases the question, "how can its traditional categories of response function?" (105).

An anxiety of a different order, though, seems also to be aroused by the scene of a cross-dressed man going into the ladies' room and asking the attendant to pin up a fallen fold of his skirt (and, we should note, as many magazine columns did, the multiply draped and folded skirts of 1870 were especially liable to fall and need pinning): that all of them—the "real" ladies and the drag queens—are doing strange, unnecessary, incomprehensible, and maybe untoward things with dresses in that room, that not only cross-dressers, but dress itself, might disrupt or slip outside of the balance of gender relations that undergird heterosexuality. Cohen posits that the great anxiety Boulton and Park arouse in the public imagination is that its most susceptible sector— the young, female one—will, through too-easy access to the seamy details of gender and sex crimes, "have their minds polluted by half-understood hints of vices of which they had previously no conception." I want to suggest that another anxiety—quite converse to (which is not to say incompatible with) this one—lurks around and behind it: that those volatile young women are in fact already too close to those vices; that the fashions and affectations shared by the drag queens and the "girl of the period" cement a space of deviant affiliation between girls and queers, a space of affiliation bounded by a category of knowledge—the knowledge of fashion's language, of its forms—that is inaccessible and exasperating to men. What this threatens, then, is the emergence of a generation of girls so enwrapped in artifice, so in thrall to faddish materialism, and so inimical to the claims of heterosexual courtship that they had might as well be—may, in the further corners of paranoid fantasy, actually be—men in petticoats.

Voluminous Behinds: The Bustle and Anal Eroticism

"There seems such a peculiar fascination to gentlemen in the idea of having a beautiful creature, such as an ordinary observer would take for a beautiful lady, to dance and flirt with, knowing all the while that his inamorata is a youthful man in disguise."

—*Sins of the Cities of the Plain* (1891)

In his 1930 classic *The Psychology of Clothes*, J. C. Flügel claims that "perhaps the most obvious and important of all the variations of fashion is that which concerns the part of the body that is most accentuated. Fashion, in its more exuberant moments, is seldom content with the silhouette that Nature has provided, but usually seeks to lay particular stress upon some single part of feature, which is then treated as a special centre of erotic charm" (160). Over the course of the nineteenth century, the Empire style's showcasing of breasts (1810s–1820s) was followed by an "accentuation of the hips" (1830s–1860s), which peaked "in the later forms of the crinoline" and "gave place to that of the posterior parts, and in the seventies and again in the eighties, women were wearing a creditable imitation of a tail" (161). More recently, Harold Koda describes "the collapse of the hoop skirt" as bringing with it "an increased focus on the derriere . . . The exaggerated focus on the ever expanding bustle . . . gave the buttocks unprecedented emphasis" (130). Few Victorians could be so direct; yet a salacious recognition of the awakening of a new erogenous zone is evident in certain bits of arch critique of what the *Pall Mall Gazette* calls the "mode hottentote" ("La Mode," April 28, 1869)—referring to the infamously exaggerated proportions with which the European imagination endowed the buttocks of African women.[10] "A new fashion has been devised of a cushion or hump worn prominently about eight inches below the waist, its position being indicated on the outside of the dress behind a large bow of ribbon, to which the still more suggestive designation of a 'pincez moi cela' [pinch me here] has been given," says a "Ladies' Column" in June 1868, typically resorting to French to simultaneously censure and propagate an object—and a term—at which "many people will be terribly shocked" (*Manchester Times*, June 27, 1868).[11]

Doreen Yarwood, in her survey *English Costume*, traces the fashion juncture in which I have been dwelling: "The skirt was indubitably the centre of attraction and the focus was turned more and more to the back as time passed. . . . Skirts became extremely complicated in draping . . . with layers of fringe, lace, accordion pleating, ruching, and flounces decorating all edges" (227). Her language is indicative. The renovation of the fashionable silhouette, as we have seen, encompassed the renewal of the body's lower and rear hemispheres as sites of structural and ornamental "complication"; almost inevitably, then, it motivated the activation of skirts, of ornament, and of backsides as focal points of anxiously fixated "attraction," attention, contention. The newly enhanced posterior emphasis of the emerging bustle silhouette is viv-

DRESS AND THE LADY.

FIGURE 1.6: "Dress and the Lady." *Punch*, August 23, 1856. *Picture Collection, The New York Public Library, Astor, Lenox, and Tilden Foundations.*

idly documented in the fashion plates through which its trajectory is perhaps best understood: their figures begin here to more frequently turn backward; to draw the viewer's gaze attentively, arousingly, to the voluminously expanded and decorated surface of the dresses' backsides and, beneath them—simultaneously obscured and hyperbolically outlined—the body's.

Caricatures of the period, recalling Flügel's comparison of the bustle to an "imitation of a tail," reveal a preoccupation with the unnaturalness—the uncanny animality—of "the last new thing in dress . . . a 'puff petticoat,' which sticks out in a bunch, and causes the female form divine to look rather like the Gnathodon or the Dodo" (*Daily Telegraph*, 1868).[12] Satirizing the crinoline, *Punch* had relied on scenarios of revelation, whether of the (allegedly absurd) materiality of the object itself or of the body concealed, precariously, beneath it. Describing a famous cartoon from 1856 (fig. 1.6), Julia Thomas writes that it "becomes a metaphor for the way that Punch as a whole attempts to lay the crinoline bare, to reveal its secrets. . . . It panders to fantasy, giving spectators

FIGURE 1.7: Cartoon showing the bustle as a snail. *Punch*, August 20, 1870. *General Research Division, The New York Public Library, Astor, Lenox, and Tilden Foundations.*

the illusion that they are able to see through a woman's clothes, even as she takes a stroll through the park" (89).

A different, possibly darker flavor of ridicule permeates Punch's take on fashion in the bustle period. In images like the example here (fig. 1.7), which depicts the bustle shape as a gigantic snail, the garment isn't a permeable screen but an impermeable shell, and the body it conceals doesn't seem open to the denuding gaze, or desirable to it: the half-human, half-creature bodies here are not merely absurd but grotesque; the ambiguously placed shells might be articles of clothing or they might be parts of the body, implying a permanent metamorphosis of the fashionable female body into some kind of monster.

This view of the post-crinoline form as something repellant works on other levels too. "For many years of late," writes a disgruntled critic in the *Pall Mall Gazette* in April 1868, "women surrounded their lower limbs with innumerable steel circlets of great strength and vast dimensions. To sit near, or to

walk close by the side of, the object of your affections was nearly impossible."
Recent developments held brief hope, and then squashed it:

> It is true: those barriers are now discarded: but fashion has invented
> in their stead a cunning system of earthworks. Trains are thrown out
> in every direction, by which the ground is so undermined beneath
> men's feet, and is rendered so shifting, unstable, and dangerous that
> unoffending persons are at any time . . . liable to be dragged along,
> overthrown, deprived of their just standing . . . and overwhelmed
> with unmerited disgrace. ("Fashion," *Pall Mall Gazette*, April 18, 1868)

Both the previous silhouette and the current one, according to this pecu-
liarly but compellingly literalized anecdote, are antithetical to heterosexual
interaction: but where the former works to block it—a blockage that inherently contains an acknowledgment—the latter wipes it out altogether. Male
viewers, more perplexed than ever by the vagaries of the "garments in which
the sex array themselves," are not merely denied access to the female body
but are thrown out of the viewing area: deprived of erotic gratification and,
the paranoid punning on "their just standing" implies, of masculine privilege
itself.

The crinoline silhouette was in no sense "natural," but its unnaturalness
was of a kind whose lines—the skirt surging out in unilateral, ostentatiously
demure circularity from a correspondingly miniaturized waist—arguably
emerged from and adhered to those of the Victorian heterosexual imaginary.
The bustle silhouette, on the other hand, does something quite different:
bringing the dress closer to the body in some areas, it then de-naturalizes it
anew and more extremely than ever. Its scopic delineations are sent outward
and backward, accentuating hips and buttocks but exaggerating them in a way
that disarticulates them from the confounded heterosexual gaze: through a
piling-on of ornament that is unappealing to a (masculinist) aesthetic that
prizes "natural" or streamlined design but of exciting expressive potential for
a queer eye moved by artifice and prosthesis, by shine, by fleeting and lavish
gestures of accretion.

There is compelling reason here to make a leap that a psychoanalysis of
fashion would seem to suggest, and that I will in conclusion gesture toward:
a connection between the bustle silhouette's sudden emphasis on the feminine posterior—the backside's extravagant emergence as the site of visual,

structural, decorative, discursive, and highly ambivalent erotogenic interest—
and, delving beneath their ladies' bustles, the marking of Fanny and Stella's
effeminate-homosexual anuses.

From the start of the juridical proceedings, the matters of dress and anal-
ity were intertwined. Dr. James Paul, the police doctor whose brutally inva-
sive examination on the night of the arrest precipitated the sodomy charges
and thus the whole saga, later admitted that his recent readings of "foreign
works" in the just-emergent field of sexology had inspired the suspicion "that
men so attired might commit unnatural offences" ("Men in Petticoats," *Reynolds's Newspaper*, May 22, 1870).[13] In the weeks after their arrest, Boulton and
Park were examined several more times, by doctors whose testimony is hard
to read, both because of the horror we must imagine the prisoners endured
and because of the simultaneously numbing and grotesque specificity it offers.
John Gibson, surgeon to the Gaol at Newgate, stated that he had examined
Boulton and found "an abrasion on the posterior part of the anal opening
extending from the interior backward; there were within the anal opening 4
or 5 small condylomatous spots—a sort of warty spot." As for Park, "the folds
on the left side of the anus did not exist in [him], but they did on the right
side." Gibson affirmed that, to his knowledge, "dilation of the sphincter, and
the destruction or removal of the folds around the anus" would result from
"the commission of the crime" (quoted in Crozier 95[14]). But Drs. Le Gros
Clark and Henry James Johnston, who testified for the defense, contested the
findings as well as the interpretations of the prosecutorial witnesses: "I took
a very powerful magnifying glass," the latter testified of his examination of
Boulton, "and a speculum of the rectum in order that the examination should
be as searching as possible. I discovered no sign of anything that might suggest
anything unnatural" ("Trial," *Reynolds's Newspaper*, May 14, 1871).

Ultimately, all of this exhaustive search for signification yielded only uncertainty. Opinions differed too drastically for revelation to stick: as William
Cohen writes, "apparently straightforward medical questions—what was the
condition of the defendants' behinds and what did this condition signify—
issued in hopeless irresolution" (81). As with the question of their "kind of
dress," resolution is hindered by the court's epistemological limitations when
faced with a cultural field of emergent discourse and material indeterminacy. As with the cataloging and display of their wardrobes, the examination
and diagnosis of Boulton's and Park's bodies produces masses of insinuative
stuff—bizarre and perplexing detail; manifold strange markings, openings,

foldings—but no convincing argument in which to contain it. There's no way to know whether any of those spots or dilations discovered by the doctors were really there and, if so, whether they bore any connection to "unnatural connexions," no way to know if, in fact, Boulton's and Park's bodies carried any signs of their sexual practices. We could imagine that they may have—and, if so, we could attempt a transvaluation of those markers as signifiers of pleasure rather than shame. (It is worth noting here that Dr. Paul told the court Boulton's "penis and scrotum were of an inordinate length" and that Boulton is said to have smiled at this.) But I want to conclude by claiming that their clothes, in ways vastly more materially recoverable, did carry such signs. Worn by Fanny and Stella, and other queer men in women's clothing, the radically new dresses of the late 1860s supplemented, or stood in for, whatever may have been visible or invisible underneath them. Drawing the eye to the backside, where it shows off swelling contours and intricate geometries, bold colors and lavish ornament, the sodomite's bustle carries the thrill of gender-crossing, claims membership in a feminine community of fashion's knowledgeable acolytes, hints at a disdain for the priorities of phallic heterosexuality, and divulges (or arouses) anal eroticism. In its queer materiality, it bespeaks the "unspeakable" strains of identification and desire that precipitate the emergence of Victorian homosexuality.

NOTES

1. A note on sources: Most of the Victorian newspapers cited in this essay (*Illustrated Police News*, *Manchester Times*, *Pall Mall Gazette*, and *Reynolds's Newspaper*) were accessed through the 19th Century British Library Newspapers database, http://gale.cengage.co.uk/product-highlights/history/19th-century-british-library-newspapers.aspx. I accessed the *London Times* through the Times Archive, http://www.thetimes.co.uk/tto/archive/. I read the *Daily Telegraph* on microfilm provided by the Center for Research Libraries.

Magazines (*Englishwoman's Domestic Magazine*, *Le Follet*, *Punch*) were accessed through the 19th Century UK Periodicals database, http://mlr.com/DigitalCollections/products/ukperiodicals/.

2. For an exploration of the year-long delay between the arrest/arraignment and the trial, see Upchurch, "Forgetting the Unthinkable."

3. The trope of the fashion magazine as an object of interest, and/or a site of identification, for queer and proto-queer boys is familiar in popular culture. In the 2006 film *The Devil Wears Prada*, for instance, the character Nigel, a gay editor at a Vogue-like

magazine, explains to the recalcitrant heroine the vital importance of this allegedly insipid media: "You think this is just a magazine? This is not just a magazine. This is a shining beacon of hope for—oh, I don't know . . . let's say a young boy growing up in Rhode Island with six brothers, pretending to go to soccer practice when he was really going to sewing class, and reading *Runway* under the covers at night with a flashlight." Relevant critical thought includes Moon, *A Small Boy and Others*, and Sedgwick, *Tendencies*.

4. See Julia Thomas's chapter on "crinolineomania" in *Pictorial Victorians*; Christina Walkley, *The Way to Wear 'Em*.

5. Reprinted in "The Ladies Column," *Manchester Times*, June 27, 1868.

6. *Daily Telegraph*, May 11, 1871.

7. Trial, 18–19. All quotations from Martha Stacey's testimony, unless otherwise noted, are from this same source.

8. Alison Gernsheim and other fashion historians confirm this: "The more or less undisguised application of additional hair, even by young women, is a curious feature of the period" (*Victorian and Edwardian Fashion*, 61).

9. Most relevantly, this happens in *Sins of the Cities of the Plain*, in which a character based on the real-life Boulton seduces a young milliner with the story that he is a "hermaphrodite" and that his penis, though functional, cannot impregnate her.

10. As in the infamous case of Sara Baartman, the South African woman showcased as "the Hottentot Venus" in London and Paris in the early nineteenth century. See Clifton Crais and Pamela Scully, *Sara Baartman and the Hottentot Venus*.

11. This item appeared originally in the *Pall Mall Gazette*, a few days earlier.

12. Quoted in De Marly, *Worth: Father of Haute Couture*, 91.

13. The work Paul referred to was probably Ambrose Tardieu's *Étude médico-légale sur les attentats aux moeurs*.

14. Gibson's testimony is quoted from the trial transcriptions held in the National Archives Public Records Office, DPP4/6.

2

An Epitome of Times and Fashions

Temporality and Textiles in Nathaniel Hawthorne's House of the Seven Gables

Babak Elahi

Textiles and Time in Hawthorne's United States

Nathaniel Hawthorne wrote and published during a time marked by social acceleration. In *The House of the Seven Gables*, the heirs of the Pyncheon estate, Clifford and Hepzibah, leave their mossy house to board a moving train that hurtles them into physical and social spaces unknown. Hawthorne's description of how two domestic characters are unmoored by locomotion tells us something about the changing pace of culture and society in the early 1800s: "At one moment, they were rattling through a solitude; the next, a village had grown up around them; a few breaths more, and it had vanished, as if swallowed by an earthquake" (II, 256). The train replaces the house as the moving locus of society: "The spires of meeting houses seemed set adrift from their foundations. . . . Everything was unfixed from its *agelong rest*, and moving at *whirlwind speed* in a direction opposite their own" (II, 256; emphasis added). The contrast between agelong rest and whirlwind speed epitomizes broader social trends. On the car taking them away from the aging seven-gabled house, Hepzibah and Clifford experience not just the acceleration of technology but the speeding up of culture and society: "New people continually entered [the train car]. Old acquaintances—for such they soon grew to be, in this *rapid current of affairs*—continually departed" (II, 257; emphasis added). The "rapid current of affairs" was not simply a function of transportation technology, or of technology per se. The speed of social intercourse of Hawthorne's time was a broader transformation of how people lived. It included changes in industry and technology, to be sure, and in rates of production and consumption, but was lived socially and culturally.

John Kasson, among others, has ably discussed Hawthorne's critique of

America's "faith" in technology as demonstrated in stories like "The Celestial Railroad." However, this acceleration of American society could be witnessed not only in the dramatic image of the railroads, but also as it was reflected and embodied at the much more diurnal and immediate level of dress (Kasson 1976, 49). Clothes were being made more rapidly and were being replaced more frequently than before. Indeed, as I will discuss later, *The House of the Seven Gables* also contrasts the stagnation of homes with the dynamisms of dress. In reading Hawthorne's depiction of dress in *The House of the Seven Gables* as well as in his sketches and journal, we can gain a deeper understanding of the relationship between textile and temporality in the first half of the nineteenth century.

Like transportation technologies, the process of industrial manufacturing was speeding up. Although the contexts of industrialization "varied widely," ranging from large-scale factory production in rural Massachusetts to the concentration of small-scale producers in New York and Philadelphia, it is clear that both production and consumption of goods was speeding up (Licht, 21–22). The later industrial changes of the 1880s would increase the scale of production, but the first half of the century had already increased its pace. The fastest growing industry was textile production. As Walter Licht has put it, "for all intents and purposes the so-called 'industrial revolution' of the late eighteenth and early nineteenth centuries was a revolution in textile production" (25). The period between the teens and the 1840s introduced the tape measure, allowing for standardization of measurement and innovations in cutting. This same period saw the growth of large-scale mechanized textile production along with the proliferation of small-scale urban fabric and clothing production. The period also ushered in the sewing machine and established retail emporia like Boston's Oak Hall as a new way to sell clothes (fig. 2.1). Even today the Oak Hall label has been borrowed by clothing manufacturers with no connections to the original store, suggesting the name's lingering association with clothing manufacture. For instance, twice a year many North American academics are reminded of the association of the name Oak Hall with clothing when they see the Oak Hall label (now appropriated by a company in Salem, Virginia) on the academic regalia they don for annual opening ceremonies in the fall and graduation day in the spring. Established by George W. Simmons, an early innovator in American advertising as well as retail clothing sales, Oak Hall is emblematic of the wider appeal of clothing emporia that catered to a growing middle class in the middle of the nine-

FIGURE 2.1: Oak Hall Exterior Illustration. Oak Hall Clothing Store, Boston, North Street. *Author's collection.*

teenth century. I will have more to say about Oak Hall later, as Hawthorne makes direct reference to it, but would like to suggest for now simply that the clothing retailer is representative of the rise of such textile emporia in the early to mid-nineteenth century in North America. These emporia embody the transitional moment in clothing production as many of them sold both cloth for tailored men's clothing as well as ready made apparel.

An important conceptual shift in these accelerated modes of production was a contraction of how the production process was imagined. By this I mean that the act of making was itself being reimagined. When a thing can be made quickly, it can also be consumed quickly without the sense of loss one might associate with something that took a long time to create. Clearly the twentieth century witnessed an even more striking hegemony of disposability as even "income" became disposable. But by the same token, the early nineteenth century witnessed a shift away from durability to impermanence. A coat was less likely to be mended and patched in 1850 than it was in 1800 because it could now be more easily replaced. Of course, this is to a certain extent a function of class: wealthier people could afford to buy new clothes or have them tailored. But it is also a function of a modern relationship to property, expressed in Clifford Pyncheon's oft-quoted remark about real estate (especially in contrast to the speed and dynamism of locomotion) in *The House of the Seven Gables*: "What we call real estate—the solid ground to build a house on—is the broad foundation on which nearly all the guilt of this world rests" (II, 263). What is less often quoted is Hawthorne's younger character's response to this statement: Holgrave (from the Matthew Maule side of the novel), as I will explore in further detail below, contrasts the multigenerational persistence of architectural property with the disposability of clothing. Like Clifford's contrast between houses and trains, Holgrave's contrast between homes and habiliments is one between stagnation and acceleration.

Historians have noted the shift from homespun to ready-to-wear in terms of class and society, but few scholars have considered how this shift in textile production is related to conceptions of time. Among the few who have considered this link, Peter Corrigan makes an interesting claim regarding the impact of industrialization on the temporality of textiles. He argues that because the shifting cycle and increasing rapidity of sartorial change (fashion) vary, "a given garment begins to appear not as the solid product of the here and now, but rather as the meeting place of a number of different historicities" (Corrigan 51). More specifically, he argues that industrial society "saw not only the elaboration of a linear time of industrial production alongside the more traditional cyclical time of agricultural production, but also a mapping of these very different sorts of time onto men's and women's clothes respectively" (54). The industrial revolution created a tension, argues Corrigan, "between serving the public understood as ever-changing consumers and serving enduring ideals such as God, the Law, medicine or whatever" (61). This shift from "enduring ideals" toward "ever-changing" desires had a bearing on how the individual was imagined. While writers like Thomas Carlyle and Henry David Thoreau imagined "a nicely settled authentic identity, where our clothing would transparently display our true selves," to quote Corrigan's paraphrasing of these two nineteenth-century commentators on clothes, any such transparent or transcendent authenticity is ultimately impossible. Rather, in the nineteenth century the "long-wave cycles . . . associated with the self as a public participant in the culture of production" are replaced by "shorter waves [associated] with the self as a private participant in the culture of consumption" (54). The individual's place at the center of materiality and temporality was shifting, becoming less enduring, more protean.

Some scholars have associated the emergence of "fashion" as such with the rise of the Burgundian court, and here again time seems to be an important factor in understanding fashion (Hunt 45). Fashion allowed for rapid change in the sartorial symbols of privilege, thus allowing the wealthy not only to stay above the poor but ahead of them in time. As competing ideologies of dress began to clash in the late eighteenth century, the temporality of fashion became one of its most important stratifying functions, especially in emerging republics ostensibly founded on notions of equality and Protestant ethics of merit. In its early development, fashion was based on individuation and, in fact, with inequality. Fashion was luxury, and luxury was an expression of status. Alan Hunt defines luxury—in its association with fashionable dress in particular—as socially divisive and inducing of weakness (79). It is the play between these two discursive definitions of fine dress as luxury (an idea dating to the sixteenth century) and weakness (a republican ideal of the eighteenth century) that marks the dynamic politics of fashion. On one side is the notion that luxury (as expressed through fashion) is a necessary symbol or emblem of status. On the other is the notion that fashionable dress is an indication of weakness. The rise and fall of sumptuary laws can be read as the dynamic dialectic between these two discursive conceptions of fashion. On the one hand, fashionable dress is a necessary part of societies based on hierarchy. On the other hand, and particularly for a Puritan capitalistic ideal, fashion (as indicative of luxury) weakens the individual and collective ethic of frugality and hard work. What complicates both of these discursive notions of luxurious dress (fashion) is the emergence of a middle class with the ability to imitate the landed aristocracies of the past. The element of time—of ephemerality—resolves the conflict between the desire to retain social stratification and the rhetoric of equality. Inequality—or hierarchy—as expressed through dress begins to have an expiration date. As codified sumptuary laws begin to give way to self-governance, rapid change in fashionable dress imposes an increasingly short time frame on what is fashionable. Inequality as expressed through dress is increasingly fleeting. At the same time, the strength of a society (as opposed to the induced weakness of luxury) is located in some golden age—a simple past marked by stability. One way this stability is expressed is through simplicity of dress—clothing that serves simple practical purposes, or simplified and stable symbolic purposes. Thus, by the modern era (the eighteenth and nine-teenth century) temporality is a key component of the discourse of fashion.

Certain theories of fashion read it as social imitation, but even here a con-sideration of time and its relation to the individual complicates such theories. Fashion is a matter of staying one step ahead, as expressed by the aristocrat Lady Paget in 1883: "The reason why fashions change so rapidly now is because they at once spread through every stratum of society, and become deteriorated and common" (quoted in Corrigan, 68). What is interesting about Paget's observation is how it reflects not just a different view of textiles but a different view of textiles' relationship to time in that the "deterioration" of clothing is not its physical dilapidation but, rather, its symbolically threadbare state in an increasingly rapid pace of change in styles. What wears clothes out is not material deterioration but, rather, their descent down the social scale. Hunt has argued that this "imitation theory" is not enough. Rather, he argues that imitation (initially by the bourgeoisie of the landed aristocracy and later by the working class of the upper class) is a case of transformative emulation in which yesterday's and even today's styles are recombined, deconstructed, and reclaimed. Hunt's attention is focused particularly on that period between the rise of sumptuary laws in the early modern era, and their eventual "dis-appearance" in the modern era. I will have more to say about sumptuary laws later, but for the current discussion it is important to note that this dynamic of fashion change has a significant temporal component. Hawthorne's fiction deals precisely with this historical shift between an era when, for example, a man's ruff seemed to have a certain stable symbolic meaning held in place partly by sumptuary laws and an era when times and fashions shifted more rapidly and the symbolic meanings of style were much more in flux, governed not by written sumptuary laws but by dynamic social expectations. Fashion in the post-sumptuary era of modernity, as Hunt explains in *Governance of the Consuming Passions*, "attempts to stamp an identity on the present" (157). These attempts to understand the temporality of dress and fashion can help us ex-plain the ways in which Hawthorne's historical fiction uses clothing as one important way both to portray a foreshortened view of the past when clothing was part of long cycles in which identities were seen as solid and constant and to depict a striking view of the present when identities and their sartorial pub-lic presence were in rapid flux.

How does the body's relationship to time change when clothes—once made slowly, mended, and worn for a long time—are made quickly and replaced more frequently? Before the 1820s, the production of clothing was seen to encompass a long process from agricultural and domestic labor to home manufacture. This process encompassed the growing of the grass that feeds the sheep that provide the wool for weaving the cloth that was cut into clothing. By the 1840s, production was envisioned in a more contracted time frame, beginning with the processed materials in hand. On the one side, a Jeffersonian agrarianism saw the cost of a wool coat as including "the value of the grass which sustained the sheep, the labour and support of the shepherd whilst tending the flocks, the labour of the manufacturers in spinning, weaving, dying and dressing the cloth, including the support of their families whilst they were employed in these various processes" (Alexander Stuart, quoted in Zakim, 39–40). On the other hand, a Hamiltonian corporate industrialism argued that "until the goods of the [cloth importer] have passed through the [tailor's] hands, their value is in a dormant state, and they contribute nothing to the embellishment or the utility of life" (George P. Fox, quoted in Zakim, 41). Again, though much has been written about how these processes democratized clothing, less is understood about how this shift away from the use value of agrarian homespun to the exchange value of ready-made dress was a shift in embodied temporality. By 1850, "making clothing was an appropriation of the value already manifest in the production of cloth. It was, at best, a commercial elaboration" (Zakim, 40). Clothes began to be seen not as disposable but as having a more limited longevity than in the past, when homespun was part of domestic production. This more ephemeral relationship to the production of clothes—the product of a broad social-industrial revolution— had implications for the relationship to the purchase and donning of clothes. Easy access to the purchase of ready-made clothing shifted, I would argue, the personal sense of time, especially for the growing middle class in the United States. Stores, where men, especially, could purchase clothes conveniently, changed the temporal relationship to property, giving it less permanence. The less permanent relationship to clothes affected the wearer's relationship to time.

As Michael Zakim has observed, large ready-made clothing stores had become popular by the 1850s and were part of the urban landscape of New York and Philadelphia. In these cities, men like James Burk, Samuel Whitmarsh, John Williams, and Henry Brooks opened the first men's apparel warehouses. Though Zakim does not mention it, Oak Hall was just as important in Boston as these other establishments were in New York and Philadelphia. As Steven

Allaback has shown, Oak Hall can be remembered for the advertising innovations of its founder, George W. Simmons, and references to it in Henry David Thoreau's writing. The son of a tailor, Simmons was an entrepreneur who elaborated the retail space where clothing was sold and developed new kinds of advertising. While Allaback notes the appearance of Oak Hall in Thoreau's work, no one, to my knowledge, has commented on its appearance in Hawthorne's writing. Hawthorne would have been keenly aware of the transformation going on around him: of clothing being transformed from a product of household labor with a particular use value to a product of industrial manufacturing with an exchange value measured both in monetary price and social worth. Hawthorne referred to Oak Hall not only in "Main Street," but also in a key passage in *The House of the Seven Gables*, as I will discuss below. In a book published in 1854, George Simmons touted, in illustrations, stories, and verse, the benefits his clothing store was bringing to the men and boys of the nation (fig. 2.2).

The acceleration of production and consumption can only partly be explained by technological or industrial determinants. The main drivers of this acceleration were political and social. The political force, as Michael Zakim has explained, was the democratizing ideology that drove the ready-made revolution. The ready-made revolution was not merely a technological or organizational speeding up; it was, rather, part of a deeper set of economic, social, political, and cultural motives. As T. Walter Herbert puts it in his reading of Hawthorne in relation to the "making of the middle-class family," Hawthorne's era was marked by "several interconnected new realities," including the creation and destruction of credit at times of boom and panic, new party political formations, "frequent" and "rapid changes of fortune" arising from the "instability of status in society," and the "scramble" for wealth and more wealth (89). Herbert identifies broad societal motivators that pushed American society toward the "new," the rapidly changing, and a scrambling population in quest of wealth. Hawthorne, claims Herbert, "asserts fresh democratic energies against a corrupt 'Past,' but the ogre of the discredited old order represents emerging features of American society" (90). This battle between "fresh" versus "old" energies arising from an expanding middle class that blurred old lines can be read in Hawthorne's novels at the site of manners and dress.

Thus, the social and cultural motivators of this acceleration complicate the political and economic forces. The sociocultural side of the equation is

FIGURE 2.2: Interior of Oak Hall Clothing store. George W. Simmons, *Oak Hall Pictorial* ("Respectfully Dedicated to the Juvenile Patrons of Oak Hall"), Boston: Damrell & Moore, Printers, 1854. *Collection of Richard Sheaff.*

related to the rise of what Richard L. Bushman calls "vernacular gentility." In tracing the dissemination of "refinement" from a social elite influenced by England into a growing North American (and particularly New England) middle class, Bushman shows that imitation of aristocratic refinement could be found in the forms that cities, houses, and persons—including the clothes of those persons—took in the eighteenth century. Between roughly 1690 and 1850, the historical sweep of time that Hawthorne was most concerned with, the middle class in the United States espoused a protestant ethic of merit and modesty, and yet wanted to retain certain class distinctions. Americans were encouraged and instructed by emerging forms of print literature to emulate the tastes and accoutrements of elite refinement based on aristocratic societies Americans claimed to displace. John F. Kasson has documented the abundance of advice literature in the nineteenth century, pointing to the paradox of making "gentility increasingly available as a social desire and a purchasable style and commodity" (1990, 43). And according to Karen Halttunen, the ideology espoused by etiquette books of this era (1830s to 1860s) privileged politically the ideal of the middle class, characterized by the happy medium between the excesses of luxury and the burdens of physical labor. For the middle class, ideas are not "contracted by laborious occupations, nor its mental powers annihilated by luxury," as Catherine Sedgwick, a writer of sentimental literature and contemporary of Hawthorne's, expressed this middle-class ideology (quoted in Halttunen, 95). As Bushman puts it, "Nineteenth-century etiquette books, among the foremost guides to gentility, contained rules written for countries centuries earlier. At a time when the Revolution had ended and principles of monarchy and aristocracy and the forces of capitalist enterprise were leading Americans into industrialization, Americans modeled their lives after aristocratic society that was supposedly repudiated at the founding of the nation" (20). Yet, this anachronistic grammar of taste (refined tastes for a rough nation) became, paradoxically, popular. It became a vernacular.

This vernacular gentility was aided and abetted by the emergence of ready-made production and consumption. The emergence of ready-made clothing for men (as opposed to women, for whom the availability of ready-made clothing came later) coincided with Hawthorne's coming of age and the unfolding of his literary career between the 1830s and 1850s. As Michael Zakim shows, this period saw a sequence of developments that contributed to the availability of men's ready-made dress at a broad level. Dry-goods establishments specializing in supplies for men's clothiers emerged in the 1830s; these gave way in the 1840s to men's clothiers having direct control over their supply of raw material; and by the 1850s the demand of clothing emporia and men's ready-made producers, not the supply of textile producers, drove the textile industry (Zakim 65–67). This availability of men's ready-made dress, then, coincided not only with Hawthorne's career, specifically, but with the focus of both etiquette books and sentimental literature on refining American manners, including modes of dress. In fact, Bushman suggests that fiction "was better suited than etiquette books to reach a broad public if only because the authors told stories about real life" (308). Hawthorne, thus, developed his literary style, one similarly focused on "real life," at a time when a discourse of vernacular gentility and men's ready-made clothing were both becoming important aspects of American society. An important component of vernacular gentility was time itself. Hawthorne's backward historical glance allowed him to place his own and his contemporaries' accelerated rates of production and consumption in a longer process of the dissemination of refinement. Hawthorne seems to have been aware that class is not a static structure but a dynamic process. By the 1830s vernacular gentility had blurred the lines between aristocratic social elites and a middle-class social hegemony. The lens of historical narrative had the potential to bring the different sides of that line back into focus. The temporal significance of text and textiles allowed Hawthorne to see precisely how this change had been wrought, how refinement had become common. Dress, I would argue, was key to Hawthorne's understanding of this dynamic shift.

Throughout his work—from the tale "The Artist of the Beautiful" to his last novel, *The Marble Faun*—Hawthorne commented on the difference between the work of the individual artist and the product of industrial labor. Late in his career, for example, in *The Marble Faun*, Hawthorne contrasted an enduring aesthetic view of the world in Italy with a dynamic industrial view of the world in the United States where flowing water is immediately put in the service of turning "the machinery of a cotton mill" (IV, 146). Space does not permit a thorough analysis of Hawthorne's sketches, journals, and other novels here, but in any reading of sketches such as "Howe's Masquerade," "Main Street," "Old News," or "The Gray Champion," or in reading the Custom House essay introducing *The Scarlet Letter*, it becomes clear that Hawthorne not only explored sartorial themes but quite often used the image of old and new fashions as temporal tropes, as narrative devices meant to indicate time-bound events, and events that have a lingering bearing on the present in which and to which he writes.

I would suggest that Hawthorne's narrative time is intimately related to his representations of dress, most vividly demonstrated in his sketch "Old News," in which the narrator uses newspapers from the Puritan and revolutionary eras to make the past present. In trying to *present* the past, Hawthorne realizes that dress is the perfect material representation of bygone manners. Old manners are made manifest by materials, time regained through textile. In "Howe's Masquerade," for instance, Hawthorne introduces a key symbol of ancestral sin: the bloodstained ruff. The young Miss Joliffe, granddaughter of the old Colonel, who has the longest living memory at this event, asks her grandfather about the eminent men he seems to recognize as the governors and rulers of "the old original democracy of Massachusetts": "Why had that young man a stain of blood upon his ruff?" to which the grandfather answers: "Because in after-years . . . he laid down the wisest head in England upon the block for the principles of liberty" (IX, 248). As we shall see, it is a similar blood-stained ruff that marks the ancestral wrong of the Pyncheons in *The House of the Seven Gables.*

A fuller account of how Hawthorne develops these sartorial literary devices in his overall oeuvre is beyond the scope of this essay. However, it is important to note that in sketches like "Old News," Hawthorne makes links not only between textiles and time, but between textile, time, and text, as the old rags of newspapers resonate with the old rags of outmoded fashions. These themes, tropes, and motifs that he develops in his sketches come to be significant in his novels, particularly in *The House of the Seven Gables.*

THE COARSE AND THE FINE: VERNACULAR GENTILITY

Hawthorne identifies in the 1830s what Richard L. Bushman has more recently described as the refinement of America. Contrary even to some of his own representations of the gray or black puritan aesthetic, Hawthorne identifies a pre-revolutionary foppery, gaudiness, and flamboyance to which, presumably, the modern taste that militated against such foppery arose during the Revolution. Bushman has identified a paradox between republican ideals of equality and a generalized desire for refinement among a growing middle class. In *The Refinement of America*, he outlines an entire aesthetic (almost an ethic) of taste based on the dichotomy between smooth and rough, or fine and coarse: "People of the lower end of the scale wore rough homespun and coarse osnaburgs and fustians, establishing in effect a textural polarity between rough and smooth" (96). Hawthorne's narrator, in "Old News," reflects precisely this kind of binary between coarse and fine in examining the very material of the newsprint—both the *textual* and the *textural* polarity between rough and smooth. He extends this both to the roughness of the content (the writing) in some of these old newspapers and to the fineness of the clothes advertised in those pages. Cloth and paper were spoken of in the same ways as either coarse or fine.

Looking at the paper of the broadsheets of the revolutionary period, Hawthorne's narrator/authorial persona writes:

> The material of the sheet attracts our scorn. It is a fair specimen of rebel manufacture, thick and *coarse*, like wrapping-paper, all overspread with little knobs, and of such a deep, dingy blue color, that we wipe our spectacles thrice before we can distinguish a letter of

the wretched print. Thus, in all points, the newspaper is a *type of the times*, far more fit for the rough hands and democratic mob, than for our own *delicate*, though bony fingers. Nay; we will not handle it without gloves!" (XI, 155; emphasis added)

Hawthorne was already recognizing (as Henry James defended him as doing), problems contemporary to his time, not only part of the legendary history he outlines. A post-revolutionary American middle class pursues precisely the kind of refinement that the Americans of the Revolution eschewed. The democratic coarseness of the text (the type, the print, the paper) is contrasted with the vernacular gentility and refinement of the textile: the gloves that protect the delicate hands of Hawthorne's contemporaries.

A brief history of sumptuary law in North America, and particularly in New England, can show clearly the dynamic social tensions that accompanied the emergence of an American middle class whose ideological self-representation had to deal with the tension between the democratization of material access to affordable clothing and a lingering social hierarchy that aimed to govern apparent (and appareled) differences between social groups. According to Alan Hunt, "sumptuary regimes that were initiated in most . . . of the New World colonies were initiated at a time when the sumptuary impulse in Europe, and in particular in England, was showing sings of flagging" (38). For instance, in 1619 "the first representative assembly held in Massachusetts approved an enactment 'Against Idleness, Gaming, Drunkenness and Excess in Apparel.' . . . Much Sumptuary energy was directed against the interconnected evils of luxury, fashion, and dressing above one's rank" (Hunt 38–39). Important laws were passed in Puritan New England in 1638 and 1651, establishing prohibitions on "gold or silver lace, gold or silver buttons, silk hoods or scarves, and 'great boots' to those with annual income of less than £200" (39). These laws covered not only dress, but other forms of luxury and idleness, with a law against theatrical entertainment being passed as late as 1750. According to Hunt, the "sumptuary regime in some of the early New England colonies was premised on the belief in a natural society of rank that had been imported from Europe with its hierarchy intact, but stripped of its formally designated ranks" (102–103). Puritanism in New England retained a fairly "traditional view of the social order" (103).

Hunt goes on to say that sumptuary legislation arises when hierarchies come under pressure or are perceived to be fragile, and that it is precisely at the moment when feudal societies are in decline that such regimes against the threat of fashion and luxury run amok emerge. However, Hunt argues that these sumptuary regimes arrived too late, and that they were transformed, in many cases, through processes of modernization away from official public legislation and toward unofficial private governance. Relying on a Foucauldian view of governmentality and surveillance, Hunt argues that a kind of policing of one's neighbors emerged to replace written sumptuary laws that declined and were less frequently enforced. Hunt documents the gradual decline in sumptuary law enforcement in Massachusetts and Connecticut after a flurry of such cases brought mostly against women in the 1650s to their total disappearance by the middle 1700s. His key point in this discussion is that the enforcement of sumptuary legislation in New England was marked by the application of the laws intended to moderate the consumption and luxury of the upper classes to the merchants and artisans who dared to dress above their station—or, more precisely, whose wives dared to dress beyond their station.

Zakim claims that the "last historic attempt at legislative prescription on dress . . . was actually made at the Constitutional Convention" of 1787 where George Mason protested "the extravagance of our manners . . . and the necessity of restraining it'" (31–32). This concern never made its way out of committee, as it were, and did not, of course, make its way into the Constitution. However, what Zakim calls a "homespun ideology" did replace the sumptuary regimes of the Puritan past. By the early nineteenth century, the link between class and dress was not made in legislative and political discourse but in commercial and social discourse, and that link was no longer a sumptuary regime of stratification of class but rather a homespun ideology that linked simplicity in dress not to frugality but to the rewards of self-sufficiency. Quoting from New York's Society for the Promotion of Useful Arts, Zakim offers an emblematic statement from 1807 about the link between prosperity, patriotism, and fashion. According to this industrial and commercial organization, the independent American farmer "will take pride and pleasure in being dressed in clothes whose softness and pliancy give warmth to the body, and pleasure to the touch, and grace to the wearer. And they will be doubly proud of this, if it is the product of their own farms, and the industry of their wives and daughters" (32).

Thus, between the passage of sumptuary laws in Puritan New England in the 1650s and the commercial expression of a homespun ideology in the early nineteenth century, we witness a gradual shift from a threatened social order using religious and natural rank to ward off the pressures of social change from below to an ascendant commercial class using nationalistic rhetoric to espouse the emerging values of a new patriotic nationalism rewarded with the luxuries of fashionable simplicity.

As an emerging American middle class began to adopt vernacular gentility, writers like Hawthorne, whose own standing in society depended on earning a living rather than inheriting a fortune, began to represent the extremes of wealth and want, and to privilege a middle ground that avoided the extremes. But in order to retain a sense of social propriety, Hawthorne had to gesture to an aristocratic past. Vernacular refinement in the present was underwritten by a gesture toward the aristocratic refinement of ancestors in the past. Thus, in representing textiles through time, Hawthorne attempts to solve the dilemma of aristocratic refinement in an egalitarian society. By the time Hawthorne is writing about a fallen aristocracy in *The House of the Seven Gables*, the earlier distinctions between gentility and common folk—first established legally under English sumptuary laws in the sixteenth century and policed during Puritan times by strict differences in dress—had already begun to blur and disappear by the mid-eighteenth century. *The Scarlet Letter* is probably the most famous instance of Hawthorne's exploration of textile, as Hester's labor as seamstress gives her a certain power and access in the Puritan society. Hester "incurred no risk of want" because she could provide women and men of higher rank with "the finer production of her handiwork" (I, 82). Public events demanded refined clothes: "Deep ruffs, painfully wrought bands, and gorgeously embroidered gloves, were all deemed necessary to the official state of men assuming the reins of power; and were . . . allowed to individuals dignified by rank or wealth, even while sumptuary laws forbade these and similar extravagances to the plebian order" (I, 82). Given her talent with the needle that inscribes the text of her own sin, Hester provides the textiles of power: "There was a frequent and characteristic demand for such labor as Hester Pryne could supply" (I, 82). Hawthorne's novel perfectly exemplifies Bushman's historical arguments about the dichotomy between coarse and fine textiles as emblematic of a deeper and broader social distinction between coarse and fine culture, as Hester's own dress is "of the coarsest materials" and she provides "coarse garments for the poor" (I, 83). I would note here, as well, that his last published novel—*The Marble Faun*—included a long disquisition on the art of the needle and its place in the lives and character of women, suggesting that a "needle is familiar to the fingers of them all" (IV, 39).

FIGURE 2.3: *Paul Revere,* 1768. John Singleton Copley, American, 1738–1815. Oil on canvas, 89.22 x 72.39 cm (35⅛ x 28½ in.). Museum of Fine Arts, Boston. Gift of Joseph W. Revere, William B. Revere, and Edward H. R. Revere. 30.781. *Photograph* © 2014 *Museum of Fine Arts, Boston.* (Plate 2.)

In *Fanshawe* as well, Hawthorne observes the contrast between refined and coarse society but examines it in a much more contemporary context, already taking note of the blurring of the lines so clearly drawn in the sumptuary laws of the Puritan era. As Bushman puts it, "Despite . . . ingrained distinctions, the visitor walking up High Street in Philadelphia in the middle of the eighteenth century might not always have been able to distinguish commoners from genteel people of fashion. Plain people doubtless fell heir to clothing once worn by ladies and gentlemen, and the irresistible urge to emulate people in power moved lesser men and women to wear cheaper or shabbier versions of fashionable dress" (98). In introducing the students of Harley College, Hawthorne notes the distinctions between the "rustic dress" of the new arrivals and the "more classic cut" of "those who had begun *to acquire* the polish" that the college would import to them (III, 335; emphasis added). In fact, the balance of refined and rustic dress is the measure of the length of the student's residence at college. The "union of classic and rural dress" showed that a young man had "but lately become a student of Harley" (III, 381). The historical distinctions of sumptuary laws explored in *The Scarlet Letter* and the contemporary intermingling of styles observed in *Fanshawe* are brought together in the foreshortened historical narrative of *The House of the Seven Gables*, which explores the historical shift from sartorial hierarchy to democratization of dress, resolving the dilemma in the hybrid costume of one of its central characters, Uncle Venner, as I shall discuss below. Hawthorne's attention to the representations of dress in both portraiture and statuary (or at least engraved figures) bears some commentary here, as it relies on the same kind of representation that historians rely on. Indeed, Richard L. Bushman's own study of refinement in America must turn to images painted to faithfully represent not merely the sartorial and physical presence of the subject but the person's social standing. For example, in analyzing a John Singleton Copley portrait of Paul Revere (fig. 2.3), Bushman comments on the unbuttoned waistcoat as a sign of democratic dress. Revere's lack of refinement in the portrait is intentionally affected to signal an egalitarian ideal opposed to gentility, an ideological position conveyed through dress and posture:

> A coatless man with a free-flowing shirt and an unbuttoned vest would be instantly identified as a tradesman or a laborer, never a gentleman. The flowing shirt or smock freed the arms to reach, lift, and swing, as was necessary for the work of commoners but un-

necessary and unsuitable for gentry. A gentleman would no more appear with his vest unbuttoned than he would laugh aloud with mouth wide open. Copley pictured Paul Revere with his shirt loose on his body, his vest open, with no coat to confine his shoulders, and so stripped him of all pretensions to gentility, at least for the purpose of the picture. (Bushman 66)

By contrast, we can see how Hawthorne identifies buttoned vestments as the sign of refinement in a journal entry on September 7, 1835, in which he describes traveling to Ipswich, Massachusetts, where he sees the one-third life-size monument of Reverend Nathaniel Rogers, down to the representation of his dress in nice detail. Hawthorne, in fact, lingers on the minute detail in which the reverend's buttons had been carved. What is most interesting about his observation is that it comes shortly after he has noted the disheveled dress—at the bosom—of a woman who greets them at one of the local homes: "a dark old house" (VIII, 9). First, he points to the informal dress of the contemporary woman, in the flesh: "Walking about town, we knocked, for a whim, at the door of a dark old house, and inquired if Miss Hannah Lord lived there. A woman of about thirty came to the door, with rather a confused smile, and *a disorder about the bosom of her dress*, as if she had been disturbed while nursing her child. She answered us with great kindness" (VIII, 9; emphasis added).

By contrast to this disheveled woman in the present, Hawthorne presents us with the very tightly bound bosom of the formally dressed man of the past, Reverend Rogers (fig. 2.4):

Entering the burial-ground, where some masons were building a tomb, we found a good many old monuments, and several covered slabs of red freestone or slate, and with arms sculptured on the slab, or an inlaid circle of slate. On one slate grave-stone, of the Rev. Nathl. Rogers, there was a portrait of that worthy, about a third of the size of life, carved in relief, with his *cloak, band, and wig*, in excellent preservation, all the *buttons of his waistcoat being cut with great minuteness. . . .*" (VIII, 9; emphasis added)

Hawthorne comments on this ability of the skilled sculptor to capture sartorial detail in his later work, when in *The Marble Faun* he acknowledges the skill of sculptors who are able to render "the nice carving of buttonholes, shoe-ties, coat-seams, shirt-bosoms, and other such graceful peculiarities of modern

FIGURE 2.4: Detailed close-up of colonial tombstone. Rev. Nathaniel Rogers, Ipswich, MA, ca. 1700. Photographic print image of colonial tombstone, Library of Congress Prints and Photographs Division, photo by Allan Ludwig, [195-?]. *Used with permission of Allan Ludwig.*

costume" in contrast to the flowing lines of ancient nude sculpture (IV, 135). The foci of Hawthorne's attention in this passage from his journals translate well into a reading of his novels. He is concerned, on the one hand, with the realities of everyday domestic life in his own time. The "dark old house," the woman's "confused look," and the "great kindness" she shows, despite her confusion: these are images that will reappear in *The House of the Seven Gables.* At the same time, the "old monuments" of the graveyard, and the access that the carved relief of Reverend Rogers gives him to the spirit of the past also animate some of the narrative concerns in *House*. Most importantly, we have the "disorder about the bosom of [the woman's] dress" contrasted with the tightly buttoned bosom of the antiquated "worthy." These same dual and overlapping contrasts between different forms of dress and different historical eras are central to *House*'s storyline.

Old and New Clothes in *The House of the Seven Gables*

By the 1840s the contrasts Hawthorne observed between then and now and between different classes had begun to converge. In the period that spans the Revolution to the first half of the nineteenth century, understatement was increasingly the key element of New England men's fashions. This understatement was a sign of refinement: "A bright silk suit on an ordinary Boston merchant would have been a breach of good taste and decidedly ungenteel. The wearer of the plain brown suit was no less genteel for this lack of color. The principle of gentility almost required that the use of bright colors should be more restrained in the clothing of the American gentry, who, by English standards, were only upper-middle-class" (Bushman 95). It is this social standing—upper middle class—that Hawthorne explores in *The House of the Seven Gables* as two ancestral lines approach it from opposite ends of the social divide. The Pyncheons and the Maules establish an early divide, one wrought by injustice but sustained both by continued injustice and by a kind of New England noblesse oblige that anticipates its Southern variant in William Faulkner's "A Rose for Emily." While condemning the original sin, Hawthorne seems to want to salvage a contemporary nobility that he wishes to place squarely in the "upper middle class," a class formed by the downward movement of the Pyncheons toward mercantilism in the form of Hepzibah's general store, and also shaped by the Maules' upward mobility into art, technology, and reform in the person of Holgrave, the daguerreotypist whose modern idiosyncrasies are laughable, but whose philosophy of mobility (both physical and social) is laudable.

Both of these extremes—the old wealth gotten through murder and lies, and the new ideas emerging out of technical innovation and social heterodoxy—are represented through clothes. The dress of Judge Pyncheon is not simply represented as refined, but as anachronistically aristocratic, a remnant, so to speak, of the Puritan dress of old Colonel Pyncheon visible in his portrait. By contrast, Holgrave's clothes are modern, overly simple, and ill fitting. Somewhere between these two lies the hybrid sartorial style of Uncle Venner, a Pyncheon relative who avoids both his ancestors' pretense to privilege as well as the uprooted reform of Holgrave. As a man marked by the patches on his clothes, Venner avoids falling into either of the two extremes by patching together elements from both.

Hawthorne carefully outlines the historical social divide in *The House of the Seven Gables* through careful attention to dress: "Velvet garments, somber but rich, stiffly plaited ruffs and bands, embroidered gloves, venerable beards, the mien and countenance of authority, made it easy to distinguish the gentleman of worship, at that period, from the tradesman, with his plodding air, or the laborer, in his leathern jerkin, stealing awe-stricken into the house which he had perhaps helped to build" (II, 12).

The wealthy class of this Puritan past is, it is clear, marked not by gaudy ostentation but by fashionable understatement that draws attention to the richness and fineness of the clothes, rather than their showiness. By contrast, the "laborer" is marked by a "leather jerkin," underscoring his acquaintance with the coarseness of life.

Hawthorne's use of clothing to establish the broad social contours of the past is matched by his use of dress at the very heart—both symbolically and narratologically—of this novel: the stain of blood on the ruff of the ancestor, a motif already established in "Howe's Masquerade." In *The House of the Seven Gables* he presents this image early in the story:

> A little boy—the Colonel's grandchild, and the only human being that ever dared to be familiar with him—now made his way among the guests, and ran toward the seated figure; then pausing halfway, he began to shriek with terror. The company, tremulous as the leaves of a tree, when all are shaking together, drew nearer, and perceived that there was an unnatural distortion in the fixedness of Colonel Pyncheon's stare; that there was *blood on his ruff*, and that his hoary beard was saturated with it. . . . The ironhearted Puritan, the relentless persecutor, the grasping and strong-willed man, was dead! Dead, in this new house! (II, 15–16; emphasis added).

The "little boy" is, of course, Clifford, who will bear the trauma of having seen his grandfather dead. The ruff is a key sign of wealth and distinction, but it is marred by the wearer's desire to accumulate material wealth. It reappears in the long, almost still-life passage that describes Judge Jaffrey Pyncheon's corpse sitting in the empty Pyncheon house after Clifford and Hepzibah have fled. And in establishing this sin-stained past of the Pyncheons, he also establishes the poverty-stricken history of the Maules, again using dress as its emblem: "The mantle, or rather the ragged cloak, of old Matthew Maule had fallen upon his children," and, of course, among these descendants is Holgrave, whose talent as a daguerreotypist might be the manifestation of the Maule "family eye [which] was said to possess strange power" (II, 26).

The clothing of Hawthorne's characters in *The House of the Seven Gables* points toward the past. Most of these figures are prisoners of the past, and their clothes show it. Judge Jaffrey, Clifford, and Hepzibah Pyncheon are dressed in garments that reduce them to ghosts, out of place in a culture of rapidly changing fashions. Holgrave and the deceased Jaffrey, junior—the estranged and "dissipated" son of the Judge whom we see only fleetingly in the novel—represent a younger generation of men. Each is dressed in a variant of more modern dress, with reform-minded Holgrave in the "ill-fitting" manner of American reformers and degenerate young aristocrat Jaffrey in imitation of European styles. Holgrave's modern dress distances him from the past only, however, to disconnect him from the grounding gravity of history. It is a seemingly secondary character—Uncle Venner—who embodies in his garments the perfect melding of privileged past and populist present. He is both venerable and avuncular, and his clothes weave past with present as well as refinement with equality.

In describing Judge Jaffrey Pyncheon's underlying guilt as something "covered up" by the "splendid rubbish" of his life, Hawthorne offers a long list of habits, actions, social positions, and accouterments—in a brilliant syntactical train of clauses—associated with the wealthy descendent of Colonel Pyncheon. This manifestation of all the things that hide the sin and ease the conscience of the Judge includes his "judicial character," his "public service," his presidency of the Bible society, his interest in horticulture, his forgiveness of his "dissipated son" on the son's deathbed, and, in one of the longest clauses of this complex and compound sentence, his clothes (II, 230–31). Garments allow Judge Pyncheon "to cover up" his guilt: "the snowy whiteness of his linen, the polish of his boots, the handsomeness of his gold-headed cane, the square and roomy fashion of his coat, and the fineness of its material, and, in general, the studied propriety of his dress and equipment" are key material expressions of the "splendid rubbish" that helps him deal with the sin of his fathers and his own injustices toward others, including his own brother,

Clifford (II, 231). Clearly, these clothes exemplify the kind of refinement Bushman identifies with an old American aristocracy (and a newly forming middle-class who aspired to it). The white linen, the "polish" of the boots reflecting the polish of manners, and the material "fineness" of the coat embodying the presumed fineness of character and breeding. However, this is a fineness of the past. This is a refinement paid for by an old American privilege that the novel challenges by associating that privilege with a ghostly history that haunts the present.

Most importantly, this inherited refinement is stained—literally and metaphorically—with blood. In the chapter that describes Judge Pyncheon's death in a macabre tableaux vivant, Hawthorne uses two motifs that run not only through the novel but that he had already experimented with in sketches that demonstrate his awareness of dress and its social significance: a blood-stained ruff and a parade of costumed characters, and, in particular, ghostly figures. Both these images, again, historicize dress and its cultural implications. Hawthorne describes Judge Pyncheon sitting stock still in the Pyncheon house now temporarily deserted by his siblings, Hepzibah and Clifford. He is expected at a dinner held by his political supporters, who want to see him elected governor so that he can protect their wealth. The narrator speculates as to the reaction of this dinner party if Judge Pyncheon were to arrive in his current state: "Neither would it be seemly in Judge Pyncheon, generally so scrupulous in his attire, to show himself at a dinner table with that crimson stain upon his shirt bosom" (II, 275). Not only does Hawthorne revive this image first introduced in "Howe's Masquerade" and connected in this novel to Pyncheon's ancestors Colonel and Gervayse Pyncheon, but he also uses one of the key signifiers (second, perhaps, only to snow-white linen) of refinement in the eighteenth and nineteenth century: the neatly buttoned coat or waistcoat: "the wisest way for the Judge is to button his coat closely over his breast" (II, 275). Recalling perhaps, among other things, the image of Reverend Nathaniel Rogers on his tombstone, Hawthorne imagines a specific and dated symbol of refinement and propriety: the buttoned coat that would cover up any stain, including that of guilt.

Hawthorne also uses in the same chapter of *The House of the Seven Gables*, titled "Governor Pyncheon," a narrative contrivance he deploys elsewhere—including "Howe's Masquerade," "Old News," and "Main Street"—that is, a parade of characters from distant and recent historical periods to show both continuity and change. In this case it is a parade of Pyncheons from the Colonel himself to the dissipated son of the Judge, all of them dead. And as with these and earlier uses of the motif, the characters are to be recognized by their clothes: "First comes the ancestor, in his black cloak, steeple hat, and trunk breeches, girt about the waist with a leathern belt, in which hangs the steel hilted sword" (II, 279). Hawthorne's parade of Pyncheons continues with "aged men and granddames, a clergyman with the Puritanic stiffness still in his garb and mien, and a red-coated officer of the old French War" (II, 279). These two periods—the Puritan past and the more recent wars with the French—also figure in the earlier sketches. There is also the "shopkeeping Pyncheon of a century ago, with the ruffles turned back from his wrists" (II, 279). We see Gervayse, the "periwigged and brocaded gentleman" of Holgrave's story told in an earlier chapter (II, 280). Even Matthew Maule makes an appearance in "leather jerkin and breeches" (II, 280). The temporality and historicity of these ghostly figures is shown clearly through their dress. Textile and time serve the narrative purpose Hawthorne wants to pursue. The significance of this time-bound representation is brought home when the narrator describes the one exception to these historical ghosts: the very modern clothing of Judge Pyncheon's dead heir. The narrator points out that among "those ancestral people there is a young man, dressed in the very fashion of today: he wears a dark frock coat, almost destitute of skirts, gray pantaloons, gaiter boots of patent leather . . ." (II, 280). The appearance of young Jaffrey Pyncheon Jr., the Judge's "only surviving child," confirms that, in fact, his is not a surviving child at all because he walks among these ghosts. The absence of long skirts for his coat, and his pantaloons, which had come to replace breeches by the late eighteenth and early nineteenth centuries, captures the historical moment. Finally, this dance macabre concludes with the Judge himself, whom we recognize not only by the crimson stain on his neckcloth but by the slightly antiquated style of his clothes: "Can we believe our eyes?" asks the narrator. "A stout, elderly gentleman has made his appearance; he . . . wears a black coat and pantaloons, of roomy width, and might be pronounced scrupulously neat in his attire, but for the broad crimson stain across the snowy neckcloth and down his shirt-bosom" (II, 280). The width and roominess of Judge Pyncheon's clothes suggest that he has a slightly dated wardrobe, as the styles of the early nineteenth century tended toward a fitted cut, both in frock coats and pantaloons. Judge Pyncheon has entered a world of garments and ghosts.

If Judge Pyncheon's clothes hint at antiquity, Clifford Pyncheon's are downright old fashioned. As he approaches the Judge and his sister, Hepzibah, who stand talking in Hepzibah's shop earlier in the novel, Clifford appears out of place and out of time. The narrator describes him from Hepzibah's point of view: She seemed to behold his gray, wrinkled, yet childlike aspect, in the old-fashioned garments which he wore about the house" (II, 247). Clifford is described as dressed in a "cloak—a garment of long ago" (II, 250). Though very much alive, he seems as ghostly in these clothes as those we see later in the parade of dead Pyncheons. His and Hepzibah's clothes seem especially out of place on the train, and it is here that they become self-conscious of their outmoded and displaced selves. Hepzibah suffers from the "womanish and old-maiden-like misery arising from a sense of unseemliness in her attire" (II, 255). Interestingly, Hepzibah begins to disappear entirely behind her clothing: she hopes that she can make "people suppose that here was only a cloak and hood, threadbare and woefully faded, taking an airing in the midst of the storm, without any wearer!" (II, 255). These descriptions give us a vision of Hepzibah and Clifford as they are leaving the House of the Seven Gables and heading toward the train. Their faded, threadbare, and aged dress becomes abundantly clear in their contrast to modern accelerated technologies and cultures.

In introducing Hepzibah, Hawthorne's narrative links time with clothes. Hawthorne does this by representing dress through three temporal images. The first is the image of Hepzibah in the present, but with signs of decline in her dress. The second is the image of her brother Clifford in the past: a miniature portrait of him in the style of Edward Greene Malbone, which the narrator describes with careful attention to the artist's representation of dress. Thirdly, another portrait represents Colonel Pyncheon, the original patriarch of the dynasty, which is decorated with some of the same fashions (including Bible and sword) that Hawthorne uses elsewhere, as in *The Scarlet Letter*, to signal New England's questionable origins. These images underscore the relationship between textile and time; they chart the decline of gentility and the concomitant rise of a middle class, or vernacular gentility.

First, as Hepzibah prepares for her first day as a shopkeeper she must earn a living through mercantile trade rather than inherit wealth and refinement. She is characterized by "a rustling of stiff silks," the stiffness of the silk indicating, perhaps, its age and decay (II, 31). The narrator asks, "How can we elevate our history of retribution for the sin of *long ago*, when, as one of our most prominent figures, we are compelled to introduce—not a young and lovely woman, nor even the stately *remains* of beauty, storm-shattered by affliction—but a gaunt, sallow, *rusty-jointed* maiden, in a *long-waisted silk gown*, and with the strange *horror of a turban on her head!*" (II, 41; emphasis added). Not only does this passage contrast the decayed present with the "long ago," it does so through the materiality and metaphor of clothing: the long-waisted silk gown, the horror of the turban—an image that is repeated throughout the novel as an indicator of Hepzibah's decline, but in some instances as a sign of her ultimate survival, like the hens that populate her garden. In the act of setting up shop, Hepzibah displays the signs of declining gentility, of aristocratic decline in the rise of democratic values.

While Hepzibah is the epitome of a decaying gentility, Judge Jaffrey Pyncheon, the more direct heir of both the Pyncheon fortune and the Pyncheon sin, is marked by a fastidiously preserved gentility in the face of democratizing social and material changes. Despite the growth of a vernacular gentility, Judge Pyncheon wishes to hold on to a persistent aristocracy. This is expressed through descriptions of his clothes:

> He himself, in a very different style, was as well worth looking at as the house. No better model need be sought, nor could have been found of a very high order of respectability, which, by some indescribable magic, not merely expressed itself in his looks and gestures, but even *governed the fashion of his garments*, and rendered them all proper and essential to the man. Without appearing to differ, in any tangible way, from other people's clothes, there was yet a wide and rich gravity about them that must have been characteristic of the wearer since it could not be defined as pertaining either to the cut or material. (II, 56; emphasis added)

Although Hawthorne seems to be attributing a kind of magic to Pyncheon's oneness with his clothes, there may be something more mundane at work. This might be what Bushman refers to as "polish" or "finish." Bushman argues that acquiring expensive (or expensive-looking) garments was not enough to give the wearer the kind of distinction associated with gentility. The carriage of the body, the manners in movement and action were as important, and this may be what Hawthorne is getting at when he says that "a wide and rich gravity about [the clothes] must have been characteristic of the wearer."

Along with Hepzibah's actual and present-day poverty and Jaffrey's refinement, the narrator also presents a vivid image of earlier wealth by referring to a miniature portrait of Clifford, Hepzibah's brother, who seems to suffer from what we might today call Alzheimer's. The image—described as "done in Malbone's most perfect style"—indicates social standing through dress: "It is a likeness of a young man, in a *silken dressing gown of an old fashion*, the *soft richness* of which is well adapted to the countenance of reverie, with its full, tender lips, and beautiful eyes, that seem to indicate not so much capacity of thought as gentle and voluptuous emotion" (II, 31; emphasis added).

The miniature portrait Hawthorne describes might have been similar to the one of Dr. Elisha Poinsett, in which Malbone pays careful attention to the form and even texture of the linen around Dr. Poinsett's throat (fig. 2.5). This would have been a key indication of refinement and genteel standing. Like this image, the one of Clifford reflects what Bushman has associated with "refinement" in America. The soft richness of the silken dressing gown is the outward and material emblem of a deeper refinement achieved through a "capacity for thought."

In contrast to the decaying refinement of Hepzibah, Jaffrey, and Clifford, Hawthorne presents the emerging fashion of Holgrave. The antiquated dress of Colonel Pyncheon, seen not only in a dimming portrait but also in the dimming person of Judge Pyncheon; the modern dress of Holgrave, who mistakes the old with the useless; and Uncle Venner, whose patched and mended clothes indicate a third way that attempts to retain the old along with the new. Holgrave's class trajectory has been the opposite of Hepzibah's and Clifford's. Their ancestral wealth is in decline, whereas Holgrave is upwardly mobile, and linked to a new form of technology that can be contrasted to the portraits in Hepzibah's rooms. As a man rising up into the middle class, and a man whose ideological position might be characterized as that of a "reformer," at least in so far as he speaks against inherited wealth, he potentially challenges an old social stability. Holgrave's reform-mindedness, even his radicalism, can be contrasted to Venner's more measured ideology of social evolution rather than revolution. Holgrave's social and ideological position is made manifest through reference to his clothes: "As for [Holgrave's] dress, it was of the simplest kind; a summer sack of cheap and ordinary material, thin checkered pantaloons, and a straw hat, by no means of the finest braid. *Oak Hall* might have supplied his entire equipment. He was chiefly marked as a gentleman—if such, indeed, he made any claim to be—by the rather remarkable *whiteness and nicety of his clean linen*" (II, 43; emphasis added). Here Hawthorne is clearly aware that

FIGURE 2.5: *Dr. Elisha Poinsett* by Edward Greene Malbone.
Smithsonian American Art Museum, Bequest of Mary Elizabeth Spencer.
(Plate 3.)

the emerging clothing stores—the early precursors of the grand department stores of the later nineteenth century—were beginning to sell and in some cases manufacture cheap clothing. Not quite as low in the scale of men's fashions as slop shops, stores like Oak Hall manufactured cheap garments for the middle and lower middle classes. An Oak Hall advertisement from this period gives a sense of the kind of men's clothing, and perhaps even the kind of

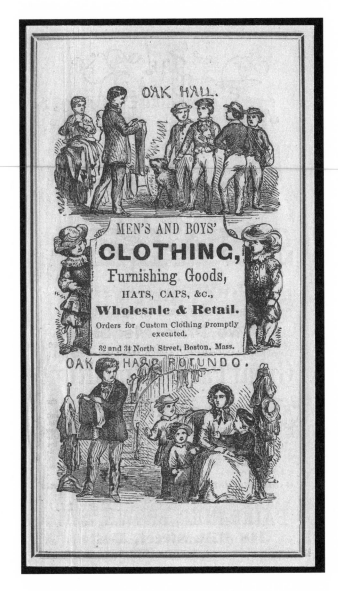

FIGURE 2.6: Oak Hall advertisement from Boston Almanac, 1854, reproduced in George W. Simmons, *Oak Hall Pictorial* ("Respectfully Dedicated to the Juvenile Patrons of Oak Hall"), Boston: Damrell & Moore, Printers, 1854. *Collection of Richard Sheaff.*

clientele, associated with this new kind of establishment (fig. 2.6). Holgrave's pantaloons, reminiscent of the ones Mother Rigby puts on old Feather-top in Hawthorne's story by that name—as opposed to breeches or trousers—are an important indication that he was acquiring refined tastes (Waugh 116), but they are also important in that they are available to him through a place like Oak Hall. His dress is the epitome of vernacular gentility and middle-class aspirations to refinement.

Most important, Hawthorne points to one of the key sartorial indicators of refinement and gentility in the seventeenth and eighteenth centuries: clean white linen. As Bushman puts it in his history of vernacular gentility: "The genteel . . . were required to wear clean, fine linen at throat and wrists." Bushman, relying in the twentieth century on the same portraits as primary sources for his history that Hawthorne consulted to write his novel, turns to images of the American middle class to support his claim: "Every male and female portrait shows fine white fabric at these points" (95). Writing about the Ridgely family of Delaware who provide the case study for his history, Bushman writes that "although Nicholas Ridgely had only two suits when he died, he had nine fine Holland shirts." Even George Washington is noted to have "packed nine white shirts and white stockings" on a visit to Belvoir. Bushman writes that the "genteel image required fine white fabric where skin met suit or dress, revealing that the immaculate body was covered by a film of white cloth" (95). Thus, Hawthorne's characterization of Holgrave as a gentleman requires certain material emblems, and the key sartorial emblem of refinement is the "remarkable whiteness and nicety of his clean linen."

However, the way Holgrave wears linen, and its sociocultural implications in the early nineteenth century, point to a certain ambiguity of the fabric's social meanings. The linen trade, a global phenomenon involving Indian and African raw materials, Irish and Scottish production as well as global markets, including American import, served both cloth and paper production needs. Linen production spans the personal and global. Clean, white linen was the mark of English and American gentility, and it was also the result of a global political economy. Strikingly, in his 1864 history of linen, *The Linen Trade: Ancient and Modern*, Dundee merchant Alex J. Ward devotes only a few pages to the American linen trade: "There are more linens used in the United States, in proportion to the population, than in almost any other country" (345), and yet "the greater portion of linens consumed being imported" (346). Writing during the Civil War, Ward was aware that linen consumption in the United States had spiked in 1862 as a result of the war, and the question of the future remained open. What was clear to him was that in the first half of the century, the United States was not producing linen independently but was part of global colonialist networks. By drawing attention to fine linens, Hawthorne points to the fact that the United States was anything but independent. Linen was mostly imported rather than produced domestically in the United States well into the middle of the nineteenth century, because flax was raised mostly for its seed, making it poorly suited for textile production (Ward 346). Thus, wearing linen was not an indication of American independence from old world aristocracy or London foppery as Hawthorne explores elsewhere. Even though Holgrave's linen might have looked rakishly ill fitting in a kind of anti-aristocratic way, it was materially *not* connected with American notions of democratized dress.

By the same token, despite his acquired gentlemanliness, Holgrave is also associated with a certain subset of the emerging middle class, whose outlandish style undermined whatever might have been positive in their ameliorative outlook on the present and future. Holgrave is described as associating with "men with long beards and dressed in linen blouses, and other such newfangled and ill-fitting garments" (II, 84). These men, from Hepzibah's point of view in her declining gentility, are "reformers, temperance lecturers, and all manner of cross-looking philanthropists; community-men, and come-outers, as Hepziabah believed, who acknowledged no law, and ate no solid food, but lived on the scent of other peoples cookery, and turned up their noses at the fare" (II, 84).

The newfangled and ill-fitting garments these men wear reflect what Nicola Nixon has identified as the debate over the "dandiacal body" emerging out of the publication, with Ralph Waldo Emerson's help, of Thomas Carlyle's *Sartor Resartus*. Carlyle's book, along with Thackeray's essay, "Men and Coats," "took aim at the sneering of unapologetic, exclusivist Regency aristocrats at the middle classes" (Nixon, 363). Emerson was eager, Nixon suggests, to make available what he saw as "Carlyle's assault on the tyranny of fashion" (363), and so anything that challenged the requirements that a certain kind of linen had to be worked with a certain kind of silk or broadcloth, would have resonated for this reformist viewpoint. To wear a linen blouse rather than a linen shirt under outer garments was to upset certain forms and manners that the "middle class was . . . busy codifying . . . [for] correct genteel society" (364). What the emerging middle class in the American North, in particular, wanted to convey was that "refinement was far more likely to be a product of cultivation and self-fashioning than to be the result of birth" (363).

The "reformers" and "temperance lecturers" Holgrave associates with are reminiscent of the utopianists Hawthorne describes in *The Blithedale Romance*. Like Holgrave's linen-bloused company, the communitarians at Blithedale, from Miles Coverdale's point of view, are identifiable not just by their clothes but by their attitude toward clothes:

Arcadians though we were, our *costume* bore no resemblance to the be-ribboned doublets, silk breeches and stockings, and slippers fastened with artificial roses, that distinguished the pastoral people of poetry and stage. In outward show, I humbly conceive, we looked rather like *a gang of beggars* or banditti, than either a company of honest laboring men or an enclave of philosophers. Whatever might be our points of difference, we all of us seemed to have come to Blithedale with one thrifty and laudable *ideal of wearing out our clothes.* (III, 63; emphasis added)

This notion of wanting to wear out one's clothes not only echoes an earlier statement Coverdale makes about changing clothes, it echoes Henry David Thoreau's comments on changing clothes in Walden. Hawthorne writes, in *The Blithedale Romance*:

The very substance upon my bones had not been fit to live with, in any better, truer, or more energetic mode than that of which I was accustomed. So it was taken off me [by illness] and flung aside, *like any other worn out unseasonable garment*; and after shivering a little while in my skeleton, I began to *be clothed anew*, and much more *satisfactorily than in my previous suit.* In literal and physical truth, I was quite another man. (III, 61; emphasis added)

As Thoreau puts it in *Walden*: "Perhaps we should never procure a new suit, however ragged or dirty the old, until we have so conducted, so enterprised or sailed in some way, that we feel like new men in the old, and that to retain it would be like keeping new wine in old bottles" (278). Hawthorne presents Coverdale's commentary as a satire of the Thoreauvean ideal:

Coats with high collars, and with no collars, broad-shirted or swallow-tailed, and with the waist at every point between the hip and armpit; pantaloons of a dozen successive epochs, and greatly defaced at the knees by the humiliations of the wearer before his lady-love;—in short, we were a living *epitome of defunct fashions*, and the very *raggedest* presentment of men who had seen better days. Often retaining a scholarlike or clerical air, you might have taken us for the denizens of Grub-street, intent on getting a comfortable livelihood by agricultural labor; or Coleridge's projected Pantisocracy, in full experiment; or Candide and his motly associates, at work in their cabbage-garden; or anything else that was miserably *out at elbows*, and most clumsily patched in the rear. We might have been sworn comrades to Falstaff's ragged regiment. Little skill as we boasted in other points of husbandry, every mother's son of us would have served admirably to stitch up for a scarecrow. And the worst of the matter was, that the first energetic movement essential to one downright stroke of labor, was sure to put a finish to these poor habiliments. So we gradually flung them all aside, and took honest homespun and linsey-woolsey, as preferable, on the whole, to the plan recommended, I think, by Virgil—'Ara nudus; sere nudus'—which, as Silas Foster remarked when I translated the maxim, would be apt to astonish the women-folks. (III, 63–64; emphasis added)

If Holgrave, as T. Walter Herbert has suggested, "envisions a wholesale social renovation" (91) in the style of Jacksonian progressivism, then Hawthorne must be presenting this at least in part as a lampoon of radical notions of reform that destroyed the virtues of the past in their attack on the sins of the past.

For Hawthorne, the spatial relationship of social classes above and below is transposed onto the temporal relationship of past and future, with the Pyncheon household in the aristocratic past and Holgrave in some utopian democratic future. In the story that he tells (a distinctly Hawthornian narrative device of a placing a fantastic legend within a realistic novel that he also employs in *The Blithedale Romance* with the Fauntleroy story), Holgrave's tale includes references to the past that are repressive of the present and haunt his characters. In the story that Holgrave tells Phoebe Pyncheon, one destined for the pages of *Godey's* or *Graham's*, he describes objects that map time onto class. Again, dress is key to this temporal mapping of class: "There were two objects that appeared rather out of place in this very handsomely furnished room. . . . a large map, or surveyor's plan . . . dingy with smoke . . ." and "a portrait of a stern old man, in a Puritan garb, painted roughly but with a bold effect and a remarkably strong expression of character" (II, 193). The man in the portrait is Gervayse Pyncheon, and his "coat was of blue velvet, with lace on the borders and at the button holes; and the firelight glistened on the spacious breadth of his waistcoat, which was flowered all over with gold" (II, 194).

Fashion historian Norah Waugh describes the waistcoat as "the most decorative article of men's nineteenth century dress." For eveningwear, waistcoats were black or white, and so a flowered waistcoat would have seemed ostentatious to Hawthorne's readers. T. Walter Herbert describes this as "effeminate" dress, presenting a "denatured manhood" in contrast to Matthew Maule as the "manly man" (92). The ostentatious refinement of the past haunts the modestly dressed people of the present. In contrast to the ill-fitting linen of Holgrave and company, the velvets and silks of these portraits indicates excess. The tale focuses on the image of Alice Pyncheon, an earlier cousin in the family, who is put into a mesmeric trance by Matthew Maule, becoming a "telescopic medium" (II, 206). Alice, while in a trance or "telescopic medium," sees three figures: first, an "aged, dignified, stern-looking gentleman, clad as for a solemn festival in *grave and costly attire*, but with a great *bloodstain on his richly wrought band*." Second, "an aged man, *meanly dressed*, with a dark and malign countenance, and a *broken halter* about his neck." And third, "a person not so advanced in life as the former two, but beyond the middle age, wearing a *coarse woolen tunic* and leather breeches, and with a carpenter's rule sticking out of his side pocket" (II, 207; emphasis added). The sartorial signs of social standing are clear. "Costly attire" is clear enough, but the "richly wrought band" is an even more specific indication of social class.

Holgrave sees the future trapped by these lingering elements of the past, particularly architectural manifestations of the past—the house of the title. In arguing against real estate dictating destiny, Holgrave contrasts shelter from clothing. The narrator explains that "the true value of [Holgrave's] character lay in that deep consciousness of inward strength, which made all his past vicissitudes seem merely like a change of garments" (II, 180). This notion of experience and change over time seeming like a "change of garments" is reinforced by the contrast between shelter and clothing, between home and habiliments that Holgrave outlines for Phoebe: why do we hold on to real estate (home as property) for generations, when we would never dream of passing down our shirts and pants from one generation to the next? As Holgrave says later, "We shall live to see the day, I trust . . . when no man shall build his house for posterity. Why should he? He might just as reasonably order a durable suit of clothes—leather, or gutta-percha, or whatever lasts longest—so that his great-grandchildren should have the benefit of them, and cut precisely the same figure in the world that he himself does" (II, 183). We change our clothes; we should likewise change our homes. This brings us back to the acceleration of social life in Hawthorne's time. The accelerated mode of life, in some respects, brought the United States more fully into its promise. However, it is not entirely clear if Hawthorne advocates a Holgravian view of the world. In fact, I would argue that between the backward-looking Jaffrey and the forward-leaning Holgrave lies a third way charted by Uncle Venner.

An Epitome of Times and Fashions: Uncle Venner's Patches

While a figure like Holgrave might have been championed by someone like Emerson, that character was the creation of Hawthorne who was less inclined to follow the utopian and egalitarian claims of the middle-class reformer, as he makes clear in his critique of the philanthropist's dogma in his portrait of Hollingsworth in *The Blithedale Romance.* Holgrave, though far less dogmatic than Hollingsworth, still has certain viewpoints that lead him to abstraction. Holgrave, for one thing, is militantly dismissive of the past: "It seemed to Holgrave . . . [as to the hopeful] that in this age, more than ever before, the *moss-grown* and *rotten past* is to be torn down, and lifeless institutions to be thrust out of the way, and their dead corpses buried, and everything to begin anew" (II, 179; emphasis added).

Holgrave is like other young men of his generation who seem so promising but who fade and make nothing of themselves: "Like certain chintzes, calicoes, and ginghams, they show finely in their finest newness, but cannot stand the sun and rain, and assume a very sober aspect after washing day" (II, 181). Hawthorne might have made this observation based on some of the cheaper types of cloth coming onto the American market in the 1820s and beyond, as competition between ready-made shops pushed merchants to produce in increasing quantity. Holgrave embodies, perhaps, the kind of person Walt Whitman imagined in *Song of Myself:* an individual who is "not contained between hat and boots." Whitman writes, "I see through the broadcloth and gingham," suggesting that he saw through "the stale and discarded" elements of culture to the natural body (34). The analogy between Holgrave and cloth reflects the transformations of men's dress that Hawthorne so closely observed throughout his writing career. Indeed, the specific types of prefabricated cloth to which Hawthorne compares Holgrave was flooding the market in the first half of the nineteenth century. "In the fall of 1826," explains Michael Zakim, "the market was flooded with English blue cloths, 'beautiful to the eye,' [but] which turned reddish brown after a few days exposure to the air." This was not lost on contemporary commentators on the industry: "It was representative of the general state of things, protested *Niles' Weekly Register*, a situation that victimized American tailors who were then 'compelled to take back the clothes made of these goods' . . ." (Zakim, 46). Hawthorne was well aware of these compromises in quality and saw them as an apt metaphor for the compromised characters of many of his own generation. In those decades between the 1830s and the 1860s, clothing went from being created from raw materials whose own production was observable, to end products that seemed simply to appear on the rack. The latter seemed to lack the quality of the former. Hawthorne seemed to be suggesting that the character of men was suffering a similar decline in quality.

A key theme of the novel is each character's relationship to time, a relationship embodied in each figure's dress: Hepzibah, Jaffrey, and Clifford seem to be prisoners of the past; Holgrave is the prisoner of the future; only Venner seems to blend past and future, traditional and modern aspects of American refinement. He embodies an emerging middle class. In his attacks on the past, Holgrave throws out the baby with the bathwater, or perhaps the body with the garments. The "main point . . . [that] better centuries . . . are to come . . . was surely right," but Holgrave's "error lay in supposing that this age, more than any past or future one, is destined to see the *tattered garments of antiquity exchanged for a new suit*, instead of gradually renewing themselves by *patchwork*" (II, 180; emphasis added). Clearly this passage presents the three relationships to time that the novel explores, relationships themselves expressed through clothes, particularly the notion of *patchwork*, a material and social characteristic associated with Uncle Venner, "the man of patches," as the narrator calls him at one point (II, 287). The metaphor of the "tattered garments of antiquity" and the "new suit" of the future reflects the descriptions of characters, with Clifford (as well as Judge Jaffrey Pyncheon) dressed in old clothes, or at least echoes of old fashions. Clifford is trapped in those old clothes—the clothes so long on the peg, clothes that when he puts them on make him ghostlike and prevent him from crossing the threshold of the House of the Seven Gables to enter the world of contemporary society (II, 170). Jaffrey *does* walk into society, but his clothes seem to be connected more to the dress of old Colonel Pyncheon in the portrait than to the modern fashions worn by Holgrave and his friends, who dress in "newfangled and ill-fitting garments."

Somewhere between the ghostlike fashions of Jaffrey and Clifford on the one hand, and the newfangled incongruity of Holgrave and company on the other, Uncle Venner appears as the pragmatic and reasonable embodiment of neither past nor future, but of a present that evolves and adapts. The fact that he mends and patches his clothes suggests that he is neither trapped by the past nor dazzled by the future. In a time of ready-made garments, when replacing one's old clothes was becoming more affordable, and when fashion imposed a kind of amnesiac temporality, Venner represents a strong middle ground. The "venerable Uncle Venner" appears "in a *clean shirt*, and a *broad-cloth coat*, more respectable than his ordinary wear, in as much as it was *neatly patched* on each elbow, and might be called an *entire garment*, except for a slight inequality in the length of its skirts" (II, 154; emphasis added). Uncle Venner's clothing includes two-cloth trousers, which point to an earlier fashion, and a hat that seems out of place. His clothing is marked by its "cast-off" and "miscellaneous character," and is patched together not only from different fashions, but from different times:

> This patriarch now presented himself before Hepzibah, clad in an old blue coat, which had a fashionable air, and must have accrued to him from the cast-off wardrobe of some dashing clerk. As for his trousers, they were tow cloth, very short in the legs, and bagging down strangely in the rear, but yet having a suitableness to his figure which his other garment entirely lacked. His hat had relation to no other part of his dress, and but very little to the head that wore it. Thus, Uncle Venner was a miscellaneous old gentleman, partly himself, but in good measure, somebody else; patched together . . . of different epochs; an epitome of times and fashions. (II, 61–62)

In a novel concerned with time, decay, modernity, and newness, Venner marks a slip zone, a time warp or woof in the novel's narrative context.

The fact that Venner has the final word of the novel is also telling, in that the novel seems to privilege Venner's middle ground—between past and future, and between the wealth of Jaffrey and the want of Hepzibah. He also occupies a middle ground between the fast fall of Clifford and the rapid rise of Holgrave. He embodies a steady middle class at a time of rapid change. The closing scene, in which Venner exchanges farewells with Phoebe Pyncheon, once again makes reference to his clothes, specifically his buttons. Even though the question of buttons points to distinctions between coarseness and fineness or patchwork and polish, the ultimate contrast is a contrast in time.

Patched old Venner tells Phoebe that he is "a great deal better, the longer [he] is kept" (II, 318). Here, he is making a distinction between himself and a younger man, who might not appreciate the attention given to him by a young woman like Phoebe. He tells her, "if you were to speak to a young man as you do to an old one, his chance of keeping his heart, another minute, would not be worth one of the buttons on my waistcoat! And—soul alive!—that great sigh, which you made me heave, has burst off the very last of them!" (II, 317). As noted above, the buttoned waistcoat was a key sign of refinement in the postrevolutionary period in the United States. This image of Uncle Venner, whose attire is undone by his emotion, humanizes him, and thus humanizes the descendants of an old aristocracy whose wealth was built on social injustices and economic privilege. The uncle softens that aristocratic past into a venerated descent. Uncle Venner embodies, perhaps, the kind of attitude associated with Hawthorne's own uncle, Robert Manning, who supposedly told Nathaniel to "mind your mother, don't look cross, hold up your head like a man, and keep your cloths clean" (Wineapple 24). Hawthorne seems to have been keenly aware of the important relationships between clothing and time. His narratives explore social class not as a static structure but as a dynamic relationship between materiality, history, and representation. His representations of an emerging middle-class identity in the United States documented the temporality of class through its material manifestation in clothing.

3

Austen's Muslin

Laura George

> It seemed a caprice of the moment, and it has established itself as
> the emblem of a period.
>
> —F. Th. Vischer commenting on the crinoline,
> quoted in one of Benjamin's notes for *The Arcades Project*

*I*n chapter 3 of Jane Austen's *Northanger Abbey*, when Mrs. Allen asks Henry
Tilney, "And pray, sir, what do you think of Miss Morland's gown?" (21), read-
ers should be forgiven for assuming that a compliment might be forthcoming.
Henry responds: "It is very pretty, madam," said he; gravely examining it; "but
I do not think it will wash well; I am afraid it will fray." (21)[1]

Rather than pointing out details such as the blue trimmings or complimenting Catherine's appearance in the dress, Henry focuses on the material
qualities of muslin: its ability (or inability) to withstand washing and its tendency to fray. Henry's attention to the fabric[2] of which Catherine's gown is
made, taken together with his focus in the conversation on muslin's costs and
Indian origins, foregrounds the materiality of the muslin as textile rather than
the appearance of a gown or a girl. In effect, in this exchange Henry appears
to refuse the standard metonymy of gown for woman; traditionally, in complimenting the gown, one in fact compliments the woman. Instead Henry
focuses on the pecuniary and quotidian properties of the gown's fabric, behav-
ing almost as if Catherine is not currently in the gown, or as if the fabric is not
currently shaped into a dress. Here Henry is playing with the double meaning
of "gown" in Austen's period when "gown" meant not only a finished dress
but also the yards of material that could be made up into a dress. This famous
interchange establishes talk about muslin as its own conversational genre, the
conventions of which (focusing on cost, origins, use, practicality) highlight the
widespread and sudden ubiquity of muslin during Austen's period as well as
muslin's role in global trade, in the colonization of India, and in the burgeoning mass-production of textiles in northern England.[3] Using this famous pas-

sage from Jane Austen's *Northanger Abbey* as a ground, I hope to approach such perennially engaging questions as when and how does a particular fabric come to signify in fiction or in critical theory? Under what conditions can textiles come to represent eras? Characters? Cultures? What historical conditions and theoretical frameworks contribute to the signifying power of textiles? Why are certain textiles widely adopted at particular points in history?[4]

My focus will be on Austen's muslin because of the tension I see between recent critical writing on Austen's muslin and the actual appearances of muslin in Austen's novel. Austen's muslin barely signifies in our modern sense. It doesn't typify a time period to her characters. It doesn't reveal anything in particular about Catherine, I will argue here, although the chapter in which the muslin conversation appears does invite us to consider Austen's delicate handling of female desire. Retroactive theoretical analysis can suggest some of what muslin might have signified to Austen's period, but these significations don't appear to have been a concern to Austen or her characters. What muslin does signify in the muslin conversation in *Northanger Abbey* is fully material and economic: shifts in global trade and industrial production make themselves felt, literally, in the fabric's physical qualities in Austen's novel. What Theodor Adorno, in a letter to Walter Benjamin, called a fabric's "expressive significance" consists precisely of both the fabric's material qualities and the global networks of trade and labor that produce those qualities (Adorno and Benjamin, 111). For Adorno and Benjamin, a fabric's expressive significance is bound up with but not reducible to the material processes of its production. Despite the fact that Austen's characters in *Northanger Abbey* focus on muslin's materiality, associations with India, and modest costs, these aspects of the fashion for muslin that Austen knew have been underemphasized. This globalized, fully material fabric is Austen's muslin.

It has become commonplace, particularly since the burgeoning of fashion theory in the 1980s (which drew upon earlier work on popular culture and subcultures), to read dress in terms of the constructions of individual and group identities and ideologies. The widespread adoption of muslins during Austen's lifetime has been often explained with reference to neoclassical values and the republican ideals of the French Revolution in particular; what the fabric signified in Austen's time and in ours has been generally assumed to cohere. But these familiar ideational aspects of the late eighteenth-century British craze for muslin do not register in Austen's novel. Historical studies of the production, transportation, and exchange of the various textiles out of which dress can be made have also flourished in the past few decades.[5] Henry Tilney's conversation with Mrs. Allen clearly suggests that the global, industrial, and everyday life experiences of muslin in Austen's time were central to the textile's expressive function. For Henry and Mrs. Allen, the fabric of Catherine's gown signifies the impact of global trade and of the mass production of textiles on the everyday use of a newly inexpensive and fragile fabric with an immediacy that, as industrial capitalism has advanced and decayed, we have lost. I'll spend the bulk of this essay elaborating this point and investigating its implications, but I will also be addressing the hint of another sort of muslin signification in Austen: the possibility that muslin's notorious fragility and, as seen in contemporary discourse, its transparency, hint at Catherine's own transparent desire for Henry.

CONVERSING ABOUT MUSLINS

The conversation between Henry and Mrs. Allen occurs in chapter 3 of *Northanger Abbey*. This chapter opens with Henry's introduction to Catherine, continues with Henry mimicking an array of genres of social discourse, including clichéd gambits of social chitchat and ladies' diaries, and concludes with what is apparently the only footnote to appear anywhere in Austen's fiction. In short, the entire chapter opens conventionalized discourses to both mimicry and analysis, and in this way it can be read as an epitome of the narrative strategies of *Northanger Abbey*. *Northanger Abbey* is famously parodic generally, as well as being Austen's most explicitly metafictional novel, but at the opening of the novel the parody is firmly located in the narrator's voice. In chapter 3 Austen appears to start channeling some of her parodic impulses through a particular fictional character: Henry Tilney. Henry's participation in the muslin conversation—the longest and most detailed of his performances in this chapter—is thus intimately bound up with the texture of Austen's novel as a whole. The entire chapter, in particularly concentrated form, dramatizes *Northanger Abbey's* explicit interest in conventions, genres, textuality, and intertextuality from Henry's initial parodic performances to Austen's final footnoting of Samuel Richardson's claim that a young lady should not fall in love with a gentleman until that gentleman's preference for her is explicitly declared. While muslins do not themselves directly signify in Austen's novel, the conversation about muslins does signify. The conversation itself signifies something about Henry's character as a possible suitor for Catherine: he will be able to see Catherine's desire for him long before Samuel Richardson would think proper. Henry's participation in the conversation about muslin also signifies his ability to see through conventionalized conversational genres in general and conventionalized conversations about muslin in particular. Henry demonstrates his ability to speak in feminized genres in ways that signal his keen awareness of the working of generic conventions in a chapter that ends with a hint—not fully realized until the conclusion of the novel—that the narrator is equally adept at seeing through the conventions that held that a woman must be desired before daring to desire. Seeing through muslin, Henry observes the global, technological, and economic conditions of the fabric, just as seeing through the conventional genres that structure much of Catherine's understanding enables Henry to perceive her (culturally unsanctioned) desire. Muslin might seem a simple thing, a suddenly ubiquitous fabric that can signify Austen's fictional worlds, but seeing through muslin gives Henry access to understanding where both fabrics and stories come from.

The muslin conversation between Henry Tilney and Mrs. Allen takes up fewer than two pages in most editions of *Northanger Abbey*, but it has nevertheless attracted outsize critical attention, perhaps because for us, reading centuries later, muslin has increasingly figured metonymically for Austen's period. Almost certainly, the most famous and most quoted line in the conversation is Mrs. Allen's startled exclamation: "Do you understand muslins, Sir?" (20).[6] Henry replies, "Particularly well" (20) and proceeds to demonstrate that understanding muslins in this context means being conversant with muslin's materiality, its texture, its fragility, and its costs above all. Muslin's rapid and widespread adoption as the reigning textile of fashion suggests that the material properties of the fabric, as well as its association with southern Asia, spoke to and for British subjects in particular ways. In a famous letter to Walter Benjamin of 1935, responding to Benjamin's "Exposé of 1935," Adorno wrote: "With regard to the construction of the passage on fashion . . . the idea of the 'changeant' occurred to me—the shot fabric which seems to have had great expressive significance for the nineteenth century and was presumably bound up with certain industrial processes. Perhaps you will pursue this idea one day" (111).[7] Adorno sees the "expressive significance" of the changeant fabric (shot silk, with the warp and woof in different colored threads so that the fabric shimmers and shifts in color as it moves) in mid-nineteenth-century fashion as inextricable from the industrial processes of its production, which in turn are inextricable from the materiality of a fabric's weight, color, and finish.[8] We tend to read the exchange between Henry and Mrs. Allen through our own vocabulary of fashion history and fashion theory, but putting Austen's passage in the context of the development of fashion historiography helps us recover some of the less familiar ways the muslin operates in this text. When Mrs. Allen asks Henry whether he "understands muslins," she is responding to his first remark to her. She has just complained about a pin tearing a hole in her muslin, a favorite "though it cost but nine shillings a yard." Henry responds: "That is exactly what I should have guessed it, madam" (20), making his first intervention into the muslin conversation one about muslin's costs. Muslin may signify Austen's period for us, but Austen's characters focus on the economics of muslin.

The ability to produce domestic muslins in tandem with early developments in mass production meant that the fabric could suddenly be obtained fairly cheaply. Henry, keenly attentive to habituated verbal patterns, also notes that the phrase "muslin can never be said to be wasted" is frequently reiterated: "But then, you know, madam, muslin always turns to some account or other; Miss Morland will get enough out of it for a handkerchief or a cap, or a cloak.—Muslin can never be said to be wasted. I have heard my sister say so forty times, when she has been extravagant in buying more than she wanted, or careless in cutting it to pieces" (21).

While Henry is likely being mischievous here, neither Catherine nor Mrs. Allen seem surprised by the behavior he describes. It was a novel thing in Britain that a fabric could be inexpensive enough to be carelessly cut or bought in unnecessary excess. As W. J. T. Mitchell puts it, "when new objects appear in the world, they also bring with them new orders of temporality, new dialectical images that interfere with and complicate one another" (243). Muslin was not a new object, but relatively easy access to less expensive, domestically produced muslins (as opposed to more expensive imported "true Indian" muslins) reshaped the clothing world of Britain. The introduction of industrially produced and more affordable muslin fabrics established not only new temporal but new geospatial orders. Was muslin an exotic product of a warmer climate? A familiar fabric produced at home? Was its draping close to the female body, suggesting curves and buttocks and revealing the movement of legs, thoroughly modern or a quotation of classical style? Gillray's famous cartoon, "The Three Graces in a High Wind," suggests both the confluence and

FIGURE 3.1: James Gillray. "The Three Graces in a High Wind." © *Victoria and Albert Museum, London*. (Plate 4.)

the tensions involved in modern Graces promenading in Kensington Gardens (fig. 3.1).

Dialectical tensions—between domestic and foreign, ancient and modern, clothed and naked, northern and southern, British and Indian—saturated discourse about muslins. Traces of these dialectical tensions make themselves felt in *Northanger Abbey*, and reading the muslin conversation in the context of these tensions can make these traces visible to us.

The passion for lightly colored and simple dresses that characterized Austen's period has often been explained as resulting from enchantment with the ideas of liberty associated with the early days of the French Revolution and with a desire to emulate classical Greece and Rome, thus locating the fashion's origins firmly within Europe.[9] However, Henry's pride in his acquisition of "a true Indian muslin" for "but five shillings a yard" (20) is a reminder that cotton was well understood to be a product of the tropics, as is the fact that

British commentators on the fashion for muslin often complained that British women were inexplicably dressing for the wrong climate. In caricatures and social commentary, it is also apparent that muslin gowns were often read as sheer and "clear" fabrics; the lack of ornamentation in female fashions caused complaints that large numbers of women were stepping out into public settings in their underwear.[10] The polarities inscribed in representations of muslin (domestic/foreign, modern/ancient, clothed/naked) manifested in multiple representations of the new fashion. As Adorno argues in the August 1935 letter to Benjamin: "dialectical images are not social products, but objective constellations in which the condition of society finds itself represented" (110). Muslin enabled a profound reshaping of the social imaginary of Austen's time, and its global and economic impacts were simultaneously elided and registered in everyday interchanges.

The changeant fabric that interested Adorno serves as a useful reference point for understanding how visually startling and anomalous the pale, matte, columnar gowns made out of soft muslins would have been in Austen's time—a relatively brief interregnum between periods of mass and color in women's dress. Figures 3.2–3.4 present three images highlighting the extent to which the muslin gowns of Austen's period differed in shape and color both from those that preceded them and those that followed them. Figure 3.2 shows a yellow sack-back gown from 1760; the gown's volume and opacity are immediately apparent.

Figure 3.3 shows a white muslin gown from 1800. The Victoria and Albert Museum in London (where this gown is held) notes that the fabric for the gown was made in Bengal, although the gown itself was made in Britain.

Figure 3.4 shows a shimmery satin gown of 1842, dramatizing the return to opaque color, volume, and light-reflecting fabrics after muslin's relatively brief reign.

Assuming that these images are representative (as standard fashion histories hold), we can see how strikingly different the dresses of the turn of the nineteenth century were from those of 1760 and 1842. The silhouettes are columnar, as the waists are considerably higher, and the predominance of white and light colors make the dresses read as much less substantial than the darker, heavier, and bulkier gowns that preceded and followed them. As I have mentioned, this visually new and popular textile generated frequent complaints that women were inexplicably dressing for the wrong climate and

FIGURE 3.2: Sack Back Gown, 1760. © *Victoria and Albert Museum, London.*
(Plate 5.)

walking around in public half naked. In talking about the fabric's fragility, how much it costs, how it can be used, Henry and Mrs. Allen are talking about how this fabric, newly accessible and newly inexpensive due to mechanized domestic production, shapes the practices of everyday life around shopping for, making, washing, sewing, and mending clothes.

Despite the frequency with which Austen scholars have written about

FIGURE 3.3: White Muslin Gown, 1800. © *Victoria and Albert Museum, London.* (Plate 6.)

the exchange between Henry Tilney and Mrs. Allen, gowns themselves do not particularly signify in Austen's fiction. In his mock lady's diary entry in chapter 3, for instance, Henry mentions that the fabric of Catherine's gown is a sprigged muslin and that it has blue trim, but he says nothing about the cut or style of the dress (even though here at least he is obliquely complimenting Catherine's appearance). References to muslin do appear in Aus-

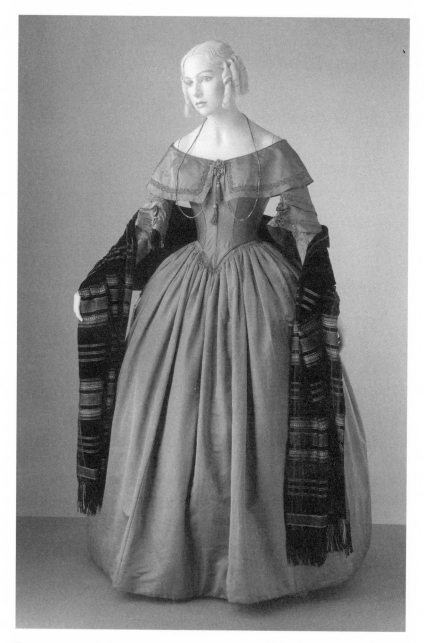

FIGURE 3.4: Satin Dress, c. 1842. © *Victoria and Albert Museum, London.*
(Plate 7.)

ten's other novels.[11] The most famous passage besides the one from *Northanger Abbey* is Lydia Bennet's request in *Pride and Prejudice* to have the "slit" in her muslin gown repaired before her clothes are sent on after her elopement. Jill Heydt-Stevenson, in fact, opens her introduction to *Austen's Unbecoming Conjunctions* with this claim: "In *Pride and Prejudice*, Lydia intimates that her virginity has already been lost when, on the eve of eloping with a scoundrel, she explains that 'I will send for my clothes when I get to Longbourn; but I wish you would tell Sally to mend a great slit in my worked muslin gown, before they are packed up" (1).

In this instance it is the slit that does the primary signifying work rather than the fabric itself, although, as Heydt-Stevenson notes when she discusses this passage at greater length, "the word 'muslin' carried sexual connotations" (87).[12] While Heydt-Stevenson's reading of the sexuality of the slit is persuasive, the preoccupation with muslin being fragile or torn runs through Austen's novels and is rarely sexualized in and of itself. In *Sense and Sensibility*, for instance, Miss Steele says to Elinor, "La! If you have not got your best spotted muslin on! I wonder you was not afraid of its being torn," (313). More important for my concerns here, muslin's delicacy is a constant preoccupation of Mrs. Allen in chapter 2, when Catherine makes her first social appearance in Bath. Mrs. Allen moves through the throng "with more care for the safety of her new gown than for the comfort of her protégée" (13). As she and Catherine sit, bereft of any acquaintance, Mrs. Allen "congratulated herself . . . on having preserved her gown from injury. 'It would have been very shocking to have it torn,' said she, 'would not it?—It is such a delicate muslin.—For my part I have not seen anything I like so well in the whole room I assure you'" (14).

While any sexual implications in relationship to Mrs. Allen are not particularly marked here, the desirability of a very "delicate" muslin certainly is—as well as the impact on the tasks of everyday life involved with wearing such a delicate fabric. As the muslin conversation in *Northanger Abbey* itself makes clear, such a delicate fabric would be completely impractical if it were not for its relatively low price, made possible by burgeoning domestic mass production of the textile.

Although muslin shows up more than once in Austen's fiction (and shows up more than any other fabric), the gown that Catherine wears when she meets Henry Tilney does not signify anything in particular about her or about the assembly other than that it is the fabric that everyone, including Mrs. Allen, wears. But this isn't always easy to see because of the extent to which costume dramas and Janeite sewing patterns have ensured that muslin gowns represent Austen's period for us today. Ideas about fabrics and fashions signifying much more than rank and status were slow to arise even as the last sumptuary laws faded from the books. The idea of a particular fabric signifying a certain historical moment had scarcely begun to be formulated in Austen's time; the first instances of fashion historiography appear in the late eighteenth century, and the study of fashion's histories doesn't really start coming into its own until the twentieth century.

In *The Art of Dress: Fashion in England and France 1750–1820*, Aileen Ribeiro notes that Thomas Jefferys' 1757 *A Collection of Dresses of Different Nations, both Ancient and Modern, and more particularly Old English Dresses after the designs of Holbein, Vandyke, Hollar and others* includes "a brief history of dress, one of the first attempts to define a chronology of the subject" (183). According to Ribeiro, "The first really comprehensive study of the history of dress in England was undertaken by Joseph Strutt" (184) with the *Complete View of the Manners, Customs, Arms, Habits &c of the Inhabitants of England* (1774–1776) and *Complete View of the Dress and Habits of the People of England* (1796–1799). Strutt, however, never speculates about why fashions change; he only notes exhaustively that they have. Lou Taylor, in *Establishing Dress History*, calls Strutt "the founder of British dress history" (90) and notes that James Laver believed that Strutt exemplified "the dawning historical sense" of dress history in the late eighteenth century (Laver, quoted in Taylor, 23). In short, Austen's period witnessed the very first attempts at a historiography of fashion. While muslin may well signify Austen's period to us, Henry's comments, and Mrs. Allen's concerns about protecting her gown, don't suggest any particular analysis of the fashion or its "meanings." Austen's letters demonstrate how attentive she was to the details of and shifts in fashion, but these shifts just happen; for Austen, as for other contemporary commentators, fashions may have "sources" (that is, the progress of a style may be tracked, most often from London to the provinces), but they do not have "meanings" in our modern sense. Austen does not speculate about causes or effect of particular shifts or the "meaning" of fabrics or styles.

In the *Northanger Abbey* conversation, we're referred insistently to muslin as a made thing, a commodity. In a world that offered many different muslins (of different weights as well as colors and patterns), Henry's concern about how well a particular fabric would stand up to washing forcibly reminds us of the challenges and inconveniences of living with and wearing this fabric, so dramatically delicate in relation to the woolens and fustians and calicos that had dominated everyday dress in previous generations. The muslin conversation in *Northanger Abbey* suggests how prevalent muslins had become, which certainly explains the strong association between the gowns and Austen's period (and Austen herself), but it would take later developments in the consciousness of fashion and fashion change (an awareness made possible by mass

production not only of textiles and clothing but of prints and publications)
to make the association of particular fabrics with particular cultural and historical periods fully legible. While Austen is not in any historical position to
make muslin signify either Catherine Moreland's time period or her individual identity, she does take some pains to remind us of muslin's fragility and
delicacy.

Mrs. Allen first interrupts Henry and Catherine in chapter 3 out of concern for the integrity of her muslin gown: "'My dear Catherine,' said she, 'do
take this pin out of my sleeve; I am afraid it has torn a hole already; I shall be
quite sorry if it has, for this is a favourite gown, though it cost but nine shillings a yard'" (20). Henry first and above all demonstrates his understanding
of muslin by demonstrating his understanding of its costs: "'That is exactly
what I should have guessed it, madam,' said Mr. Tilney, looking at the muslin"
(20). In fact, throughout the conversation, Henry speaks most frequently of
the costs of muslin and his skill in shopping for it: "I always buy my own cra-
vats, and am allowed to be an excellent judge; and my sister has often trusted
me in the choice of a gown. I bought one for her the other day, and it was pronounced a prodigious bargain by every lady who saw it. I gave but five shillings
a yard for it, and a true Indian muslin" (20).

As Claire Hughes reminds us, "In decoding this conversation from a modern standpoint, we must recall that muslins were to the late eighteenth and
early nineteenth centuries what synthetic fibers were to the mid-twentieth
century—they transformed life" (188). There are clear historical reasons why
the cost and material properties of muslin should have been of paramount
importance at this time. The perceived and real fragilities of Austen's muslin
are inextricable from the processes by which muslin was made. Obviously, the
British had only very recently developed processes that enabled the domestic
production of muslin. Although the fineness of handspun cotton thread and
hand-woven muslins produced in India had long provoked British envy, it was
only with Crompton's development of the spinning mule in the 1770s that
British textile producers had access to a domestic thread that was both fine
enough to form a muslin and strong enough to withstand the pressures of textile machinery. These technological developments dramatically increased the
demand for imported cotton and, eventually, encouraged the development of
cotton agriculture in the New World. Domestically producing textiles from
imported raw materials offered a new business model, one that, among other
effects, provided strong motivation for Britain's increasing colonial domi-

FIGURE 3.5: Promenade Dresses, 1809. *Author's personal collection.*
(Plate 8.)

nance in India. The reference point for the fabric itself, though, even when
domestically produced, was typically India; in ways that are no longer immediately recognizable to us, the fabric's very fragility and light weight were themselves allusions to India and the tropics.

It is hard to overstate the extent to which the new muslin gowns registered as sheer to nonexistent in contemporary discourse. Sir Walter Scott
opens *Waverly*, for instance, with a brief mention of the "primitive nakedness
of the modern rout" (4); Lord Byron, in *Don Juan*, remarks on "that hour, called
'half-hour,' given to dress,/ Though ladies's robes seem scant enough for less"

FIGURE 3.6: Wirgman Dressmaker, Afternoon Dress for July 1801. *Author's personal collection.* (Plate 9.)

(canto 15, stanza 5). Determining what people were looking at is less simple. Certainly some fashion prints of the period emphasize shorter, more delicate skirts that hint at the female shape, as can be seen in the August 1, 1809, print of promenade dresses from Ackermann's Repository of Arts (fig. 3.5).

However, the majority of the fashion prints from the period that I've seen don't emphasize the angles or shape of the female figure nearly to this extent. See, for example, Wirgman, Dressmaker's 1801 print of afternoon dresses for July (fig. 3.6).

As Anne Hollander reminded us in *Seeing Through Clothes*, "The way clothes

look depends not on how they are designed, but how they are perceived"
(1993, 311).

Expressive Significance and Industrial Processes: Muslin's Histories

While I believe muslin's material qualities and histories to be paramount in *Northanger Abbey*, Austen's novel does suggest aspects of the demand side as well. What hints of demand-side desires do appear here seem focused primarily on the fabric's delicacy, low cost, and Indian associations. However, most modern histories of the fashion for pale, columnar muslin gowns have tended to focus on just a few dimensions of how muslins spoke to and for Austen's time, often citing both neoclassicism and the egalitarian ethos of the French Revolution as important sources.[13] Both twentieth-century fashion historians and contemporary commentators have associated the popularity of muslin gowns with the French Revolution and with nakedness more or less simultaneously. James Laver, for example, lays the reason for this change at the door of the French Revolution:

> Like all great social upheavals, this had a profound effect on the clothes of both men and women. The dress of the Ancien Régime was swept away. Suddenly there were no more embroidered coats or brocaded gowns, no more wigs or powdered hair, no more elaborate headdresses, no more talons rouges. "Return to Nature" was the cry, but in the matter of costume this is never quite possible, unless people are willing to adopt the nudity of the savage. (148)

Mrs. Mackie, in *A Picture of the Changes of Fashion*, her privately printed memoir of 1818, makes a related observation:

> How surprised would the English ladies have been had they heard that, in a few years, <u>they</u> would appear in the <u>costume</u> of those <u>figurantes</u> on whom they looked with so much contempt. It was in fact a term of reproach, and, when a woman's petticoats were too short or too scanty, it was usual to say, "you look like a <u>figurante</u> at the Opera." Yet this dress, Alas! has not only been imitated but exceeded, and (painful to remark) it was from a nation of murderers that the fashion was taken, and its date was the French Revolution. (14; emphasis original)[14]

Engraved for the Lady's Magazine.

London Walking & Full Dress.

FIGURE 3.7: London Walking and Full Dress. C. 1790–1805. *Author's personal collection.* (Plate 10.)

In *The Culture of Fashion*, Christopher Breward locates neoclassicism as a determining cause of the late-eighteenth-century craze for muslin: "The predominance of pale, floating textiles and the new emphasis given to the forms of the body, underpinned by an academic and popular interest in the classical world, lead to the simple neo-classical lines of the turn of the century, rejecting padding and ingenious cut for the basic shift-like chemise gathered under the bust" (122). There are certainly reasons, as figure 3.7 suggests, with its references to peplos and chlamys, to locate "liberty" and "the classical world" as key reference points for this sudden and dramatic shift in women's fashion, but both refer strictly to the ideational dimensions of "expressive significance"; neither is "bound up with certain industrial processes"—or processes of colonization, importation, or cultural mimicry.

Both "neoclassicism" and "the French revolution," are catch-all terms for enormously complex sets of images and associations, and these two axes of expressivity continue to structure many recent discussions of the fashion for muslin. Benjamin and Adorno, attentive above all to questions of class and labor, of industrial processes in the manufacturing of fabric, remind us to be attentive to the labor needed to grow cotton in tropical regions, transport it to Britain, and process it into thread and then fabric in textile mills. Any discussion of "expressive significance" must be bound up with material processes of production. And in this instance, crucial aspects of the "expressive significance" of muslin as well as of "the industrial processes bound up in its production" all lead back to India via Manchester, as the muslin conversation in *Northanger Abbey* clearly registers.

Cotton in all its popular variations—calico, understood to be named for Calicut; muslin, understood to be named for Mosul—was widely recognized as a fabric with global origins and implications in eighteenth- and nineteenth-century Britain. Cotton was well understood to be an agriculture of the southern hemisphere (most likely indigenous to India and the Americas and of ancient cultivation in the Middle East, the states around the Black Sea, and northern Africa). The muslin gowns that may seem to Austen fans so thoroughly British were, in fact, intimately part of British commercial interests in southern Asia, and often conjured up specifically non-British associations for those at the time. William Wordsworth, for instance, when he depicts wandering through London in Book 7 of *The Prelude*, sees "Negro ladies in white muslin gowns" (228). In contrast, his British female characters are clothed most frequently in russet (wool dyed with woad or madder). Joseph Inikori's *Africans and the Industrial Revolution in England* does a good job of summarizing the importance of wool to the English and later British economies and the texture of everyday life prior to the importation of cotton textiles and raw cotton. He argues that "the sheep was to medieval and early modern England what crude oil is to contemporary Saudi Arabia" (26). The importation of first cotton fabrics and then raw cotton disrupted these very long-standing economic and cultural patterns; cottons were *always* recognized as at least partly "not from here."

The accusations of nakedness that arose when women started wearing muslin gowns in large numbers further connected the fabric to exotic and poorly clad peoples in hot climates. Laver emphasizes the striking visual change in fashion that muslin represented: "Perhaps at no period between primitive times and the 1920s had women worn so little as they wore in the early years of the nineteenth century. All the female attire seemed to have been designed for tropical climates, and yet the climate of Europe can have been no different in 1800 from what it was in 1850, when women wore ten times as many clothes" (155). Like associations with the classical world or the French Revolution, associations of the fabric with a hot climate date back to the period, particularly in persistent observations that modern women in Britain were risking catching horrible diseases through being cold. In *A Mirror of the Graces* (1811), A Lady of Distinction complains that "some of our fair dames appear, summer or winter, with no other shelter from sun or frost, than one single garment of muslin or silk over their chemise—*if they wear one!*" (77; emphasis original) and notes that "to wear gossamer dresses, with bare necks and naked arms, in a hard frost, has been the mode in this country; and unless a principle is made against it, may be so again, to the utter wretchedness of them, who, so arraying their youth, lay themselves open to the untimely ravages of rheumatisms, palsies, consumptions, and death" (76). In 1803 an outbreak of influenza was known as the "muslin disease." As the writer of the anonymous *The Age We Live In: A Fragment. Dedicated to Every Young Lady of Fashion*, noted in 1813:

> But what says the rude month of March? Why, the three graces came to pay me a visit, in the likenesses of Maria, Augusta, and Anne St. L—. A cold month for those naked goddesses to go themselves abroad in; but they have been so long used to go without clothes that I suppose they are hardened to all weather. It is, doubtless, to imitate these unadorned beauties that we have got rid of so many superfluities within the last twenty years. Nay, so much do we display of our own proper figures, and so little did our grandmothers, that were they to step out of their tombs to look about them they would conclude the world to be inhabited by a different race of beings, of quite another make to themselves. (88–89)

In an 1801 letter to her sister Cassandra, Jane Austen wrote, "Martha and I dined yesterday at Deane to meet the Powletts. . . . Mrs. Powlett was at once expensively and nakedly dressed; we have had the satisfaction of estimating her lace and Muslin" (To Cassandra Austen, Thursday 8–Friday 9 January 1801, *Jane Austen's Letters* [70]). Generations of Janeites and Georgetteites have ensured that these dresses are at least as familiar as the generally much darker, bulkier, and more ornamented hooped and panniered dresses that preceded them and the similarly darker, bulkier, and more ornamented hooped and crinolined dresses that followed them; the gowns' very familiarity to modern readers of Austen has made the extent to which the craze for them represented for many a disturbing departure as hard to see for us as, according to contemporary accounts, they were literally hard to see for some of the fashion's viewers. The repeated references to nakedness offer evidence of the widespread association of muslin fabrics with the primitive, the naked, and the foreign. While important, associations with the classical world or the French Revolution reinforce a far too Euro-centric reading of the fashion's associations.

The dominance of muslin in Austen's England was not the first time cotton fabrics had roiled the experience of everyday life. The "calico controversies" of the late seventeenth and early eighteenth centuries involved protectionist legislation (to protect domestic woolen and silk industries) banning the importation of printed calicos from India. While this phase of demand for Indian cottons can perhaps be explained in purely domestic ideational terms—in terms of long-standing associations of color and pattern with status—they were, of course, Indian. While the early eighteenth-century demand for brightly printed cottons may be understood with recourse to long-standing associations between ornamented fabrics and privilege, the late eighteenth-century demand for white, pale, and discretely ornamented muslins is harder to explain. The craze for pale muslin could not have happened without British mastery of chemical dyeing techniques, of course, but supply-side technological innovation in itself cannot create demand. In fact, as Chandra Mukerji has argued, it takes a materialist culture to generate supply-side innovation. In India for thousands of years, and in England of the early eighteenth century, fabric was bleached through a complex process of souring and being staked out in the open air for months. Berthollet's discovery of chlorine bleach and Watt's development of a process to mass-produce bleached cotton were sine qua nons of the late eighteenth century passion for pale muslins. Equally, without Crompton's mule, which was able to produce cotton thread both fine enough to serve for muslin and strong enough to serve as warp, the muslins that enabled British ladies to look like Greek statues (or Creole ladies) would simply not have been available in large quantities. With Crompton's mule, the British were able to mass-produce cotton fabrics almost as fine as those the Indians with their many years of practice were able to make by hand. Nevertheless, the ability to cheaply produce light-colored fabrics or delicate fabrics is not, in and of itself, enough to create a popular fashion.

The aspiration to mimic the very fine, hand-spun textiles of India was likely an important motivation for a number of late eighteenth-century innovations in textile production. Edward Baines's 1835 *History of the Cotton Manufacture in Great Britain* is stocked with quotations from British travelers amazed, over the centuries, by the fineness and whiteness of India's best muslins. This quote represents what British artisans saw themselves as aspiring to duplicate:

> The white calicuts . . . are woven in several places in Bengal and Mogulistan. . . . Some calicuts are made so fine, you can hardly feel them in your hand, and the thread, when spun, is scarcely discernible. There is made at Seconge a sort of calicut so fine that when a man puts it on, his skin shall appear plainly through it, as if he was quite naked, but the merchants are not permitted to transport it, for the governor is obliged to send it all to the Great Mogul's seraglio and the principle lords of the court, to make the sultanesses and noblemen's wives shifts and garments for the hot weather; and the king and the lords take great pleasure to behold them in these shifts, and see them dance with nothing else upon them. (57–58)

In creating fine muslins, the British knew they were mimicking Indian textiles, a knowledge that frequent references to wrong climates and fragile fabrics and near nakedness all allude to. The muslin conversation that Austen includes in *Northanger Abbey* assumes these associations as a matter of course. But in Austen's hands the muslin that Catherine Moreland and Mrs. Allen wear is not sexualized (or at least not overtly; I'll return to the final footnote of chapter 3 at the end of this essay). Instead the fineness and delicacy of the fabric (at least as compared to traditional woolens) refers us to the hazards of walking across crowded assembly rooms, managing mistakes in sewing, and living with fabric no longer valuable enough to serve as a capital good for the middle ranks of society.

When in her early piece "Frederic and Elfrida," Austen has Frederic, Elfrida, and Charlotte effusively praise Rebecca for her "sentiments so nobly expressed on the different excellencies of Indian & English Muslins, & the judicious preference you give the former" (*Juvenilia*, 6), she reminds us that

British consumers of the period knew they were shopping in a globalized marketplace and that references to India were inextricably part of the reception of domestically produced muslin. As Suzanne Daly notes of Victorian novels in *The Empire Inside: Indian Commodities in Victorian Domestic Novels*, "Cotton's foreign origins are often gestured at, but never quite emerge from the background to become a part of the narrative. In other words, cotton emerges as a text despite relentless efforts to make it into context" (37). The fact that a "true" muslin and an "Indian" muslin are the same thing in Henry's account suggests a certain definitional tie that will take years to fade from view.

Neither Benjamin nor Adorno were interested in reducing the expressive significance of fabric and other commodities merely to the material bases of their production. In a later letter of November 10, 1938, Adorno chastises Benjamin for connecting, as he sees it, the expressiveness of Baudelaire's celebration of intoxication to taxes on wine: "I regard it as methodologically inappropriate to give conspicuous individual features from the realm of the superstructure a 'materialist' turn by relating them immediately and perhaps even causally, to certain corresponding features of the substructure. The materialist determination of cultural traits is only possible if it is mediated through the *total social process*" (283; emphasis original).

As Adorno puts it a bit later in the same letter, "The direct inference from the duty on wine to *L'Ame du Vin* imputes to phenomena precisely the kind of spontaneity, tangibility, and density which they have lost under capitalism" (283). In capitalist societies characterized by omnipresent alienation, commodities like muslin can no longer directly signify the labor that went into their production. Arguably, one way this loss of spontaneity, tangibility, and density has manifested itself is in our ability to thematize material objects—to see them as fundamentally symbolic—not as emblems of rank in the older sense but as signifiers of individuals and cultures, as speech. It is as a result of the increasing tendency to take fashion for speech (individual or collective) that we find it harder to register the ways that the immediacy of a fabric's textures and costs were unmediated and apparent concerns in the early days of the Industrial Revolution. The fashion for columnar muslin gowns cannot be reduced to the struggles around the importation of cotton textiles or technological innovations—but these material realities do find expression in the genre of muslin talk as Austen records it in *Northanger Abbey*. This is not to deny the ideational aspects of demand as we can read them looking back. No doubt both the convulsions in France and Enlightenment neoclassicism contributed to the historically brief but intense revulsion against darker colors and highly ornamented fabrics that innovations in cotton spinning and bleaching could sustain, but muslin's associations with the south and east, with the exotic others of northern Europe were equally present in the reception of Britain's newest textiles.[15] The connection of muslin to India is assumed in Austen's muslin conversation in *Northanger Abbey* and was part and parcel of the everyday economics of living with muslin.

A DELICATE FABRIC

As I noted at the start of this essay, chapter 3 of *Northanger Abbey* concludes with the narrator's stern reminder that Catherine absolutely must follow Richardson's dictum. On the night of her first meeting with Henry Tilney and the night of the muslin conversation, we watch Catherine settle in for bed.

> Whether she thought of [Henry] so much, while she drank her warm wine and water, and prepared herself for bed, as to dream of him when there, cannot be ascertained; but I hope it was no more than a slight slumber, or a morning doze at most; for if it be true, as a celebrated writer has maintained, that no young lady can be justified in falling in love before the gentleman's love is declared,* it must be very improper that a young lady should dream of a gentleman before that gentleman is first known to have dreamt of her. (22)

The asterisk after "declared" leads to this footnote: "Vide a letter from Mr. Richardson, No 97. vol. ii. Rambler" (22). In this letter Richardson had written, "That a young lady should be in love, and the love of the young gentleman undeclared, is an heterodoxy which prudence, and even policy, must not allow." In footnoting a source for the narrator's observation, Austen does two things. First, she gives what in the narrative proper would have stood as a general statement of truth (for the world of the novel or perhaps any world) an author and a location. Rather than being merely the observation of a disembodied narrator, the convention that Catherine should feel no desire for (or even curiosity about) Henry is credited to an authority outside the world of the novel. Rather than being universal, it is specifically localized. Second, by including any footnote at all, Austen dislocates the reader temporarily from the diegetic world of the fiction and into the intertextual world outside it. Just as Henry's parodic impulses undermine the authority of conventional chitchat and conventionalized diary entries and reveal the contours of conventional muslin conversations, here Austen's text hovers between undermining the authority of the narrator and her fictions and undermining Richardson's sententious statement.

Austen's narrator, of course, fully discredits this interdiction at the end of *Northanger Abbey*. As Henry proposes to Catherine, we are told:

> She was assured of his affection; and the heart in return was solicited, which, perhaps, they both equally well knew was already entirely his own; for, though Henry was sincerely attached to her, though he felt and delighted in all the excellencies of her character and truly loved her society, I must confess that his affection originated in nothing better than gratitude, or, in other words that a persuasion of her partiality for him had been the only cause of giving her a serious thought. It is a new circumstance in romance, I acknowledge, and dreadfully derogatory of an heroine's dignity; but if it be as new in common life, the credit of wild imagination will at least be all my own. (252–53)

We've been reminded throughout the novel of Catherine's wildly apparent (if not to her) attachment to Henry; here the narrator reminds us that without this clear and evident attachment, Catherine might have had no chance to be a heroine at all. Is it a coincidence that the Richardson footnote, part of Austen's explicit undermining of Richardson's claim that women must lack desire until chosen, that this wholly atypical footnote occurs at the end of the chapter with Austen's most extended focus on muslin? There's no way to rule coincidence out, of course, but as we've seen, muslin's transparency (at least to late eighteenth- and early nineteenth-century viewers whose eyes were accustomed to much heavier and more opaque fabrics) was insistently sexualized in Austen's period if not necessarily by Austen herself. It's just after the muslin conversation that Austen is moved to include a footnote about female desire, footnoting a claim that she explicitly repudiates at the end of her novel. Catherine's gown may not be transparent, but it is not fully visible to Henry, who seems to see primarily the fabric itself and the fabric's origins and costs. Catherine herself, though, is transparent, as is her desire, and her desire sparks Henry's own.

The rich and intricate world of fashion theory has helped us see ornaments and textiles in literature with new eyes over the past few decades. Virginia Woolf's famous complaint will likely not resonate for future generations of scholars: "Speaking crudely, football and sport are 'important'; the worship of fashion, the buying of clothes 'trivial.' And these values are inevitably trans-ferred from life to fiction. This is an important book, the critic assumes, be-cause it deals with war. This is an insignificant book because it deals with the feelings of women in a drawing-room" (73). Fashion and its significations are now recognized as important via academic journals, conferences, and books, and rich discourses exist with which to articulate the potential meanings of cut and color, shape and fabric. Although Austen was writing before these discourses began to cohere, her careful attention to the nuances of conven-tionalized conversation helps us see the patterns in the muslin conversations of her time.

Austen, writing more than a century before Woolf's famous lectures, and at a time when the investigation of "fashion" as laden with significance had barely begun, nevertheless reveals the extent to which muslin's connections to India and to industrial manufacturing were never far from sight. The modern theoretical understanding of fashion does not find a place in *Northanger Abbey*, but muslin's fragile materiality does, as does the extent to which that materi-ality was imbricated with India, global trade, and British manufacturing. For the characters in Austen's novel, materiality in both senses—the sense of the challenges of living with such a relatively delicate fabric and the sense of that delicacy as part and parcel of a global economic order—constitutes the ex-pressive significance of the fabric for her time. We, of course, are still working out what the materiality of Austen's muslin means for ours.

Notes

1. I will be using the Cambridge Edition of the Works of Jane Austen throughout this essay. While there has been some controversy about the choice of the second edi-tions of *Sense and Sensibility* and *Mansfield Park* as copy-texts for the Cambridge editions of those novels, these controversies don't concern *Northanger Abbey* or any of the brief passages from other Austen novels that I will be using here. As Jane Aikens Yount notes in her review essay, "Jane Austen Scholarship: 'The Richness of the Present Age'": "If textual editing took center stage in Chapman's edition nearly one hundred years ago, annotation steps forth as the protagonist of the Cambridge edition" (95). In keeping with contemporary interests among Austen scholars, a significant proportion of these annotations refer to textiles and fashions. The Cambridge edition is thus the obvious choice for scholars interested in Austen's place in fashion history and theory.

2. I'll be using the word "fabric" here in the modern sense, but it's helpful to remember that in Austen's period the word was applied to anything "fabricated"—manufactured. It only became synonymous with textiles later in the nineteenth century, suggesting the extent to which textiles were associated with manufacturing processes by this point.

3, In attempting to use close reading of fiction to produce material histories, this essay is particular indebted to Bill Brown's 1996 *The Material Unconscious: American Amusement, Stephen Crane, and the Economies of Play.* Bill Brown is now known for his role in what he has called Thing Theory and I have learned from all his work, but *The Material Unconscious* was helpful at an early stage of this research. A passion for "things" continues to coalesce and gather steam in a number of academic disciplines—from developments in object-oriented ontology in philosophy to a wide range of thing-oriented studies in literary studies, art history, history, and popular nonfiction. One watershed moment in this web of intellectual developments was the appearance of a special issue of *Critical Inquiry,* edited by Bill Brown, which appeared in 2001 (later reissued in expanded book form in 2004) that included an introduction by Brown entitled "Thing Theory." In the 2001 introduction to the journal issue, Brown acknowledges the importance of the work of both Benjamin and Adorno to this new project of Thing Theory, noting that "because Benjamin devoted himself to such explanations [those that focus on "how things are part and parcel of society's institution"] he assumes particular authority in the following pages" (11). In a more recent essay, "Objects, Others and Us," Brown puts it this way: "Whereas Marx recognized a history of human labor that lay congealed in every human artifact (accounting for its value), Benjamin recognized multiple histories congealed there together: a history of production, but also of circulation and consumption and use, thus also a history of collective fascination, apprehension, aspiration" (188). Benjamin's evocative processes of collage in *The Arcades Project* have made his work ceaselessly inspiring, but in the original "Thing Theory" essay Brown also gives important credit to Adorno: "Indeed, Theodor Adorno, arguing against epistemology's and phenomenology's subordination of the object and the somatic moment to a fact of consciousness, understood the alterity of things as an essentially ethical fact. Most simply put, his point is that accepting the otherness of things is the condition for accepting otherness as such" (12). To read more on Adorno's ethics of things, see Wilford's "Toward a Morality of Materiality" and Haynes's "To Rescue Means to Love Things: Adorno and the Re-enchantment of Bodies." While I hesitate to use the very loaded term "unconscious" for my text packing (as opposed to "unpacking") project here, I have taken inspiration from Bill Brown's early remarks in *The Material Unconscious*: "Like any unconscious, it must be analytically *produced* by a certain kind of attention, concentration, or inhabitation that is unwilling to understand the seemingly inadvertent as genuinely unmotivated" (14; emphasis original).

4. Probably the closest analogue in our time to the intense use of muslin in Austen's time would be the use of denim in ours. For current work on denim see the Global Denim Project (http://www.ucl.ac.uk/global-denim-project), which poses a version of my question: "Our research suggests that on any day the majority of the world's population is wearing just one textile—Denim. We want to know why."

5. Beverly Lemire's work has been absolutely essential for this project, from her earlier work on British domestic consumption of cotton to her more recent work revitalizing contemporary awareness of the extent of the Indian Ocean trade in cottons prior to Vasco de Gama and the continuing importance of East-West as well as North-South trade in cottons through to our own time. See, in particular, *Fashion's Favourite: The Cotton Trade and the Consumer in Britain, 1660–1800; Dress, Culture and Commerce: The English Clothing Trade before the Factory, 1660–1800; Cotton*; "Fashioning cottons: Asian trade, domestic industry and consumer demand, 1660–1780;" "Fashioning Global Trade: Indian Textiles, Gender Meanings and European Consumers, 1500–1800;" "Domesticating the Exotic: Floral Culture and the East India Calico Trade with England, c. 1600–1800;" and, with George Riello, "East and West: Textiles and Fashion in Early Modern Europe." Chandra Mukerji's *From Graven Images: Patterns of Modern Materialism* has also been a foundation text for all my work on fabric and clothing.

6. Not one but two recent articles have borrowed Mrs. Allen's question as titles for their essays. In addition, the recent BBC movie adaptation (Jon Jones, 2007) of *Northanger Abbey* not only has Mrs. Allen ask this particular question, but the script has her say twice more in the film, "And he understands muslin!" which does not happen in Austen's novel. In the film script, phrases about Henry understanding muslin become a leitmotif and important character signals for both Henry and Mrs. Allen. Jackie Reid-Walsh's (2009) "'Do You Understand Muslins, Sir?': The Circulation of Ball Dresses in *Evelina* and *Northanger Abbey*," argues that both *Evelina* and *Northanger Abbey* can be read as "fictive ethnographies" (215); that is, they can be mined for ethnographic information about women's dress despite the fact that they are fiction. Judith Wylie's 2007 "'Do You Understand Muslins, Sir?': Fashioning Gender in *Northanger Abbey*" argues that in the famous conversation in chapter 3 Henry demonstrates "transvestic identification with the woman as spectacle" (141). A wide range of other essays have addressed this particular scene without using Mrs. Allen's question in the title, including Nigro's "Estimating Lace and Muslin: Dress and Fashion in Jane Austen and her World" (2001), Hughes' "Talk about Muslin" (2006), and Forgue's "The Mighty Muslin" (2010). Clearly the first decade of the twenty-first century has witnessed an efflorescence of scholarly work on Austen's muslin. Surprisingly, a number of these readings seem to assume that Henry is being quite genuine in his interest in muslin, despite the narrator's return at the end of the exchange: "Mr. Tilney was polite enough to seem interested in what [Mrs. Allen] said; and she kept him on the subject of muslins

till the dancing recommenced. Catherine feared, as she listened to their discourse, that he indulged himself a little too much in the foibles of others" (21). Readings that take Henry's interest as sincere also tend to fly in the face of Henry's pronounced tendency to parody conventionalized social discourses throughout the novel. As Jill Heydt-Stevenson points out, Henry "performs and parodies the feminine role when he discusses with Mrs. Allen the cost of muslin by the yard, his frequent choice of a gown for his sister, the fabric of Catherine's dress which he 'gravely' predicts will not 'wash well,' and the recycling of extra muslin to worthy purposes" (113–14). It may be that Henry's parody here has become harder for some readers to spot as memories of the conventionality of muslin conversations of this era have faded.

7. Adorno is responding to the following passage from Benjamin's "Paris, the Capital of the Nineteenth Century" (also known as the "Exposé of 1935"): "Fashion prescribes that ritual according to which the commodity fetish demands to be worshipped. . . . Fashion stands in opposition to the organic. It couples the living body to the inorganic world. To the living, it defends the rights of the corpse. The fetishism that succumbs to the sex appeal of the inorganic is its vital nerve. The cult of the commodity presses such fetishism into service" (Benjamin, *Arcades Project*, 8).

Benjamin wrote and rewrote versions of this passage several times; in each iteration the link between "fashion" and the inorganic is assumed. Adorno, in the same letter, also advises Benjamin to detach from the concept of "the organic" and replace it with the category of "the living"—that is, "not with some superior nature" (*Benjamin and Adorno: The Complete Correspondence*, 111). Although Benjamin doesn't explore this in his work on fashion, the fashions of nineteenth-century France were far from inorganic as we might use the term in the wake of the mass production of plastics and synthetic fibers—all their textiles derived from plants or animals in some way, as did most objects used for ornamentation. It might be more accurate to say that fashion couples the living body to materials that once were living or part of living beings.

8. Benjamin was also interested in the idea of a particular fashion serving as a symbol or metaphor for a specific historic period more generally. In fragment B7,5 of *The Arcades Project*, Benjamin includes this note, a passage from F. Th. Vischer, cited by Eduard Fuchs in *Die Karikatur der europäiaschen Völker*. Vischer writes that the crinoline is "the unmistakable symbol of reaction on the part of an imperialism that spreads out and puffs up . . . and that . . . settles its dominion like a hoop skirt over all aspects, good and bad, justified and unjustified, of the revolution. . . . It seemed a caprice of the moment, and it has established itself as the emblem of a period, like the Second of December" (Fuchs, quoted in Benjamin, *Arcades Project*, 76).

9. In his "On the Concept of History" (more familiarly known as "Theses on the Philosophy of History"), Benjamin writes:

> History is the subject of a construction whose site is not homogeneous, empty time, but time filled full by now-time [*Jetztzeit*]. Thus, to Robespierre ancient Rome was a past charged with now-time, a past which he blasted out of the continuum of history. The French Revolution viewed itself as Rome reincarnate. It cited ancient Rome exactly the way fashion cites a bygone mode of dress. Fashion has a nose for the topical, no matter where it stirs in the thicket of long ago; it is the tiger's leap into the past."
> (*Selected Writings*, vol. 4, 395)

10. While the popularity of pale colors no doubt contributed to the perception of the "clearness" of muslin, the matte texture of muslin likely did too. The silks and satins (like Adorno's changeant) that dominated style before and after the muslin craze tended to have much more reflective surfaces as well as often heavier textures.

11. The word "muslin" does not appear in *Persuasion* or *Mansfield Park*, but scattered references to muslin do appear in *Emma* and *Sense and Sensibility*, as well as in *Northanger Abbey* and *Pride and Prejudice*. I discuss the other works above, but it's worth noting here that in *Emma*, as Harriet dithers while shopping, "hanging over muslins and changing her mind" (251), Emma finally works to "convince her that if she wanted plain muslin it was of no use to look at the figured" (253) in order to resolve the transaction. Harriet's intensity in her muslin shopping marks her as silly, much as Mrs. Allen's does.

12. Heydt-Stevenson writes, "The word 'muslin' carried sexual connotations, as in the following definitions: 'a bit of muslin' referred to 'a woman, a girl'; 'a bit of muslin on the sly' suggested illicit sexual relations" (87), citing Eric Partridge's *Dictionary of Slang and Unconventional English*. It is worth noting that according to the *OED*, the first attested usage of "muslin" in this sense occurs in 1823. The sexual connotation is logical, though; contemporary commentators frequently noted that muslin gowns strongly resembled garments that had previously served only as underwear, and the fabric's association with the sheer, nearly transparent fabrics of an exotic and sexualized culture in India only further underscored the sexual frisson. A not-infrequent modifier for muslin in the discourse of the time was "clear," apparently meaning that the fabric was unpatterned, although it could be dyed. For centuries patterned cloth had been the almost exclusive province of the aristocracy; the fact that imported calicos put patterned cloth within the reach of a much wider swath of the population seems to have driven the "calico crazes" that caused so much controversy (and protectionist legislation) in the late sixteenth and early seventeenth centuries. For more on the calico crazes, see especially Chandra Mukerji's *From Graven Images: Patterns of Modern Materialism* and Beverly Lemire's *Fashion's Favourite: The Cotton Trade and the Consumer in Britain, 1660–1800*.

13. Despite the fact that twentieth-century fashion historians have tended to associate gowns bound under the breast and falling straight to the floor with liberté, égalité, and fraternité, aristocratic women such as Marie Antoinette, Empress Josephine, and

Lady Hamilton (and their portraits) played important roles in the diffusion of this fashion. Of course, at any time aristocrats can wish to appear aligned with notions of democracy, as we see in the prevalence of blue jeans on Hollywood stars and tech giants today.

14. Note that Mackie is focused on the origin rather than the meaning of the fashion.

15. There are indications that, in France in particular, the colonial associations of the chemise dress, an important forerunner of the 1790s fashion for pale muslin gowns, had colonialist associations with the West Indies as well as the East Indies. As Valerie Steele notes in *Paris Fashion*:

> There is some evidence that the chemise dress had colonial as well as clas-
> sical and English antecedents. Much of French eighteenth-century wealth
> was based on Caribbean sugar—and Creole ladies understandably favored
> cool, light, white fashions. Both the material and the indigo that (with
> bleaching) tinted it to a striking bluish white came from the tropics, how-
> ever much they were popularly associated with the pellucid atmosphere of
> Mediterranean Greece and Rome. (39)

Jane Ashelford concurs in *The Art of Dress: Clothes and Society 1500–1914*: "Although the French Queen, Marie Antoinette, and her ladies wore clothes of extreme artificiality on state occasions, away from court they often wore robes à la créole, thought to have originated in the French West Indies, or 'chemise dresses'" (174–75).

The chemise dress, as it crossed the channel, was hardly denuded of these associa-tions. But as Ashelford points out, the dress soon became more public in England:

Although the fashion soon spread to England, the chemise dress remained an infor-mal garment, worn in the privacy of the home. The situation changed in August 1784 when Georgiana, wife of the fifth duke of Devonshire, attended a concert "in one of the muslin chemises with fine lace that the Queen of France gave me" (Ashelford 175, quoting extracts from the correspondence of Georgiana, duchess of Devonshire).

Ashelford's account complicates the notion, commonplace at the turn of the nine-teenth century, that in the wake of the French Revolution, women simply threw off their clothes and began appearing in public in their underwear. Ashelford suggests that commentators were right to associate the fashion with France, and the tumultuous events of the early 1790s probably did encourage the spread of a feminine repudiation of ornamentation, but Georgiana's revolutionary trip to the concert and the association of the chemise with Marie Antoinette and the West Indies complicate less nuanced accounts.

4

William Makepeace Thackeray's Fashionable Humbugs

Consuming National Distinctions of Dress in Vanity Fair

Amy L. Montz

*H*alf French and a conniving social fraud, William Makepeace Thackeray's scandalous "love to hate her and hate to love her" character Becky Sharp is not socially acceptable to the middle- and upper-class persons with whom she spends so much time in the novel.[1] She is, however, quite capable of constructing a charming identity because she affects the desirable characteristics of a fashionable woman as well as a Frenchwoman among the English. "Honest old Dobbin" may see through Becky's disguise and recognize "what a humbug that woman is!" but George Osborne, Amelia Sedley's husband and would-be lover of Becky, dismisses the concept of "humbug—acting!" in Becky's character, because he refuses to see through her pretense to the evident artificiality she displays (Thackeray 1985, 338). Rather, like Amelia, who becomes "overpowered by the flash and dazzle and the fashionable talk of her worldly rival" (338), George is blinded by Becky's constructed self. Her penchant for acting and her desire for fashion and worldliness mark her as a "humbug"; her clothes and her sparkle mark her as a savvy consumer.[2] It seems that Becky is all "flash and dazzle" and no real substance.

Amelia Sedley acts as Becky's foil in Thackeray's novel, and I use the word "act" in two ways: Thackeray scripts her character as a counterpoint to Becky's, and Amelia herself willingly and actively performs as Becky's opposite. The shy innocent to Becky's flamboyant coquette, the unfashionable Englishwoman to Becky's fashionable French, Amelia succeeds as the ideal woman England proclaims it desires because she looks and behaves "naturally." The first descriptions of Amelia concern her "guileless and good-natured" self, her face that "blushed with rosy health, and her lips with the freshest of smiles," and her eyes "which sparkled with the brightest and honestest good-humour" (43). Like Becky, Amelia sparkles, which *seems* to be a gift of nature rather than fashionable artifice. And Amelia's nature, is, of course, bestowed upon her by two middle-class English parents and not, as Becky's is, by an English artist and a French opera-girl. However, this naturalness is just as conscious as Becky's fashioning, marking both women as humbugs.

Thackeray's *Vanity Fair* offers a dichotomous presentation of French and English women[3] that is rooted in the consumption of fashion and of nation. Through its comparison of Becky Sharp Crawley and Amelia Sedley Osborne, Thackeray's novel exposes England's suspicions of women's conscious style and fashionable consumption. As style is associated with artificiality, purposeful and mindful consumerism, and, particularly in nineteenth-century England, France, style functions as signals of deception and deceit to the English. Therefore, Englishwomen's supposed ignorance of dress—yet continuous, seemingly accidental beauty and style—would signal that their "natural" style is rooted in the innocence and purity of their consequence of birth and not in their learned consumption and artificial construction of a fashionable self. What seems to be the unconscious self-stylizing of Amelia is in fact clumsy, feigned ignorance of fashionable dress and personal beauty; this feigned ignorance is presented in the novel as equivalent to Becky's carefully constructed and willfully gained knowledge of the same, marking them both as fashionable humbugs. When Thackeray presents both Becky Sharp and Amelia Sedley as artificially constructed, he argues that their fashion and style are the results of learned behaviors and careful articulation of artifice and manner and not, as so many would argue, the result of arbitrary national distinctions.

"NATURAL" BEAUTY AND "ARTIFICIAL" STYLE: ENGLISH AND FRENCH HUMBUGS

Becky Sharp is a dangerous woman in Thackeray's novel because despite her nation of origin and her low station of birth, she moves within the middle and upper classes with ease and comfort; through Rawdon Crawley, she marries into the aristocracy; she solicits sexual advances and marriage proposals from several high-ranking members of English aristocracy; she receives costly gifts from Englishmen that, the narrator slyly suggests, if they actually "went to gentlemen's lawful wives and daughters, what a profusion of jewellery there would be exhibited in the genteelest homes of Vanity Fair!" (352); most importantly, she conceives a child of mixed English and French blood. Throughout Thackeray's novel, both the characters and the narrator emphasize Becky's artificiality again and again, and this excessive repetition underscores the nineteenth-century panic over a woman's artificiality and its signals of foreignness. Becky invents her own ancestors (48); she is "artful" (67), a "humbug" (338), and an actress (491) with "a habit of play-acting and fancy dressing" (612). While these accusations seem in step with a novel that proclaims itself "without a Hero," the same accusations from literary critics seem almost extreme. She is painted as "an unscrupulous and greedy representative of the rising middle classes" (Zlotnick, 57), the promoter of "female chicanery" (Jadwin, 666), a "sirenlike heroine" (Dyer, 197), and, most importantly for this study, "an artist" (Sheets, 421). Robin Ann Sheets furthers the discussion of Becky's artifice and her artfulness by arguing that not only does Thackeray write Becky Sharp as an artist but that he writes an entire novel about art (420), its deceit (421), and its potential for counterfeit (422) as well. Becky's designation as an "artist" calls forth her capacity for artful deceit, her construction of her family, her self, and her feelings which are all part, as Sheets reminds us, of Becky's capacity for mimesis; the novel demonstrates, again and again, Becky's imitative skills and powers of performance (421).

As Becky's English foil, Amelia is presented as a demure, charmingly clumsy girl with seemingly so little idea of her own style and beauty that she cannot help but fail at constructing herself. Seen as a "natural" beauty, Amelia and her actions often are described with the terms "natural" (Thackeray 1985, 70), "artless" (148), or "unaffected" (148). Even contemporary literary critics fall sway under Amelia's gentle awkwardness and see it as the consequence of nature, rather than a combination of nature, nation, and, most importantly for this study, learned skills through a careful and thorough education. Judith Law Fisher, for example, argues that "Amelia's appearance is the consequence of her own nature" in that her eyes, skin, lips, and good humor create a physique as well as a personality (400). For Fisher, Amelia's appearance is directly correlated not only with the features with which she was born but also with her "good humor" and "own nature." Robin Ann Sheets reminds us that "As often as Becky is called artful, Amelia is called artless; the word refers to both her innocence and her ineptitude" (423) as Thackeray's novel presents her. Amelia's innocence often is revealed in her downcast eyes or her blushing face; her ineptitude, however, speaks to an ignorance that does not seem learned, when, in fact, it is.

This fashionable failure can be read as a "natural" mistake by a Victorian audience; it takes place because Amelia, as an Englishwoman, supposedly cannot construct artificiality. In the world Thackeray creates, as well as the world in which he writes, artfulness is contrasted with artlessness, as France is contrasted with England, and as Becky's theoretical artifice is contrasted with Amelia's theoretical naturalness.[4] These contrasts demonstrate the similarities rather than the differences between England's assumptions about its women and the women of other nations. Kit Dobson argues that Amelia Sedley is just as guilty of performance as Becky Sharp is, and that the constant repetition of the word "natural" to describe Amelia is in fact a performance of the expectations of English femininity.[5] Both the constant repetition of the words "art," "artless," and "artifice" in Thackeray's novel as well as the novel's sly acknowledgment of its interest in performance through its introduction of the stage of Vanity Fair itself expose Thackeray's awareness and purposeful scripting of his characters' performances. From small-scale stagings of friendship, familial expectation, and domestic duties to larger, subtle scriptings of nineteenth-century ideologies of, and expectations for, domesticity, nationality, class, and gender expectations, Thackeray's characters understand the value of a good performance. My interest here, however, is not solely in feminine performance—whether conscious or not—but in fashionability and style; through artifice, affectation, and those minute details of manner and of dress, Becky and Amelia possess individual styles that are, in the end, nationally ascribed.

As Thackeray's characters try to sort out what is "natural" and what is "artificial," they use the same method as their nineteenth-century reading audience: an examination of a woman's style, that individualized and socialized collection of fashion, manners, and deportment. Therefore, these presentations are rooted not only in the national but also in the fashionable, two realms that are, as we see consistently in nineteenth-century texts, intrinsically connected. For Victorian England, this was divided according to nationalist lines, and fashion critics have paid particular attention to the national distinctions the nineteenth century made between English and French women. Valerie Steele's influential fashion study *Fashion and Eroticism: Ideals of Feminine Beauty from the Victorian Era to the Jazz Age* notes that while the English continued to insist on "natural" beauty, "the French, on the other hand, often implied that natural beauty was only the beginning. A woman learned to *become* beautiful" (135; emphasis original). The assumption in England, ultimately, was that "learning to become beautiful" was an unattractive and suspicious trait in women.

These beliefs are not without historical precedent; throughout the nineteenth century, fashion and manners texts separated English and French women's approaches to dress and beauty, creating the distinction between nature and construction, between natural and artificial, as the distinction between England and France. In an 1861 text about life in Paris, the pseudonymous Chroniqueuse finds "how plain, alongside of these [Frenchwomen], appear English girls, who, with ten times more natural beauty, seem so ugly with their poke bonnets, ugly and coarse stuff gowns that cling to the figure, while the little short jackets add to the uncouthness of the *tout ensemble*! 'As badly dressed as an *Anglaise*,' has got to be a proverb among the Parisians; and surely they are right" (157). To Chroniqueuse, English girls appear "plain" alongside their fashionable French sisters, despite possessing "ten times more natural beauty." To an English-reading public, however, these girls are triumphant in their appearance abroad, as their beauty is not diminished or overshadowed by the flounces and petticoats, the artful construction that fashion—particularly French fashion—demands.

In her 1878 treatise on fashion, aestheticism, and appearance, *The Art of Beauty*, Mrs. H. R. Haweis (Mary Eliza Haweis) encompasses the prevailing Victorian attitude toward the history of dress and popular fashion trends and instructs her readers on how to choose the most becoming dress and ornamentation. While she strives to instruct all women on proper color coordination and on draping fabrics according to natural bodylines, she cannot avoid calling attention to Englishwomen's superiority in the world of beauty. As Haweis argues,

> The Englishwomen are considered by all nations to be among the most beautiful in the world, whilst the French are commonly far less gifted by nature, but a Frenchwoman understands how to hide her defects and enhance her beauties to a far greater extent than an Englishwoman—and this, not because her moral character is necessarily lower, but simply because she belongs to an artistic race, cultivating aesthetic tastes. (1978, 258–59)

Haweis presents her belief in the superiority of Englishwomen's beauty as a consequence of nature and birth. Frenchwomen, in contrast, excel in the artificial construction of beauty; their "artistic race" understands "how to hide [their] defects and enhance [their] beauties," traits Englishwomen, it seems, are not capable of. In Haweis's estimation, this is "not because [a Frenchwoman's] moral character is necessarily lower" than an Englishwoman's, but the adverb "necessarily" suggests that a lowered moral character may at least be partly responsible. By establishing a division between women's artificiality and naturalness, between standards for constructed beauty and natural beauty, Haweis reiterates Victorian England's common division between French and English. Haweis's and Chroniqueuse's texts, later in the century than Thackeray's novel, still exhibit the prevailing understandings of nationality evident in the Victorian mindset. Therefore, with the addition of Thackeray's text, we see that from the 1840s to the 1870s England still believes in the national distinctions between it and France.

FRENCH HABITS OF PLAY-ACTING AND FANCY DRESS: THACKERAY'S FASHIONABLE HUMBUG

Victorian England wanted to believe that Englishwomen were, unlike Becky Sharp, incapable of constructing a fashionable self, but as Thackeray's novel reveals, this was an unfulfilled and unrealistic desire. Characters' fashionability must be examined in conjunction with an exploration of nineteenth-century England's understanding of national distinctions in dress. Such an examination allows for an exploration of Thackeray's novel that highlights the double bind in Victorian England regarding fashionable women's clothing: to be fashionable, one must be aware of the fashions and the ideas they convey, but to be a good Englishwoman, one must pretend to be ignorant of the artificiality of fashion and persuade others of one's ignorance. When viewed with a Victorian understanding of fashion and national identification, it seems only logical that Becky Sharp, half French herself, would be obsessed with fashion. Thackeray's novel seems overly concerned with fashion as it details Becky's clothing again and again, particularly in discussions of Becky's stage acting and tableau constructing, and always in conjunction with her social climbing. Becky's concerns with fashion are the concerns of an ambitious woman, as she manipulates fashion and the common understanding and interpretation of fashion to climb the social ladder. Becky Sharp is constructed as a dangerous woman throughout the novel because she knowingly constructs herself; she is aware of the artificial nature of fashion.[6] As Ellen Bayuk Rosenman notes, in the nineteenth century fashion was deemed dangerous because it was both artistic and sexually aware (15); a woman's sophistication and self-construction in the arena of fashion speaks of secret initiations and rites. Becky not only understands this, she also revels in it. She stages tableaux in which she is the star, the figure to be admired and fawned over by her male admirers, and her clothing speaks to these desires: she is admired and fawned over because she dresses to be so. Sharon Marcus argues that "those who sell fashion, like those who produce dolls, create simulacra of femininity not for men but for *women and girls* to scrutinize, handle, and consume. To market femininity to women is to use hyperfeminine objects to solicit a female gaze and to incite female fantasy" (4; emphasis original). Marcus argues that the looking and looking back of feminine fashion is not grounded in heteroeroticism but rather in homoeroticism; thus, fashion is worn by women for the visual pleasure of other women.

This certainly holds true in Thackeray's novel, but the argument can be taken even further. The solicitation of a female gaze of which Marcus speaks is less the issue in *Vanity Fair* than the power of women to "scrutinize, handle, and consume." I believe that the marketing of femininity is not where the power of fashion lies in *Vanity Fair* but, rather, with women's consumption and the reading of fashion. Fashion is, I argue, an arena to which Victorian women are relegated because it is seen as trivial. Becky's interest in dress and, most important, her use of dress prove this belief to be false; fashion is not a trivial realm, because it can be used to promote personal agendas, convey or assume national affiliation, or, in Becky's case, to move within national class ranks. To counter this, the Victorian audience dismisses fashionable know-how as simple foreign deception; true Englishwomen would not have such arcane and dangerous knowledge. Thackeray uses Becky and England's distaste for her to highlight the hypocrisy evident in these fears.

Because fashionable women like Becky Sharp understand the artificiality of dress and the presentation of self for which it allows, they are familiar with both the consumption and interpretation of fashion. With their seemingly innate knowledge of fashion, women such as Becky are privy to skills, heretofore usually associated with men, of reading, interpreting, and consuming objects, and, most importantly, women. Becky possesses, therefore, a small piece of masculine power; it is no wonder that she is usually in the company of men in the novel, for this reason, if not for her sexual misadventures. What Becky Sharp best demonstrates and what Thackeray's novel best implies is that women's fashion and, through it, constructions of self are not dangerous only because they solicit the male or the female gaze; fashion is dangerous also because it is made to solicit any gaze at all.

To complicate the groundwork laid by previous critics, particularly Sheets and Marcus, I believe we can take Becky's power of performance and conscious, purposeful consumption of fashion one step further to examine how her artistry, her artfulness, her performance, and her mimicry are all parts of herself that Becky *enjoys*. Ultimately, what is dangerous about Becky is that she is believed to have mastered feminine secrets and has learned to enjoy her body through her hyperstylizing (discussed in the next paragraph). Because she is half French, Becky therefore has awareness of the seemingly mystical fashion knowledge supposedly unavailable to Englishwomen. But further, Becky Sharp is artificial because she chooses to be so; the reader never sees any sign that there is a real Becky beneath the façade of the performer, the flirtatious lover, the good wife, the social climber, the capricious friend, and the dozens of other roles that Becky plays throughout the novel. Like all good performances, these roles depend heavily on costume change to carry the weight of staged authenticity; or, as Patricia Marks reminds us, "Becky is nothing without her finery" (82).

Once she establishes a modicum of respectability as the wife of Rawdon Crawley, Becky no longer receives her dresses, shawls, and accouterments of fashion secondhand; her constructed self, therefore, is no longer a borrowed self.[7] She is completely aware of every ring or bracelet, of every fold or bow, and even her surroundings would never dare to clash with Becky's *ensemble*. While seated with "a party of gentlemen around her" (Thackeray 1985, 444), Becky is observed in the candlelight by Lord Steyne:

> [The candles] lighted up Rebecca's figure to admiration, as she sate [sic] on a sofa covered with a pattern of gaudy flowers. She was in a pink dress, that looked as fresh as a rose; her dazzling white arms and shoulders were half-covered with a thin hazy scarf through which they sparkled; her hair hung in curls round her neck; one of her little feet peeped out from the fresh crisp folds of the silk: the prettiest little foot in the prettiest little sandal in the finest silk stocking in the world. (445)

Becky sits on a floral-patterned sofa to match her pink dress that looked, fittingly, "fresh as a rose." The sofa and Becky match entirely too well, just as the candlelight hits her a bit too perfectly. But it is not just for the "ice and coffee . . . , the best in London" that "the men came to her house to finish the night" (444); men like Lord Steyne come because Becky has displayed herself to utmost perfection. While the "candles lighted up Lord Steyne's shining bald head" and his "twinkling bloodshot eyes, surrounded by a thousand wrinkles," demonstrating every physical fault of the aristocrat, those same candles light instead Becky's "figure to admiration" (445). In her own things and in her own home, Becky is able to fashion a self to her best advantage. By matching her clothing to her surroundings, by best situating herself in the candlelight, and by surrounding herself only with admirers, Becky ensures her social success among a small but elite crowd, a success dependent on her knowledge of fashion and her ability to display her best features.[8] The national danger here stems from the fact that not only has Becky inserted herself into the English aristocracy by marriage, and the middle class by friendship, she also has gained the admiration and attention of several Englishmen precisely *because* she has constructed a beautiful and pleasing self.

Thackeray's novel satirizes the differences between Englishwomen's and Frenchwomen's approaches to fashion in one particular scene, the confrontation of Becky Sharp Crawley and Amelia Sedley Osborne at the infamous June 15, 1815, Brussels ball the night before the Company is called off to war. This ball has been discussed greatly in criticism and history for its impact on the soldiers and its proximity to warfare, but like Thackeray's narrator's, our place is with the noncombatants (346). For Becky Sharp, the ball represents the best of such shining moments for her; her utter grasp of fashion, of self-construction through clothing, and of those stylish secrets to which she and not Amelia is privy allow her to construct a self that is, without a doubt, the belle of the ball. The narrator tells us that while Amelia's "appearance was an utter failure," Becky Sharp's "*debut* was, on the contrary, very brilliant. She arrived very late. Her face was radiant; her dress perfection" (342). She is swarmed by men and gossiped about by women, who "agreed that her manners were fine, her air *distingué*" (342), two points that Becky proves complete falsities when she walks over to Amelia and "finish[es] the poor child at once" (342). Becky's shining moment is dependent not on the clothes that she is wearing but rather on her reading and consumption of the clothes other women are wearing.[9] She reads Amelia's dress as an artificial covering of awkwardness and discomfort: "Mrs. Rawdon ran and greeted affectionately her dearest Amelia, and began forthwith to patronize her. She found fault with her friend's dress, and her hairdresser, and wondered how she could be so *chaussée*, and vowed that she must send her *corsetière* the next morning" (342). And as if this long reprimand was not enough, Becky then "left her bouquet and shawl by Amelia's side, and tripped off with George to dance" (343).

When Becky reads Amelia's ball dress, she reads not only Amelia's inability to wear fashionable clothing but also her inability to dress herself in appropriate and flattering dress. She sees through Amelia's façade to her corset; by offering to send her *corsetière*, Becky takes her reading even further to state that it is Amelia and not her clothing that is a cause for fashionable crisis.

I quote this passage at length because this scene functions as the crux of the nineteenth-century fashionable argument highlighted in Thackeray's novel: there is a distinct difference between Englishwomen and Frenchwomen that is seemingly recognizable not only through what they wear but how well they wear it. At this moment, Becky's utter artificiality and Amelia's utter naiveté at disguising artificiality are nowhere better seen. Becky's knowledge of fashion and power in the fashionable world allow for her perfect dress and radiant face; indeed, her fashionable knowledge lends itself perfectly to her evaluation of Amelia. In a discussion of snobbery and consumerism in *Vanity Fair*, Joseph Litvak argues that "in a marketplace mobbed with cool customers, the successful consumer must be able conspicuously to consume not just commodities but other consumers; or—to put it more tastefully—she must consume the *consumption* of other consumers" (63; emphasis original). Becky is, above all else, a successful consumer. Her power lies in artificiality and in recognition, in that secret French knowledge of dress that she possesses, and in her subversive ability to read, consume, and interpret.[10] At the Brussels ball, Becky not only reads but consumes, and as Litvak reminds us, she not only consumes but consumes consumption; in addition to being a siren and a humbug, Becky becomes, in this moment, a succubus, feeding on fashion faux pas. She is able to suck the life and shine out of Amelia's evening, and all because "Women only know how to wound so" (Thackeray 1985, 343). She understands that Amelia is just as artificially constructed as she is. The irony of this moment is that Amelia, an Englishwoman, is constructed poorly.

Further, Becky's knowledge of women, of bodies, and even of fashion allows her to recognize that Amelia's failure is not due to her fashionable tastes, but rather, her husband's. It is George and not Amelia who has "commanded new dresses and ornaments of all sorts" for Mrs. Osborne for the ball (341), and it is George who feels "with a sort of rage" Amelia's appearance as "an utter failure" (342). George believes that "he had behaved very handsomely in getting her new clothes" (342), but in fact, the clothes he has acquired for his wife lead to her ridicule and scorn at the hands of Becky Sharp. George's responsibility extends even to Amelia's body itself; her corset and dress fit so poorly because Amelia is, at this point in the novel, pregnant with George's child.[11] Becky sees Amelia's clothing as a façade. By calling attention to Amelia's poorly worn corset, Becky calls attention to Amelia's figure, the actual body beneath the clothed body on display for the attendees of the ball. That figure is not disguised by the corset Amelia wears; Amelia is visibly pregnant, in public, at a ball.[12] Becky understands that the female body, particularly the pregnant body, should be shaped and disguised by the corset. She recognizes Amelia's unfashionable presentation as the artificial presentation it is: a poor attempt to ape fashionable dress—acquired by her husband—and a poor attempt to disguise the growing pregnant body—also, in truth, George's fault. What we see in the character foils of Becky Sharp and Amelia Sedley is a nationalistic double standard; the Englishwoman and her knowledge of fashion and style cannot be proclaimed to be artificial, as to do so would be to acknowledge Englishwomen's understanding of the artificiality of style. Yet "natural" beauty and style do not exist, as Amelia's poor attempt to disguise her pregnant body presents. By its very construction, "naturalness" is learned, and therefore there is no such standard as "natural" style; all that remains is artificial, stylized, and learned naturalness.

ENGLISH MANNERS AND NATURAL TIMIDITY: THACKERAY'S DARLING

Only seven years after the publication of *Vanity Fair*, Frederick Audax's *A Hint from Modesty to the Ladies of England on the Fashion of Low-Dressing* urges Englishwomen not to be swayed by the lure of fashion and its many artifices. He argues that artifices are "unworthy" of the women of England (iv), particularly because

> An English woman! Who can tell her praise? Who can even most faintly trace all her excellencies? To say that she is a pattern to every country blessed with civilization, is to say nothing that is not in course. . . .
> And how beautiful! All fair and all lovely she is! In her the North and the South meet, drop every blemish, and unite their beauties in a model of Nature! (7)

Audax claims that Englishwomen are "a pattern to every country blessed with civilization," and that their domesticity, generosity, and modesty (7) are unparalleled. But Audax also takes his praise beyond his countrywomen's superior inner qualities to call attention to their outer beauty. In Audax's opinion, the Englishwoman is the result of the unification of "the North and South" into a "model of Nature." For the author, Englishwomen's beauty is dependent on the beauty of Nature; he calls attention to geographical regions to claim that Englishwomen's beauty is formed by the melding of two such regions' ideals. They have no need for artifice and fashion to make their outward appearance appealing, as Nature has already been so generous.

Yet Amelia Sedley, representative of all of these good English qualities, is a social failure, and Becky Sharp, reviled so often for her artificiality and written as the antithesis of the good Englishwoman Audax and others claim to desire, is a social success. Thackeray portrays Becky as accomplished in everything her society claims desirable for their women yet still dismisses her as false and artificial; Amelia, however, is portrayed as natural and unconscious of how to construct a fashionable self but fails again and again. Becky Sharp fulfills every obligation regarding the art of conversation, beauty, and dress set forth by fashion tracts and manners texts such as Sarah Stickney Ellis's *The Women of England* or Mary Eliza Haweis's *The Art of Beauty*, yet despite it all, the text marks her as foreign, as a "humbug," and as artificial.[13] Ellis tells her readers that "women have the choice of many means of bringing their principles into exercise, and of obtaining influence, both in their own domestic sphere, and in society at large. Amongst the most important of these is **conversation**" (119; emphasis original), a charge with which Becky Sharp most happily complies. Miss Crawley, Becky's benefactor and champion prior to her marriage to Rawdon, declares "little Miss Sharp" to be "the only person fit to talk to in the country!" (Thackeray 1985, 141). Most of Becky's charm comes from her penchant for mimicry, and Miss Crawley "laughed heartily at a perfect imitation of Miss Briggs and her grief, which Rebecca described to her" (171). But even Becky Sharp's acting and conversational skills cannot withstand the onslaught of Amelia Sedley, "who came forward so timidly and so gracefully" with a "sweet blushing face" to meet Miss Crawley that the elderly lady declares her "charming" and spoke of her "with rapture half-a-dozen times that day" (178). It is not Amelia's conversational skills or playacting that infatuates Miss Crawley, but rather the grand lady's "good taste. She liked natural manners—a little timidity only set them off" (178). For Miss Crawley, Amelia's appeal lies in her "natural manners" and "timidity," two traits that, it would seem, are inherent. Yet as the existence of so many conduct and fashion tracts attest, manners and style are learned; it is important, therefore, for a woman to learn to appear *unaware* of this knowledge.

For both women, the argument that pits artifice against naturalness is wholly dependent on recognition by the English reading—and viewing—public. The novel's presentation of Englishwoman Amelia Sedley and half-Frenchwoman Becky Sharp relies heavily on national stereotypes with particular regard to fashion. Becky's artificiality, demonstrated by her existence on credit, her hand-me-down clothes, and her humbuggery, stands in sharp contrast to Amelia's "natural" manners, seeming naiveté, and supposed unawareness of fashion. Becky's constant successes in the fashionable world are the result of the approval and admiration of men and foreign women rather than of the social arbiters: middle-class Englishwomen. When she and Rawdon go to Paris, the narrator notes that "her success in Paris was remarkable. All the French ladies voted her charming. She spoke their language admirably. She *adopted at once* their grace, their liveliness, their manner" (412; emphasis added). Becky's fashionability relies not only on her talent for mimicry and art but also on her adaptability. In England, and among the English-women in Brussels, Becky imitates their fashions and manners; among the French, Becky does the same. It is important to note here that Becky does not fall back on a supposedly natural racial instinct for French grace, liveliness, or manner, as writers like Mary Eliza Haweis might argue that Frenchwomen inherently have. Rather, she adopts her current society's manners and customs, and for this she is considered "the gayest and most admired of Englishwomen" (413). Becky's talent for reading and consuming fashion, when coupled with her mastery of staging, allows her to mimic the women of her acquaintance. In this sense, she reads the society around her not only for what its citizens are but also for what they expect their outsiders to be. As a result, in England Becky is most assuredly French, while in France she is most assuredly English. The fact that she can claim no country as her own in a social setting lends itself to her cosmopolitanism and reinforces the image of Becky as "a most artful and dangerous person" (413). She understands how to construct a personal and a national self, but she does it too well in England; Becky is free of any of the awkward gestures and innocence that Amelia supposedly possesses. This perfection of presentation, a self too put together, is what ultimately marks Becky as French.

Amelia, in contrast, is "the best, the kindest, the gentlest, the sweetest girl in England," according to George Osborne (253), and while this praise is exaggerated, it is important in its qualifications. In England Amelia is indeed ranked among the kindest and gentlest of girls, because in England Amelia is valued and praised for her submissiveness and demureness. But as we see at the beginning of *Vanity Fair*, all of these traits—style, deportment, manners, and carriage—can be learned as well as inherited. Amelia's first introduction in the novel is not through appearance but rather through her headmistress's letter to her parents: "'Those virtues which characterise the young English gentlewoman, those accomplishments which become her birth and station, will not be found wanting in the amiable Miss Sedley, whose *industry* and *obedience* have endeared her to her instructors, and whose delightful sweetness of temper has charmed her *aged* and her *youthful* companions'" (40; emphasis original). The English virtues for which Amelia is most praised are her industry and obedience, and her temper and amiability have made her a favorite among the school, but her "*deportment and carriage*, so requisite for every young lady of *fashion*" are found in need of work (40; emphasis original). While Amelia's "industry and obedience"—two personal aspects of her character—are praised, her fashionability and presentation of self are found wanting. The headmistress, Miss Pinkerton, gives instructions on how to solve this deficit in Amelia's character—use of the backboard for "four hours daily during the next three years" (40)—but never once does she suggest that Amelia cannot *learn* to acquire "that dignified *deportment and carriage*." What Miss Pinkerton's letter suggests instead is that such signifiers of fashionable awareness are, in fact, learned, and not inherited; Miss Pinkerton acknowledges the artificiality of fashionable women.

Amelia is just as affected as Becky, or as any other woman in the novel, despite the veneer of naturalness she possesses. Mrs. O'Dowd, another wife of the regiment, declares that Amelia, "a natural and unaffected person, had none of that artificial shamefacedness which her husband mistook for delicacy on his own part" (327), although, in truth, she does. Amelia's presentations of innocence appear more natural but are in fact just as artificial. When her family teases her about George Osborne, Amelia, "hanging down her head, blushed as only young ladies of seventeen know how to blush" (67). This posturing presents Amelia as modest and humble, but it, too, is a learned response of modesty and humility. Even her blush, labeled as secretive knowledge only available to "young ladies of seventeen," appears a triggered response to the mention of her young gentleman; "young ladies of seventeen," on the marriage market and aware of the effect of their appearances on the male public, would understand the effect of those blushes, as well. Mary Ann O'Farrell reminds us that nineteenth-century novels and their novelists use the blush as a means of articulation, and that "by means of its attentions to blushing as a perceived event of the body, the [nineteenth-century English] novel suggests that—in seeming involuntarily and reliably to betray a deep self—blushing assists at the conversion of legibility into a sense of identity and centrality," ultimately becoming, in this sense "an act of self-expression" (5). Seen as involuntary, the blush is a way of making the private aspects of the body public; the blush is blood rushing to the skin, a response to shock, horror, excitement, shame, and other internal markers of personal revelation. But the blush is also about knowledge; O'Farrell argues that "innocence, after all, is compromised by the knowledge that raises the blush" (18). Amelia, in the end, despite the novel's insistence in her guilelessness, *knows how to blush.* Her understanding of an Englishwoman's middle-class feminine style is a learned response to behaviors, and through the presentation of her clumsy, awkward fashioning, and pretty blushes, Amelia scripts the very artificiality Victorian England claims to despise—and it loves her, as an Englishwoman, for it.

The "artificial shamefacedness" that is not as evident on Amelia is very much evident on Becky Sharp. At Becky's first dinner with the Sedleys, Becky's innocence is dependent on "holding her green eyes downwards," on her white gown, and on her "bare shoulders as white as snow" all creating "the picture of youth, unprotected innocence, and humble virgin simplicity," implying that Becky is "very modest" (Thackeray 1985, 60). Becky's "picture of youth" is in truth a picture; it is a projection constructed by Becky's artfulness and her ability to best portray the attributes her audience desires. She understands that a successful and advantageous marriage with the laughable but wealthy Jos Sedley would lead to her social success, and Becky instructs herself to maintain the façade of innocence and attentiveness, as a blushing virgin would do: "'I must be very quiet,' thought Rebecca, 'and very much interested about India'" (60). In contrast, Amelia Sedley enjoys some fashionable success once more when Dobbin returns from India. The men in his company, "as usual, liked her artless kindness and simple refined demeanour" (698). While the men "as usual" appreciate Amelia's artlessness and simplicity, they are reiterating their desire for the traits England so desires for its women: the appearance of artlessness, and the presentation of naturalness.

Amelia appears as the celebrated Englishwoman because she exists "in contrast"; that is, we see who Amelia is through seeing who she decidedly is not.

Her "artless kindness and simple refined demeanour" stand ever in contrast to Becky's artfulness and ostentatiousness. On the honeymoon tour, Amelia "Joins *Her* Regiment" and in truth she possesses George's company with "Her simple, artless behavior, and modest kindness of demeanour" (316; emphasis added). When "it became the fashion, indeed, among all the honest young fellows of the—th [sic], to adore and admire Mrs. Osborne" (316), Amelia finds herself with "a little triumph, which flushed her spirits and made her eyes sparkle" (321). This triumph that flushes Amelia's spirits flushes her face, as well; her social successes bring a healthy blush to her cheeks and shine to her eyes. Unencumbered by the fashionable "flash and substance" like Becky Sharp might wear, Amelia's physical presentation would appear, as some nineteenth-century writers would suggest, "plain," but, rather, her careful construction of fashion and dress demonstrates how well it highlights her stylistic triumph. But by reiterating, again and again, how both are constructed artifices, and by demonstrating the façade of fashionable success—and fashionable failure—Thackeray stays quite true to his prediction that his novel is one "without a Hero." The absence of a "perfect" heroine and a "perfect" villainess helps to highlight the ambiguity and complexity of the construction of a fashionable female identity in the early Victorian era.

As an author, Thackeray himself plays fast and loose with expectations for fashion; in the illustrated version of his text, he offers us a footnote:

> It was the author's intention, faithful to history, to depict all the characters of this tale in their proper costumes, as they wore them at the commencement of the century. But when I remember the appearance of people those days, and that an officer and a lady were actually habited like this—[image] I have not the heart to disfigure my heroes and heroines by costumes so hideous; and have, on the contrary, engaged a model of rank dressed according to the present fashion. (1994, 63–64)

The image shows the slender column silhouette of the Regency era, with an exaggerated poke bonnet—the very same that Chroniqueuse mocks—that completely disguises the face of its wearer. Accompanying the heroine is a naval officer in a bicorne hat as proportionately unequal as hers. By admitting that he is, in fact, unfaithful to history, Thackeray notes that no costumes in the text are "proper." Thackeray suggests from the onset the artificiality

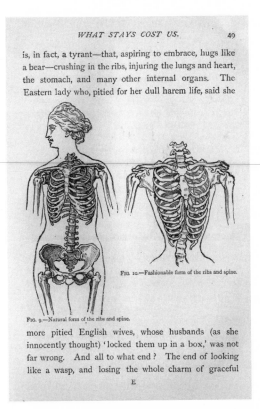

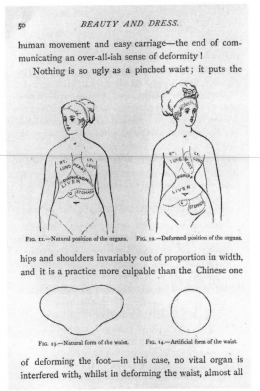

WHAT STAYS COST US. 49

is, in fact, a tyrant—that, aspiring to embrace, hugs like a bear—crushing in the ribs, injuring the lungs and heart, the stomach, and many other internal organs. The Eastern lady who, pitied for her dull harem life, said she

FIG. 10.—Fashionable form of the ribs and spine.

FIG. 9.—Natural form of the ribs and spine.

more pitied English wives, whose husbands (as she innocently thought) 'locked them up in a box,' was not far wrong. And all to what end? The end of looking like a wasp, and losing the whole charm of graceful
E

50 *BEAUTY AND DRESS.*

human movement and easy carriage—the end of communicating an over-all-ish sense of deformity!

Nothing is so ugly as a pinched waist; it puts the

FIG. 11.—Natural position of the organs.   FIG. 12.—Deformed position of the organs.

hips and shoulders invariably out of proportion in width, and it is a practice more culpable than the Chinese one

FIG. 13.—Natural form of the waist.   FIG. 14.—Artificial form of the waist.

of deforming the foot—in this case, no vital organ is interfered with, whilst in deforming the waist, almost all

FIGURE 4.1 (LEFT): Haweis, *The Art of Beauty* (1878). "Natural form of the ribs and spine." "Fashionable form of the ribs and spine."
FIGURE 4.2 (RIGHT): Haweis, *The Art of Beauty* (1878). "Natural position of the organs." "Deformed position of the organs."

of fashion and does so with his French and his English female characters interchangeably.

Mary Eliza Haweis, among other writers of her time, spent a great deal of energy and ink trying to convince her reading public that danger lurked where artificial fashions reigned. In *The Art of Beauty* she offers images similar to Thackeray's that work to exaggerate the fashions of the time in order to emphasize the problems they present to the natural female form. Her work presents women's bodies internally, with a look at the anatomical deformities that can occur with the current fashions.

When urging women to choose corsets that would be a "servant" rather than a "tyrant" in supporting the female figure, Haweis offers the following comparative illustrations (figs. 4.1 and 4.2): in examination of the skeletal frame, "Fig. 9—Natural form of the ribs and spine" and "Fig. 10—Fashionable form of the ribs and spine" (1978, 49), and an examination of the anatomical frame, "Fig. 11—Natural position of the organs" and "Fig. 12—Deformed position of the organs" (50).

These two sets of images show how the natural shape of the body has been manipulated through artificial means, namely the corset, which was first brought to England, it seems, by either "Mademoiselle Pantine, a mistress of Marshal Saxe" or "an early Norman lady" (48), making the ancestry of corsetry, in Haweis's eyes, decidedly French. Therefore, as her illustrations demonstrate, it is the French we are to blame for these artificial deformities of the natural womanly shape, just as Becky Sharp's insistence on artificial beauty stands in stark contrast to Amelia Sedley's natural, more English looks. But it is important to remember that even Haweis advocates for supportive garments; her argument is not to abandon the corset—to do so, it seems, would be to "look very slovenly" (48)—but rather to find a garment that "aspir[es] to embrace" rather than "hugs like a bear—crushing in the ribs, injuring the lungs and heart, the stomach, and many other internal organs" (49). If we were to alter Thackeray's estimation, then, we can see that only women *and* corsetry know how to wound so. Even with this supporting device that embraces, the natural shape is altered, making Haweis's suggestion one for artificiality, however slight.

To be a fashionable success, then, is to be artificial; there is no "natural" style, despite English claims. What remains important to the English reader is whether that artificiality is evident. What Thackeray's novel seems to argue— and indeed, what many Victorian novels and fashion tracts seem to suggest— is that while artificiality is an undesirable trait, women can *learn* to seem natural. Ultimately, despite England's panicked insistence to the contrary, there is no difference between the way French and English women approach fashion. *Vanity Fair* sets up a dichotomy between Becky and Amelia, and thus the dichotomy between French and English and between artificial and natural; it calls attention to the artifice of all fashionable persons and personas. When English writers claim "naturalness" for their countrywomen, they are in fact veiling artificiality and removing agency from a woman's understanding of fashion and her own body. Englishwomen should be "natural" because they should be symbolic representations of a national ideology that prides itself on the modesty and natural beauty of its women. If Amelia's "naturalness," discussed throughout Thackeray's novel, is a version of Becky's artifice, then the designation of "natural" is a false one. Thackeray's novel emphasizes Victorian England's concerns over the artificiality of women as well as its subsequent relegation of such artificiality to the French; Frenchwoman Becky Sharp is an artifice, a sham, because England needs her to be so.

NOTES

1. This essay comes from a chapter of my dissertation, "Dressing for England: Fashion and Nationalism in Victorian Novels," through Texas A&M University in 2008. It was also presented in part at the 2009 Victorian Markets and Marketing Conference in Vancouver, BC.

2. Joseph Litvak's argument about Becky's consumerism will be discussed later in this essay.

3. While Becky is only half French, the English in the novel read her as entirely French, and therefore a conniver.

4. Interestingly, Cree LeFavour's article "Acting 'Natural': *Vanity Fair* and the Unmasking of Anglo-American Sentiment" tells us that for American audiences, Becky Sharp was seen as natural. LeFavour also notes, "To be 'natural,' then, had a dual and somewhat contradictory meaning since it simultaneously signaled effortless, authentic performance of the 'self' while also indicating an undesirable absence of cultivation and domestication most damningly and shockingly linked to female sexual passion which is in turn coded black" (par. 42). Taking LeFavour's argument into consideration, we can see that unlike English readers who understood "natural" to be both authentic and a representation of English nationalism, American audiences read "natural" as racially rather than nationally charged.

5. Dobson writes, "While Rebecca's identity is often viewed explicitly as a performance, Amelia's 'appropriately' feminine and English identity, consciously or not, remains a naturalized performance—it is simply performed with far greater success" (2). Other critics argue similarly to Dobson in reading Amelia as performative. In "Female Sexuality and Triangular Desire in *Vanity Fair* and *The Mill on the Floss*," Phyllis Susan Dee reminds us that "if gender is performative . . . , Amelia's submissive, self-effacing behavior may conceal a more complex personality" (392). It is my argument, however, that while gender and femininity are important constructs to Victorian womanhood and well discussed in *Vanity Fair* criticism, we must not lose sight that fashion, dress, and style were intricate parts of women's lives in the nineteenth century, as they are today. Ultimately, these concerns are writ, first and last, in the fashionable arena.

6. Mary Hammond notes that "Becky's flattery and falsehoods are intolerable precisely because they are in danger of professionalizing—and therefore exposing to the

world—the performances by which other women secure their futures. Intolerable, too, is her genuine Frenchness. Not the gentile [sic] Frenchness of the aristocracy, but the common, dangerous Frenchness which threatens middle England" (33).

7. Earlier in the novel, all of Becky's clothes come to her secondhand, either as Amelia's cast-offs or as gifts from admirers bought at secondhand shops or auctions. One example that contradicts this theory would be Becky's presentation at court, for which she robs the Crawleys' ancestral wardrobes, picking through old dresses to secure quality brocade and lace (Thackeray 1985, 558). Here, older clothes offer Becky respectability and authenticity because they offer her the illusion of an English pedigree.

8. In "Siren and Artist: Contradiction in Thackeray's Aesthetic Ideal," Judith Law Fisher reads this scene as demonstrating "Becky's mechanical skill at arranging her portrait . . . emphasized by the theatrical lighting and careful composition of the scene" (399). Fisher contrasts what she calls "Becky's manufactured brilliance" (399) with Amelia's "genuine 'pink and white' beauty" (399) and "sincerity" (400).

9. The other women in the novel who possess Becky's power of reading and interpreting fashion are, surprisingly, the Misses Osborne, George's sisters. They often shred Amelia's confidence with their "bold black eyes" because they read through her outward appearances and find them wanting. Or, as the narrator reminds us, "the Misses Osborne were excellent critics of a Cashmere shawl, or a pink satin slip; and when Miss Turner had hers dyed purple, and made into a spencer; and when Miss Pickford had her ermine tippet twisted into a muff and trimmings, I warrant you the changes did not escape the two intelligent young women before mentioned" (150). The social power they have, while not vast like Becky's, is, like Becky's, dependent on their fashionable vision.

10. This English belief in a furtive, French knowledge of fashion can be dated as late as the 1890s, as George Meredith's title character from *Diana of the Crossways* is accused of having "'the secret of dressing well—in the French style'" (140–41).

11. I am extremely grateful to Dr. Anne Longmuir at the 2009 Victorian Markets and Marketing Conference for pointing out that Amelia is most likely pregnant in this scene, which allowed me to question further Becky's purpose in reprimanding Amelia's wardrobe choices.

12. Of interest to note is the continuing debate—well into the twenty-first century—regarding the role of the corset in Victorian women's lives. While nineteenth-century women did wear corsets during pregnancy, there was concern over spontaneous miscarriage because of tight lacing. The fact that Amelia's corset seems to fit so poorly suggests that she is, in fact, not participating in tight lacing and is being quite cognizant of the concerns corsetry might present to the health and safety of her unborn child. As always with Amelia, at the moment she is at her most natural—especially when considering her physically apparent maternal body—she is her most unsuccessful at being beautiful, despite what the characters in the novel claim. For further discussion

on the use of corsets in pregnancy, please consult any of the excellent works by Mel Davies, Valerie Steele, or Leigh Summers.

13. Even Becky's good housewifery is artificial, albeit successful. The narrator tells us that "a good housewife is of necessity a humbug" (211). In this sense, then, Becky performs an acceptable role.

5

"Such Hosts of Rags"

Transatlantic Crossings between Paper and Cotton in Melville's "The Paradise of Bachelors and the Tartarus of Maids"

Amber Shaw

"Before my eyes—there, passing in slow procession along the wheeling cylinders, I seemed to see, glued to the pallid incipience of the pulp, the yet more pallid faces of all the pallid girls I had eyed that heavy day"

—Herman Melville, "The Paradise of Bachelors
and the Tartarus of Maids"

*I*n the closing pages of his chapter on the Lowell, Massachusetts, textile mills, in *American Notes for General Circulation* (1842), Charles Dickens gestures toward comparing the quality of life of the New England mill "girls" he has observed and that of the Manchester, England, workers with whom he is "well acquainted" (154). In describing the comparative luxury of Lowell's factory system, Dickens implicitly asks his readers to recognize the inhumane working conditions of the mills in Manchester. A little over a decade later, Herman Melville uses the same rhetorical strategy in his diptych "The Paradise of Bachelors and the Tartarus of Maids," which was published in the April 1855 *Harper's New Monthly Magazine*.

Melville's story fictionalizes two visits, one to a dinner party of London bachelors in Temple Bar and the other to a desolate New England mill. As with Dickens, Melville urges his readers to translate their misgivings about the horrific mill working conditions for women across the Atlantic. Melville's Dickens-like fictionalization of transatlantic travelogues emphasizes the chiasmus of text or textile crossings. While Dickens looks to the United States as a way to critique Britain, Melville inverts the international comparison, suggesting that the idle British bachelors are an oblique commentary on American mill girls and the culture that exploits them. These two texts, of course, are not completely reciprocal, for Melville's story is fictional. Dickens's notoriety and the subsequent vogue for factory tours, however, points to the interest in cotton production at this cultural moment. Just as we might question whether it's fair to compare Lowell and Manchester, Melville's short story itself, as a piece of fiction, inherently poses the problems of eyewitness believability and supposedly factual accounts.[1] Throughout "The Paradise of Bachelors and the Tartarus of Maids," Melville highlights the discrepancy between public praise of the mills and the reality of life within the factory walls. In subtly noting these national and generic differences, Melville at once talks about—and does not talk about—the Lowell mills. By describing cotton–rag paper production instead of textile weaving and by filtering these observations through his largely ambivalent narrator, Melville emphasizes the real material—and transatlantic—connections between consumer and factory. In doing so, he underscores the relationship between the actual poor working conditions in the New England factories and the more nebulous damage from the transatlantic literary community's idealization of the Lowell mills and urges his readers to come to terms with their own complicity in the global economy.

Claiming he has "carefully abstained from drawing a comparison between these factories and those of our own land," Dickens provokes his nominally British (but, ultimately, transatlantic) audience with ethical questions about the differences between the two towns:

> Are we quite sure that we in England have not formed our ideas of the 'station' of working people, from accustoming ourselves to the contemplation of that class as they are, and not as they might be? I think that if we examine our own feelings, we shall find that the pianos, and the circulating libraries, and even the *Lowell Offering*, startle us by their novelty, and not by their bearing upon any abstract question of right and wrong. (161)

This distinction between "novelty" and ethical correctness is noteworthy in its implicit condemnation of his British readers, and it's one that lurks just beneath the surface of Dickens's entire account of his visit to Lowell. For Dickens, the amenities that Lowell workers enjoy are not just frivolous pastimes but concrete examples of the contrasts between the mills and the nations. The piano is not just a piano; rather, it's a material good that suggests the workers are treated as real human beings and not mere cogs in the factory system.

FIGURE 5.1: Engraving of Lowell, Massachusetts. ca. 1850. *Library of Congress Prints and Photographs Division.* (Plate 11.)

In fact, such effusive praise for Lowell and its mill system was not unusual; Dickens's keen interest in the cleanliness of the mills and the humanity with which the "girls" were treated are common tropes in mid-nineteenth-century representations of Lowell. Just as writers as various as Dickens, Harriet Martineau, William Ellery Channing, Horace Greeley, Emma Willard, Elizabeth Peabody, and John Greenleaf Whittier celebrated the town's almost utopian environment, contemporary images of Lowell similarly naturalize buildings that represented the city's burgeoning industrialism so that they seemed to be a part of the otherwise idyllic landscape (Eisler, 35). The distant perspective used in this color engraving of around 1850 (fig. 5.1) teases the viewer to look down at the mill town and see it as a sort of utopia. The string of brick-colored mills that draw a line through the center of the engraving divide the sky from the hillside and suggest that Lowell's utopian industrialism coincides with the much more pastoral image we might normally associate with the outskirts of a major American city such as Boston. On the surface, then, this image may look like an anti-industrial representation of what would otherwise have been rural America; however, the tropes along the frame of the engraving (the sky, the hillside, even the river), point toward the tall, square factories made famous by figures as various as Dickens and Melville but also by publications such as the *Lowell Offering*, which ultimately gained a transatlantic audience.

Most of the anecdotes in Dickens's Lowell chapter describe novelties (such as the shiny newness of the town or the "fine" names with which the girls sign their *Lowell Offering* articles), but Dickens ultimately demands his readers take seriously the "abstract question of right or wrong" by looking back across the

Atlantic toward Manchester. Writing in the conditional mood, Dickens suggests that if he were to compare the two towns, "The contrast [between Lowell and Manchester] would be a strong one, for it would be between the Good and Evil, the living light and deepest shadow" (164). The "Good" and "living light" of Lowell that Dickens catalogs only further underscores the "great haunts of desperate misery" that exist throughout Britain's textile mills, with which his British reading public would have been more than familiar (164). In putting the onerous duty of acknowledging the discrepancies between the mills on his readers—these criticisms, after all, are completely couched in conditional language—Dickens critiques the Manchester mill system indirectly, an important distinction for a writer writing for and selling to the popular marketplace. Even in this factual travelogue, the conditional mood intimates a distinction between Dickens the traveler and Dickens the author. It's both an authorial pose and a protective measure for someone as famous as he was with an audience that had varying connections to these institutions.

The narrator of Melville's diptych similarly embarks on his two separate transatlantic journeys for the novelty of the experiences. It echoes a Dickensian travelogue, too, for the unnamed narrator mixes seemingly factual reporting and thoughtful reflection. The first half of the story takes place at a leisurely dinner party of bachelors in London, which "was the perfection of quiet absorption of good living, good drinking, good feeling, and good talk" (81). The bachelors embrace the "fraternal, household comfort" of the gathering, for they've created a place where one can "give the whole care-worn world the slip, and, disentangled, stand beneath the quiet cloisters of the Paradise of Bachelors" (74). The second half of the story is set in New England as the narrator "for economy's sake, and partly for the adventure of the trip . . . , resolve[s] to cross the mountains, some sixty miles, and order[s] future paper at the Devil's Dungeon paper-mill" (84). There he observes "girls [who] did not so much seem accessory wheels to the general machinery as mere cogs to the wheels" (88). The two parts of the diptych are unrelated save the narrator's presence, but his occasional commentary illustrates how he comes to understand the "inverted similitude" of the two places, for the paper mill is "the very counterpart of the Paradise of Bachelors, but snowed upon, and frost-painted to a sepulchre" (86). While he initially considers his tour of the paper mill a "novelty" or amusing ancillary to his visit, the narrator becomes increasingly affected by what he sees. He concludes his factory tour (and the story) with a not-quite-articulated critique of the transatlantic system that implicitly facilitates the exploitation of labor in the mills and connects the two halves of the diptych.[2]

These critiques are not overt, for Melville published "The Paradise of Bachelors and the Tartarus of Maids" in *Harper's New Monthly Magazine*, the most popular American periodical and one that had just recently begun publishing American authors (Milder, viii). The magazine, according to Shelia Post-Lauria, cultivated its vast readership by covering a wide array of topics, often without taking a partisan stance (167). "Paradise," for example, was published alongside such pieces as an installment of William Makepeace Thackeray's *The Newcomes* and an article on the catacombs in Rome as well as fashion plates for men and women, so readers would have had the opportunity to peruse the latest clothing designs before (or after) reading a story that critiques the exploitive mill labor that very likely produced the cloth used to make similar garments (figs. 5.2 and 5.3).

If the story itself is a subtle correction of the transatlantic periodical culture that vaunted Lowell and its factory system, then, perhaps, we should read the juxtaposed fashion plates and stories in *Harper's* as a reflection of the world in which Melville published but also pushed against. It was also one of three transatlantic diptych short stories that Melville published in *Harper's* and *Putnam's* between 1853 and 1855, all of which, Aaron Winter explains, "are narrative experiments angling toward a 'cakes and ale' populism that [are] nonetheless flexible enough to accommodate Melville's ever-sharpening critique of American social and political values" (17). Melville's "ever-sharpening critique" was a liability in such a widely distributed magazine that shied away from controversy, but, as Robert Milder notes, "Melville found he could broadly have his say if he said things obliquely enough, assigned them to a genial or crotchety narrator, or clothed them in symbolism" (ix). In carefully characterizing his narrators, Melville, like Dickens, could both distance himself from his potentially controversial social commentary and appease "the great mass of the American people" who regularly read *Harper's* (quoted in Post-Lauria, 167).

Accordingly, Melville couches the majority of his critique in the second half of the diptych and in his narrator's seemingly neutral observations of the mill workers. In a series of fleeting reflections, he compares the work the girls perform in the mills with that of the loafing London bachelors he has just visited. Post-Lauria suggests that the editorial culture of *Harper's* muted whatever social critique Melville would have included in the diptych, and the narra-

FIGURE 5.2 (RIGHT): Fashion
plate illustration from April 1855
*Harper's New Monthly Magazine. Cornell
University Library, Making of America
Digital Collection.*
FIGURE 5.3 (BELOW): Fashion
plate illustration from April 1855
*Harper's New Monthly Magazine. Cornell
University Library, Making of America
Digital Collection.*

tor remains "ambivalent toward the horrors of the social realities portrayed"
(174). To this we should add that the narrator's muted or ambivalent reactions
throughout the story are themselves a critique of both the New England mills
and the media ecology surrounding the transatlantic cotton industry in the
mid-nineteenth century (174). British luminaries such as Dickens toured the
United States's first factory operation and celebrated what they observed in
factual newspaper articles and travelogues, but Melville uses his fictional story

to present a bleaker picture of life in the mill and how willful ignorance—even removed across the Atlantic—equally affects the exploitive system. Through his somewhat inarticulate narrator, Melville suggests life in a New England mill isn't uplifting at all.

While "The Paradise of Bachelors and the Tartarus of Maids" can be read as a call to action for transatlantic labor reform, Melville eschews any sentimental descriptions of the exploited workers. Instead, he addresses the Dickensian "abstract question of right or wrong" by calling attention both to the bodily suffering of the "maids" as they operate the machinery and to the narrator's visceral reaction during his factory tour. Rather than enjoying the comfortable mill town amenities Dickens describes in *American Notes*, the maids in Melville's story are inextricably linked to the factory itself. The first "girl" he encounters typifies the workers. "A face pale with work, and blue with cold," the girl remains mute but looks at the narrator with "an eye supernatural with unrelated misery" (87). All of the operatives he observes are similarly silent and downtrodden—almost lifeless—as they are absorbed in their labor. While the narrator usually describes the workers without editorializing commentary, his sustained attention to their weak bodies and minds and their pale complexions demonstrates he understands "through consumptive pallors of this blank, raggy life, go these white girls to death" (91). They are "their own executioners" as the very work that (however minimally) sustains them also contributes to their puny health, a far cry from journalistic reports of cheerful, thinking mill girls proud of their labor and their independence (91).[3]

The narrator's observations become even more scathing when Melville's story is read alongside contemporary accounts of Lowell and its homegrown literary magazine the *Lowell Offering*, with which Melville's contemporary audience would have been familiar. A magazine written and edited entirely by Lowell's female operatives, the *Lowell Offering* was published monthly between 1840 and 1845, and as Stephen Yafa notes, it "became an international sensation, a symbol of brave new gender equality and an ode to self-improvement" (114). Widely circulated, the *Lowell Offering* was read in middle-class homes that also subscribed to periodicals such as *Harper's* and *Putnam's*. Dickens even claimed the magazine "compare[d] advantageously with a great many English Annuals" (161). Lowell mill owners capitalized on the *Lowell Offering's* far-flung praise, marketing the periodical as an advertisement of sorts for the female-centered community they'd cultivated. Since it was "uncensored and independent," the *Lowell Offering*, as Benita Eisler points out, "provided a fortuitous medium for those two expressions of distinctly American genius: public relations and packaging" (36). Indeed, while the magazine began as a "traveling mirror to reflect an ideal system," and it was read around the world as showcasing the very amenities that other transatlantic mills such as Manchester clearly lacked, the periodical's idealism, in many ways, ultimately belied the desires of the mill operatives. A literary periodical that published a mixture of fictional stories and nonfiction essays, the *Lowell Offering* (and, later, the *New England Offering*) was marketed as avoiding social critique.[4] Instead, its editorial policy privileged pieces that were cheerfully naïve in their treatment of demanding labor, often highlighting the Puritan values at the core of the mill project.[5] The iconography of the title page, which was identical for the *Lowell Offering* and the *New England Offering*, demonstrates the manner in which the "girls" often figure as individuals among a tasteful blend of floral imagery and carefully wrought words we might not expect to be associated with machine operatives (fig. 5.4).

Here a Lowell "girl" appears magnified in the foreground while the austere-looking factory building looms behind her. The exaggerated difference between her size and the factory's size underscores the magazine's role in emphasizing the operatives as thinking people. The "girl," in fact, holds an open book on the cover of this magazine, suggesting self-conscious textual identity we'll also find in Melville's short story. Indeed, as Lowell grew, labor conditions became increasingly complicated and controversial. The literary label that "was supposed to seal it off from the turmoil of 'issues,'" according to Eisler, slowly "became a balancing act that was doomed to fail" (36). With the rise of the Ten-Hour Movement, the increasingly political voices in the magazine began to tarnish the publication's idealized image. By 1845 the magazine had ceased publication.

While the *Lowell Offering* was short lived, in many ways it determined transatlantic discussions of the cotton industry (and industrialization more generally). It also provided an insider's view of the Lowell utopia for international reformers. After her one-day visit to Lowell, Harriet Martineau was so enamored with the factory and its literary magazine that she convinced English publisher Charles Knight to reprint a selection of the mill workers' literary efforts in *Mind Amongst the Spindles* (1844), which as with Dickens's *American Notes*, brought Lowell's literary mill workers to the British reading public.[6] Highlighting only the best aspects of the American mills, Knight and Martineau took "care to choose those *Offering* artists heaviest on moral uplift,"

FIGURE 5.4: Title page for 1849 *New England Offering. Harvard University Widener Library.*

omitting any pieces that hinted at dehumanizing labor or unethical working conditions (Eisler, 34–35). Martineau similarly projects her own conclusions upon the "girls" she observes at Lowell, claiming "twice the wages and half the toil would not have made the girls I saw happy and healthy without that cultivation of mind which afforded them perpetual support, entertainment, and motive for activity" (xvi). Celebrating what she perceives as earnestness, Martineau calls attention to how distinct she believes these "girls" are from the Manchester workforce. Indeed, many writers who initially praised the industrial advancements of Lowell were by the 1850s too far away to recognize or witness its changes. As Eisler outlines, "admiration was the more intense, the farther the admirer lived from Lowell," and Lowell seemed to be most interesting to those who were not around to see the day-to-day operations of the mill (35). Living and writing in Massachusetts, Melville, unlike Dickens or Martineau, would have been aware of the increasing turmoil and social upheaval at the nearby Lowell mill, which, as we will see, had global reverberations.

Melville's story should, then, be understood as a corrective that illustrates the actual working conditions in the mills, something visitors might not experience on a routine tour. Moreover, his diptych emphasizes the importance of proximity and perspective by subtly critiquing the idle London bachelors who use distance and isolation as excuses for ignorance. The factory Melville's narrator tours, for example, is "in a very out-of-the-way corner," and as Cupid the tour guide notes, they "don't have many" visitors (95). Those who do visit believe the factory and its machinery are "a miracle of inscrutable intricacy" (95). The narrator initially complains "he cannot distinctly see," but after traveling from London to New England, he comes to understand the true crisis of the mills, confessing "the strange emotion filled [him]" as he concludes his tour (91, 96). Just as the disparate reactions to Lowell—indeed, the discourse surrounding the mid-nineteenth-century textile industry—were often directly related to geography, Melville's narrator highlights not only the stark differences between the London bachelors and the New England maids but also their more implicit connections. As the narrator comes to realize during his factory tour, the bachelors' choices to recuse themselves from worldly concerns only further emphasize their implication in global problems. The extreme of choosing isolation is, then, just as damning as promoting idealized accounts of the world.

While Melville's narrator visits a paper mill, the factory system and workers he describes in many ways directly echo the plentiful published accounts of Lowell at the height of its production. As the narrator enters the Devil's Dungeon mill, he observes "a spacious place, intolerably lighted by long rows of windows, focusing inward the snowy scene without" (88). While this initial description of the paper mill highlights the brightness and size of the factory, the space is not uplifting. Likewise, the workspace supposedly provides ample natural light for the women at work, but the narrator immediately judges the harsh light. The windows don't welcome the outside scenery into the mill; they cast an "intolerabl[e]" light across the space. Articles in the *Lowell Offer-*

ing often describe a similar physical space, but they focus on the mill's more agreeable aspects. "Letters from Susan" (1844), for example, recounts a new mill worker's "very pleasant" first impressions (Farley, 51). They are not "such dreadful places as you imagine them to be" (56). Instead, Susan describes the factory as bright and technologically advanced: "The rooms are high, very light, kept nicely whitewashed, and extremely neat; with many plants in the window seats, and white cotton curtains to the windows. The machinery is very handsomely made and painted, and is placed in regular rows" (57). The mill, then, presents "a beautiful and uniform appearance," one that's counter to stereotypical descriptions of polluted factories (57). Written in a fictional letter to be sent home, Susan characterizes the factory as cozy and domestic. This picturesque space, however, is noticeably unpopulated. Rather than describe her fellow workers, Susan focuses on the factory itself, carefully avoiding the work and the girls who operate the looms. "When the girls [are] gone," she notes, she often watches "the lathes moving back and forth, the harnesses up and down, the white cloth winding over the rollers" and thinks the independently moving machinery "beautiful" (57). The girls' absence is telling, for the beauty in Susan's "long perspective" only can be achieved without seeing the people who perform the demanding manual labor that's ultimately required to produce the finished fabric.

In "The Paradise of Bachelors and the Tartarus of Maids," however, Melville's narrator immediately perceives the relevance of not only the modern machinery but also the women who operate it. Surveying the vast room, the narrator thinks the windows have reflected the snow-covered landscape inside the factory. He quickly realizes, though, that the "snowy scene" is not a mirror image of the outside world but endless rows of silent, working girls. Filling the long, airy room, "at rows of blank-looking counters sat rows of blank-looking girls with blank, white folders in their blank hands, all blankly folding blank paper" (88). The narrator focuses on the "blank looking girls," noting their presence throughout the factory and their similarity to everything else in the room. The girls, moreover, do not possess the active minds that so enchanted Lowell advocates, for the narrator repeatedly observes the eerie similarity between the operatives and the blank paper they produce. In details such as these, Melville begins to distance the Devil's Dungeon paper mill from characteristic descriptions of Lowell. Here, even though Cupid showcases the company's newest machines, the "blank looking girls" are the true workhorses of the factory. Susan may take pleasure in the rows of "beautiful" machines, but Melville's narrator cannot take his eyes off the pale young women who produce the paper he's about to order.

Indeed, as the narrator moves through the factory, he becomes increasingly observant of both the girls' working conditions and the similarities between them and the paper. As with Martineau and Dickens, whose narratives rely on their eyewitness accounts of the mills, Melville's narrator emphasizes that "before [his] eyes—there, passing in slow procession along the wheeling cylinders, [he] seemed to see, glued to the pallid incipience of the pulp, the yet more pallid faces of all the pallid girls I had eyed that heavy day" (95). The "blank looking girls" assume the appearance of paper, but as he witnesses the actual labor involved, the narrator begins to understand that the women, too, become part of the product. The narrator rarely pauses to reflect on what he "eye[s]" in the mill, but his qualifying adjectives here—everything and everyone is "pallid" and the day is "heavy"—intimate his growing shock throughout the tour. In contrast to the suggestion of one *Lowell Offering* writer, these "pallid" girls are not "led to the reflection, that the mind is boundless, and is destined to rise higher and still higher" through their work (quoted in Eisler, 64). Instead, they're led toward death as the narrator even confuses the factory's ultimate product. Asking Cupid, his tour guide, "'You make only blank paper; no printing of any sort, I suppose? All blank paper, don't you?'" the narrator goes on to justify his question: "'It only [strikes] me as so strange that red waters should turn out pale chee—paper, I mean'" (89–90). His verbal slip—beginning to say "cheek"—intimates the gravity of their working conditions. The workers are as plentiful and expendable as the blank paper they produce, and managers such as Cupid appear oblivious to the effects of their inhumane environment.

The Lowell workers similarly experienced a high turnover rate. As Janet Greenlees explains, the physical well-being of the girls was routinely dismissed. Since most female factory workers were considered temporary labor, "reformers focused on workers' morality, rather than the physical and environmental causes of ill-health" despite the well-documented connections between mill conditions and the girls' health (184). "By 1849," Greenlees notes, Lowell doctors Josiah Curtis and Gilman Kimball believed the "main causes of operatives' ill-health were working long hours in poorly ventilated, overheated and lint-filled rooms" (180). Still more shocking, Yafa notes how "doctors frequently saw female workers vomiting up little balls of cotton"

(96). Yet, even with such concrete medical evidence, conditions in many New England mills began to "deteriorate" throughout the mid-1840s as owners established a pattern "of recognizing health risks, followed by little concrete action" (Greenlees, 181, 179). By repeatedly describing the maids' complexions as "blank," "sheety," or "pallid," Melville's narrator tacitly comments on these well-documented (but often ignored) working conditions. For him, highlighting the showy parts of the New England mills won't transform or erase their grittier realities.

It's especially notable, then, that the narrator's description of the paper mill's rag room highlights the similarities between paper and textile production: both rely on and begin with cotton. This room, too, features some of the dirtiest and most dangerous work in a mill, for cotton fluff was palpable in the air and covered the contents of the room. As a pivotal stop on the narrator's factory tour, the rag room presents him with the horrors of the mill far more graphically than the rows of blank girls downstairs:

> He took me up a wet and rickety stair to a great light room, furnished with no visible thing but rude, manger-like receptacles running all round its sides; and up to these mangers, like so many mares haltered to the rack, stood rows of girls. Before each was vertically thrust up a long glittering scythe, immovably fixed at bottom to the manger-edge. The curve of the scythe, and its having no snath to it, made it look exactly like a sword. To and fro, across the sharp edge, the girls forever dragged long strips of rags washed white, picked from baskets at one side; thus ripping asunder every seam, and converting the tatters almost into lint. The air swam with the fine, poisonous particles, which from all sides darted, subtly, as motes in sun-beams, into the lungs. (Melville, 90)

Melville's detailed description of the room intimates his implicit commentary on New England's more prominent industry. Just as the rag and carding rooms were often placed on the upper floors of textile mills (as seen in fig. 5.5, an elevation of the Boott Mill in Lowell), Devil's Dungeon features a polluted rag room that's removed from the more public spaces on the lower floors of the factory. Its confined location mimics both the controlled lives of the women who make the paper and their often idealized working conditions. Indeed, the narrator's description emphasizes the cloistered space. He compares the girls to "mares" as they stand at their "mangers" of rags, and their work

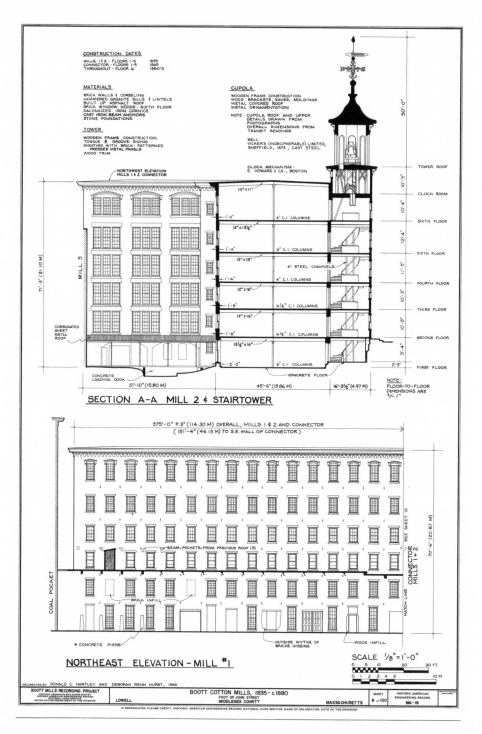

FIGURE 5.5: Elevation of Boott Mill in Lowell, Massachusetts. *Library of Congress, Historic American Buildings Survey/Historic American Engineering Record/Historic American Landscapes Survey.*

PLATE 1: The crinoline silhouette at its height. *Englishwoman's Domestic Magazine*, July 1862. *Picture Collection, The New York Public Library, Astor, Lenox, and Tilden Foundations.*

PLATE 2: *Paul Revere*, 1768. John Singleton Copley, American, 1738–1815. Oil on canvas, 89.22 x 72.39 cm (35⅛ x 28½ in.) Museum of Fine Arts, Boston. Gift of Joseph W. Revere, William B. Revere, and Edward H. R. Revere. 30.781. *Photograph © 2014 Museum of Fine Arts, Boston.*

PLATE 3: *Dr. Elisha Poinsett* by Edward Greene Malbone. *Smithsonian American Art Museum, Bequest of Mary Elizabeth Spencer.*

PLATE 4: James Gillray. "The Three Graces in a High Wind." © *Victoria and Albert Museum, London.*

PLATE 5: Sack Back Gown, 1760. © *Victoria and Albert Museum, London.*

Plate 6: White Muslin Gown, 1800. © *Victoria and Albert Museum, London.*

PLATE 7: Satin Dress, c. 1842. © *Victoria and Albert Museum, London.*

PLATE 8: Promenade Dresses, 1809. *Author's personal collection.*

Afternoon Dress for July, 1801.

Wirgman, Dress-maker, Hanover Street, Hanover Square.

PLATE 9: Wirgman Dressmaker, Afternoon Dress for July 1801. *Author's personal collection.*

Engraved for the Lady's Magazine.

London Walking & Full Dress.

PLATE 10: London Walking and Full Dress. C. 1790–1805. *Author's personal collection.*

PLATE 11: Engraving of Lowell, Massachusetts. ca. 1850. *Library of Congress Prints and Photographs Division.*

PLATE 12: Ellen Terry as Lady Macbeth, 1889, John Singer Sargent (1856–1925). © *Tate, London 2014.*

"Yet Nature is made better by no mean,
But Nature makes that mean; so o'er that art
Which, you say, adds to Nature, is an art
That Nature makes."——SHAKESPEARE.

PLATE 13: Mary Eliza Joy Haweis, frontispiece from *The Art of Decoration* (London: Chatto and Windus, 1881). *By permission of the Mark Samuels Lasner Collection, on loan to the University of Delaware Library.*

PLATE 14: Kate Greenaway, *Young Girl Waving a Rose Branch*, pencil and watercolor, 1886. *By permission of the Mark Samuels Lasner Collection, on loan to the University of Delaware Library.*

PLATE 15: Portrait photograph of Jessie Fauset. Century Art Studio, 112 W. 125th St., New York. *Library of Congress.*

PLATE 16: "Gertie Millar as Mary Gibbs in 'Our Miss Gibbs,'" by Rita Martin, published by J. Beagles & Co.; bromide postcard print, 1909. © *National Portrait Gallery, London*.

is monotonous, "forever drag[ing]" the cloth across their individual scythes. Even their menial, endless work is violent: the girls are "ripping . . . every" seam and transforming the rags into pulpy lint—almost completely destroying the cloth. In contrast to the "blank" faces and mechanical labor downstairs at the machines, the rag room, the narrator suggests, exerts an even greater physical and mental damage as the girls are valued only for their dehumanized strength and endurance.

The poisoned air associates Devil's Dungeon with contemporary textile mills even more concretely. In the second installment of "Letters from Susan," Susan begins describing the various jobs in the mill with the carding room, or "where the cotton flies most, and the girls get the dirtiest" (Farley, 51). Susan doesn't dwell on the carding room, but her account highlights the looming danger of working there: it's full of polluted air. Accordingly, Melville's narrator emphasizes just how prolific the "poisonous" fluff is in the mill (90). It "dart[s]" in the air from every direction and seems to head straight "into the lungs," highlighting the direct correlation between the physical conditions of the mill and the poor health of the workers who cannot escape the particles. The cotton fluff in the air even gains a consciousness of sorts; it appears to move with precision and seems menacing, as the humans are reduced to helpless animals, "immovably fixed" to their labor.

The seemingly metaphorical relationship between the girls' bodies and the paper they produce is made real in the rag room as the girls at once use their bodies to rip apart the cotton and inhale much of their raggy product. Daneen Wardrop similarly understands cotton fluff as an important point of connection between the imaginary paper mill and the very real textile mills. Wardrop argues, "Melville's story detailed the same lint-inhaling 'kiss of death'" that was widely discussed in contemporary social reform tracts (73). "Melville's masterpiece of social criticism," she continues, "excoriates the working conditions for women at mills where they lived unnaturally cloistered lives, breathed lint, and lost control of the ownership of their bodies" (73). His meticulous account suggests "Melville was appalled by working conditions in New England factories" (73). As the midpoint of the narrator's factory visit, the rag room and its omnipresent cotton fluff are crucial to Melville's social critique. If before visiting the rag room he is overwhelmed by the silence and seeming "blankness" of the operatives, then after experiencing its hot, polluted environment, the narrator begins to "see it now" and more clearly perceives the often obscured bodily realities of factory labor (Melville, 91).

These details and the narrator's developing perceptiveness further imply that Melville was appalled by the lack of reaction to these inhumane surroundings. When the narrator asks about the cotton fluff, Cupid dismisses his concern, claiming the girls don't cough because they "are used to it" (90). Cupid also doesn't recognize the relationship between the workers' waif-like appearance and their working environment; rather, he "suppose[s] the handling of such white bits of sheets all the time makes them so sheety," which may linguistically associate their bodies and the product of their labor but ignores the grave significance merging human bodies and textiles (91). By rejecting—or refusing to acknowledge—the dangerous link between cotton fluff and ailing operatives, Cupid resembles contemporary mill owners on both sides of the Atlantic who "refused to accept responsibility for poor mill conditions or workers' poor health" (Greenlees, 184). Indeed, when the narrator leaves the rag room, he pauses to reflect on what he's witnessed, concluding that Cupid's apathy or "strange innocence of cruel-heartedness" is far "more tragical and more inscrutably mysterious" than the awful working conditions themselves (Melville, 91).

This realization is another turning point in the story, for it's the first time the narrator articulates his nascent social criticism. It's almost an afterthought, but by verbalizing his own understanding of and discomfort with the factory managers' apathy, Melville's narrator invites similar reactions from his readers. As Sidney Bremer suggests, "Once inside the factory, Melville's narrator can no longer avoid the pressing realities of an economic system that is 'served' by the laborer as by a 'slave'" (55). He's traveled a great distance to the paper mill for the adventure of the journey and the novelty of the tour, yet the realities of the rag room make real his understanding of industrialism as a serious—and seriously flawed—business.

The actual cotton in the rag room only further connects the Devil's Dungeon paper mill with textile factories and reinforces the transnational interdependence of industrial operations. As cotton fluff fills the air and the girls' lungs, it inextricably links them to the product and to the mill itself. It also associates them and the paper they make with the bachelors in London, who may benefit materially (and perhaps even financially) from the girls' labor. The narrator is overwhelmed at the sight of so much cotton in the rag room, and he asks where the mill gets "such hosts of rags" (90). Cupid's response—" 'Some from the country round about; some from far over sea— Leghorn and London' "—seems vague (90). After all, gathering cotton from the nearby countryside as well as a cosmopolitan city across the ocean isn't exactly a precise answer. The broad geographical scope of the cotton, how-ever, reiterates the very real relationship Melville outlines throughout the dip-tych, for the fabric not only unites the two halves of the story but also aligns the Devil's Dungeon paper mill with the transatlantic textile trade. In these terms, then, Cupid's broad response is perfectly reasonable because it mimics the industry it represents.

While Cupid doesn't recognize how the rags "from the country round about" are related to those "from far over sea," the narrator specifically asso-ciates the rags that make the girls so "sheety" with the men he's met in Lon-don: " ' 'Tis not unlikely, then,' murmured I, 'that among these heaps of rags there may be some shirts, gathered from the dormitories of these Paradise of Bachelors' " (90). Instead of merely gesturing toward some metaphorical relationship between the bachelors and the maids, the narrator fancies that the cotton shirts and the cotton-rag paper they will become could be concrete products of this complex affiliation. It's all the more shocking that both par-ties are unaware of the other's existence without the narrator's hope for such a coincidence. As Winter aptly argues, these subtle yet material connections illustrate Melville's argument that "there is no life without strings attached; one chooses willful negligence and complicity with exploitation or one does not" (31). By acknowledging this global network and representing it through the cotton shirts that have traveled across the Atlantic, Melville's narrator, as Winter claims, is no longer "merely a means of uncovering ironic analogies between the two halves of the diptych"; indeed, the narrative whole depends on this unifying strand (31).

In turn, Melville—and his reading public—are "all supporting the cycle of production and consumption that consumes its own primary producers" (Winter, 55). Just as the United States shipped raw cotton to Britain through-out the mid-nineteenth century, and Britain exported tons of finished cotton for the United States' consumption, the bachelors' used shirts and the maids' exploited labor reinforce the thoroughly integrated complicity of the system. By 1860, for example, American mills made about $115,000,000 of cloth (Yafa, 120). The United States, however, still imported about $32,500,000 in finished British cotton and supplied Britain with about 80 percent of their raw cotton, or about 800,000 tons a year, all of which was slave produced (130–32). Melville's bachelors, then, may choose to be unaware of the maids and the mills across the Atlantic, but through their continual consumption and their discarded clothing they still contribute to the inhumane conditions inside the mill.

Through this circulation, the shirts become tangible connections between the two halves of the diptych—and materialize the narrator's unwitting but crucial penchant for stringing disparate scenes together through a single, double-processed global product. Indeed, the shirts are the only material objects to cross the Atlantic to witness not only London leisure but also New England toil. If they exemplify such a crucial point of intersection between Britain and the United States and between the bachelors and the maids, and if the factory the narrator tours so closely resembles the mid-nineteenth-century textile mill, then why does Melville's diptych specifically describe the production of cotton-rag paper?

During the tour of the mill, Melville's narrator seems overwhelmed by the sight of the sheer volume of paper, and he imagines its myriad future uses just as he imagined its textile-based past: "Looking at that blank paper continually dropping, dropping, dropping, my mind ran on in wonderings of those strange uses to which those thousand sheets eventually would be put. All sorts of writings would be writ on those now vacant things—sermons, lawyers' briefs, physicians' prescriptions, love-letters, marriage certificates, bills of divorce, registers of births, death-warrants, and so on, without end" (94).

Just as the narrator understands the shirts in the rag room are, perhaps, from the bachelors with whom he dined in London, he imagines the paper as another prospective transatlantic connection. These two material goods, then, epitomize not only the relationship between the bachelors and the maids but also the economic interdependence of London and New England. Moreover, the narrator twice acknowledges that the consumption and willful ignorance of the cloistered bachelors contributes to the impoverished and unfulfilled lives of the women who make the real stuff of the bachelors' daily lives—cotton and paper. The amount (and the actual material presence) of these two items emphasizes both their importance and their prevalence. While thousands of blank sheets of paper keep "dropping, dropping, dropping" from the machines, the narrator thinks about their connections to the "hosts of rags" he saw just minutes before. Just as cotton fluff swirls around in the air of the rag room and forms the paper pulp, the reams of blank paper fall endlessly around the feet of the factory operatives. Both are omnipresent, so mundane they're almost not worth noting.

It's telling, then, that Melville's narrator dwells on the paper itself since he's been so absorbed with its cotton roots. Just as Dickens hedges and teases the similarities between Lowell and Manchester (and their respective products), the implied author of Melville's diptych exaggerates the blankness of the paper in the face of a narrator whose worldly knowledge has not prepared him to realize the products as potential—and life-altering—human records. Melville suggests the paper's material worth, for when his narrator visits, he purchases paper for the "several hundreds of thousands" of seed packets his company sells (a detail that recalls the hyper-lush factory descriptions in the *Lowell Offering*) (84). The packets at once suggest a neat narrative possibility (if the seeds are cotton seeds, then the cotton-rag diptych has come full circle) and emphasize the narrator's naïve assumption that this place is generative. Many critics read these seed packets as a sexual metaphor, especially in contrast to the celibate bachelors and maids (and Cupid), but it's equally important to understand them as seeds themselves, which place the narrator within another transatlantic economy.[7]

The London bachelors, he remembers, would also have a great need for "those thousand sheets" of blank paper that continually drop from the female-operated machines. The volume of paper, too, recalls the ever-increasing textile production in Lowell (and across New England). According to Yafa, by 1834 American mills had "turned out an astonishing quantity of cheap cotton cloth—27,000,000 yards, or 15,698 miles, of it annually," an amount that only increased as the century progressed (112). In this way, Melville seems to be chronicling an industry on the brink of change, since cotton-rag paper was beginning to be displaced by cheaper, cotton-free, and easier to produce wood-pulp paper during the 1850s. Much like the idealized New England textile mills, cotton-rag paper was becoming obsolete, an object of nostalgia. The narrator's ambivalence, then, is redoubled, since the thing he sees is unclear. While we (and the narrator) see the product being made, its destination and ultimate use can only be speculation. He may travel to the remote paper mill for solitary adventure, but the decision is ultimately economic. The price of paper, the narrator admits, "amount[s] to a most important item in the general account" of his company (84). Thus, before he even sees the mill, the narrator admits his preference for inexpensive goods, even if the purchase comes at the expense of quality, morality, or human perspective.

The shift from fabric production to papermaking also underscores how Melville uses graphic descriptions of the mill and its workers to distance his diptych from other texts that merely document the "novelty" of the mill-town experience, to return to Dickens's term. The narrator's adventure of visiting the mill becomes a commentary on the vast, transatlantic literary interest in Lowell as a "New Jerusalem," modeling utopian industrial production and virtuous living (Eisler, 15). While the Devil's Dungeon paper mill produces countless sheets of blank paper, the New England textile factories were already the subjects of numerous literary and journalistic accounts by the mid-1850s. These popular publications were, much like the shirts and the rag paper in the diptych, widely circulated transatlantically. The *Lowell Offering*, of course, was popular on both sides of the Atlantic, especially after Martineau's and Dickens's vocal support in the mid-1840s. Martineau's and Knight's *Mind Amongst the Spindles* collection was first published in Britain and then in the United States one year later, so the British anthology of the Lowell girls' writing also reached readers in both nations. Moreover, Martineau's introductory letter was reprinted in the June 1843 *Lowell Offering*, again publicizing Martineau's beliefs transatlantically.

Dickens's *American Notes*, too, was originally published in Britain, but it was immediately notorious in the United States as copies were both shipped across the Atlantic and pirated by an American publisher. *Lowell Offering* editor Harriet Farley's review of the book in the January 1843 issue calls attention to Dickens's transatlantic view of the textile industry (95–96). While she applauds him for seeing "so much to please him in [the] 'City of Spindles,'" she also coyly comments on his transatlantic distinctions: "[I] regret for their sakes that so broad a line of distinction must be drawn between us and our sister operatives, across the Atlantic. Heaven speed the day when sentiments, more worthy of enlightened Britain, shall prevail among her rulers, and justice and generosity shall guide their counsels" (96). Melville's "The Paradise of Bachelors and the Tartarus of Maids," published in *Harper's*, addressed a similarly global audience, not only in content but also in its physical publication in a periodical that was read on both sides of the ocean. As this body of texts moved transatlantically, even commenting on one another, the writers engaged in a quiet generic crossing in which fiction and nonfiction critiques became almost indistinguishable.

These are just four of the most famous examples of the paper and ink devoted to the New England mills, for scores of articles and stories attempted to capture the specialness of what had been built in Lowell. And yet in many ways these accounts were as inscrutable as the blank pages produced at the Devil's Dungeon and the "blank looking girls" who made them. If these articles focus on the very best aspects of the mills, then the Devil's Dungeon paper mill, for Melville, underscores how their endless production (like the paper mill itself) is futile and even harmful for the workers. Gillian Brown similarly points to this literary ecology in her brief discussion of the story. She suggests that "the mechanical workings of the publishing industry are exposed as violations of nature" because "the health and beauty of the female paper-mill workers are subsumed into the paper they produce. . . . Industry," she concludes, "does not merely alienate the worker's labor but incorporates the worker" (240).

In turn, we should also read the shift from textile to cotton-rag paper as a critique of the Lowell advocates' belief in the intellectual fulfillment of the mill workers. While the ideal Lowell girl would have cultivated an active mind, Melville repeatedly connects the blankness of the paper with the operatives' interest (or lack thereof). The narrator even considers the maids' interiority as he observes the endless pages of blank paper: "I could not but bethink me of that celebrated comparison of John Locke, who, in demonstration of his theory that man had no innate ideas, compared the human minds at birth to a sheet of blank paper; something destined to be scribbled on, but what sort of characters no soul might tell" (94). In his final moments in the mill, the narrator again obfuscates his own thoughts, this time not by claiming blankness but by quoting John Locke, a figure who embodies the very ideas of social contract and responsibility at issue throughout the story. Locke, too, would have been the type of figure the Lowell workers would have studied in the popular "mutual improvement societies" that both Dickens and Martineau note in their essays. It's clear, though, that the Devil's Dungeon doesn't support this ideal intellectual atmosphere, and therefore the narrator's citation reads more like lip service than sincere application of his education to the experience itself.

Just as the narrator's reference to Locke's text signifies the unspoken debates over the way industrialism treats its "girls" in the mills, Melville's diptych as a whole stands in for the much more explicit rallying cry we might expect to be published in contemporary journals. For if *Harper's* resisted such potentially radical interventions, then they often needed to be veiled and couched within a fictional pretense. This exaggerated narrative obliqueness accounts for the narrator's silent yet visceral reaction to what he sees inside the Devil's Dungeon. By the end of the diptych, in fact, he applies the language of blankness to himself, which is telling because he's come to realize that the blankness he's critiqued in the girls is a painful physical reality as much as it is an apt metaphor.

As he ends his tour, the narrator feels flushed, yet Cupid says his cheeks "look whitish" (96). The narrator, then, begins to assume, if only for a moment, the appearance of both the paper he's come to purchase and the operatives he's observed. Cupid's comment, too, makes the narrator doubt the objective facts of his own body and his control over it, recalling the mill workers' own helplessness. Nevertheless, he feels sure that upon leaving the Devil's Dungeon, he "shall feel them mending," another historical resonance, for female operatives were almost always sent away from the mills to convalesce (or, more likely, die) (96). It's unclear whether he actually wants to believe that his own body is so affected by the condition of the mill and what he's witnessed. Still, the narrator's insistence that he will be better when he leaves shows how he does in fact realize that the mill determines his body and even the language he uses to describe it. By "mending" his cheeks, the narrator turns again, if coyly, to language that has potential double meanings within this space: for the girls who handle the cotton rags, "mending" would mean repairing tattered cloth, quite the opposite of what happens to the fabric in the rag room at the paper mill:. The narrator, then, comes to see his cheeks as part of a textile-like body, which has also crossed the Atlantic over the course of the story.

Despite the narrator's visceral reaction to what he sees in the factory and his need to "mend" his body, he still places an order for paper and leaves the mill without overt political comment. As he drives away "wrapped in furs and meditations," his mind is as impenetrable to us as the girls' minds are to him (96). The narrator's mute complicity is tantamount to the ignorance of the bachelors; he's witnessed the horrors of the mill and yet still participates in the economy that makes such corruption necessary. In his discussion of the end of the diptych, Winter argues, "Melville offers a narrator who posits himself in the role of a voyeur, discovers social guilt in his complicity with the exploited condition of the working class, yet in the end does absolutely nothing" (30). Winter is exactly right, and, in fact, it's not just that the narrator refuses to act.

He also refuses to say anything. This reticence to put words to thoughts makes him uncomfortable, and that's exactly what Melville's diptych is doing within literary transatlantic textual circulations on the textile industry.

The final ambivalence, then, belongs to the reader, who like the narrator must choose whether to act beyond the page and whether blankness is either morally or economically satisfying. This, of course, is where the real margins between fiction and nonfiction exist, since Melville's imagined readers are thinking, acting subjects who cannot avoid participating in the global economy. The narrator's final, most inscrutable line—"Oh! Paradise of Bachelors! and oh! Tartarus of Maids!"—is also Melville's most damning critique of the publishing frenzy surrounding the textile mills (96). It's not just that our being aware of the problem can't easily absolve us of guilt; rather, it often makes us, like the narrator, uncomfortably complicit.

Notes

1. While many critics compared Manchester's mill system and Lowell's, it's worth noting their size difference. In 1841 the Manchester mills employed around 374,000 workers. Lowell's factories, in contrast, employed only 72,119. By 1851 the discrepancy was only slightly less: 379,000 employees in Manchester and 92,000 in Lowell (Greenlees, 19).

2. The few articles or book chapters published on "The Paradise of Bachelors and the Tartarus of Maids" mainly present allegorical or generic arguments (see Gretchko and Weyler for representative examples). Even fewer critics have considered the cultural moment, particularly the parallels among Lowell, Manchester, and the paper mill in the story. Aaron Winter suggests that the story "certainly engages the picturesque as a mode of upper class delusion about the lives of workers" (29). Sidney Bremer similarly discusses the cultural relevance of the story: "Melville's story demonstrates that the traditional image of the European city cannot even account for the modern European city itself—any more than the popular mythology of neighborly rural hamlets can accurately represent the economic slavery and the life-denying mechanization of an industrialized American countryside" (56). More specifically, Robert Milder acknowledges that "on the most explicit level, the Devil's Dungeon paper mill visited by the seedsman-narrator is a representation *in extremis* of countless New England factories scattered throughout the stream-fed landscape" (xvii). Similarly, Elizabeth Schultz reads the female workers in the second-half of the diptych as "Melville's recognition of the oppression to which industrialization and the market economy in the antebellum period subjected women" ("'Bartleby,'" 82). William Spanos, in passing, reads the story

as a commentary on the mills: "Melville is clearly alluding to the Lowell project [in] 'Paradise.'" (150).

3. These observations, however, recall reform-minded poetry of the 1840s, such as Elizabeth Barrett Browning's "The Cry of the Children" (1842) and Thomas Hood's "The Song of the Shirt" (1843).

4.. For a thorough discussion of *Lowell Offering* editor Harriot F. Curtis, see Ranta.

5. Even after it ended, the *Lowell Offering* influenced other periodicals. Most notably, editor Harriet Farley ran *The New England Offering*, which published selections written by women throughout New England, from 1848 until 1850.

6. For a more detailed discussion of Martineau's interest in the *Lowell Offering* and her relationship with Charles Knight, see Frawley.

7. Winter discusses the narrator's seed packets in more detail, connecting them, albeit briefly, to the publishing industry: "Like the seedsman's envelopes, Melville's text is a manufactured paper object and therefore part of the vicious economy that it describes. As Thomas reminds us, 'the very pages we are holding might have been produced by an exploitive system' (182). And "by purchasing the fictional contents of Melville's paper envelopes, the reader becomes an unwitting participant in the economic exploitation of the factory maids" (Winter, 33).

6

Dressing the Aesthetic Woman, from "Maison Lucile" to *Midnight in Paris*

Margaret D. Stetz

Midnight in Paris (2011), written and directed by Woody Allen, deals comically with the nostalgia that second-rate or would-be artists experience, as they dream their way into times of past glory and imagine themselves being welcomed and encouraged by the greats whose works they idolize. The film presents two such "wannabes": Gil, a scriptwriter from Hollywood, who places himself at the center of Parisian modernist circles of the 1920s, and a beautiful woman named Adriana, who inhabits Gil's fantasy world but who is herself a frustrated artist, longing to go even farther back in time. She is a provincial by birth, from Bordeaux, and a dress designer manquée, who had arrived in Paris hoping to work with Coco Chanel. Instead, she has found herself consigned to the unfulfilling role of a what we might call the "triple M," as mistress, model, and muse to a sequence of masculine creators—from Modigliani, to Braque, to Picasso, to Ernest Hemingway, and potentially to Gil—and her dissatisfaction with this fate parallels that of Zelda Fitzgerald, who wanders first disconsolately and then suicidally through the 1920s sequences, after having her own artistic ambitions dismissed by her male contemporaries.

When a Belle Epoque–era carriage providentially appears in answer to Adriana's yearnings, and it spirits her away to Maxim's in the 1890s, there is a surprise in store both for her and for the audience. As the well-known figures of the period, including Toulouse-Lautrec, hover round her eagerly, we think we know what will happen next. Once again, we expect, she will be exploited purely as a decorative object, albeit now as the embodiment of the Aesthetic woman of the *fin de siècle.* Since, however, this is her own time-traveling fantasy, she is offered not an opportunity to pose but to create—to design costumes for the stage. Though the lovelorn Gil returns alone to the twenty-first century and mourns her loss, no one can blame her for accepting the invitation to become an innovator herself, for she will presumably be able to bring a modernist sensibility to the clothes that she makes for the nineteenth-century theater and thus be a designer of consequence.

It is, of course, unfair to raise questions about historical accuracy when viewing an example of cinematic fiction. Nonetheless, audiences might be forgiven for wondering how and whether fantasy and reality do intersect here. Certainly, the image of woman (often with a capital "W") was essential to the Aesthetic movement of the second half of the nineteenth century, whether we are examining Paris or London or, for that matter, New York, each of which experienced its own version of Aestheticism. The works of art most often reproduced or exhibited now, in order to represent the Aesthetic period, usually tend to be those by men, from Toulouse-Lautrec's posters of Moulin Rouge dancers, to Burne-Jones's paintings of angelic maidens on golden stairs, to Henry James's novels about women collectors of decorative furnishings. Always, the female figures in them appear dressed (or, in the case of both Oscar Wilde's and Aubrey Beardsley's veil-shedding Salome, undressed) and posed by their male creators, with their tumbling lengths of Rossettian red hair, or their Whistlerian white tea gowns, or their Beardsleyesque peacock skirts either chosen and arranged or imagined by masculine connoisseurs of particular ideals of femininity. Such a pattern holds true even in the recent exhibition *The Cult of Beauty: The Aesthetic Movement 1860–1900*, curated in 2011 by Stephen Calloway and Lynn Federle Orr for the Victoria and Albert Museum, as well as in the accompanying exhibition catalog, where women predominate as exquisite subjects of visual representation but receive scant attention as active makers of art.

Was there, in fact, room for women artists in the milieu of the late-nineteenth-century Aesthetic movement, whether these were artists whose medium was cloth, or watercolor, or photography, or the pen? Was the Aesthetic woman chiefly a being envisioned by male aesthetes, or did she have an independent existence and, moreover, exercise real power and influence? Could she, like her masculine contemporaries, make a living out of shaping and professing, rather than merely embodying, the principles of beauty? Was Woody Allen's Adriana being set up for a second disappointment by going back in time, or did she have a chance of succeeding at the turn of the century?

In the world of Aesthetic fashion, at least, the names that have survived are again largely those of men, particularly when it comes to those who designed for the theater and for its star performers. Among the most prominent of these was Jacques Doucet (1853–1929), who dressed the very actresses—Réjane and Sarah Bernhardt, in particular—whom any fan of the Belle Epoque stage would have worshiped as arbiters of style, putting them into costumes that exemplified "the fluidity, relative informality, and surface decoration of the Art Nouveau style" (Troy, 33). More than a dressmaker, though, Doucet considered himself an aesthete-collector, both of paintings and of books. As Nancy J. Troy writes in *Couture Culture* (2003), what "really excited Doucet was the creation of ensembles of objects" on a large scale—"the accumulation and display of fine and decorative art" (36), which he preferred to the role he played in fashioning the Aesthetic woman.

Yet there were opportunities for women, too, of the *fin de siècle* to make their mark through the production of Aesthetic dress and to see their work celebrated. In France, Jeanne Paquin (1869–1936) achieved such great fame that, in "1900, she was selected to preside over the Fashion Section of the Exposition Universelle in Paris, where the enormous statue of *La Parisienne* that towered over the exhibition" was sculpted, wearing a costume based on one of her designs (Troy, 130). Today, of course, Paquin's name has lost some of its luster, and it is to that "monstrous effigy" at the Exposition Universelle, "dressed in a negligee or a dressing-gown," that A. S. Byatt refers to, disparagingly, in her neo-Victorian historical novel *The Children's Book* (2009), where she also erases the designer's identity as a woman and speaks of "Paquin himself" (246).

Perhaps the best example, however, of the sort of career that Woody Allen's fictional Adriana, who is fluent in English and who goes by a first name alone, might have emulated was that of the single-named couturière Lucile, proprietor of the Maison Lucile, which opened in London in 1894 (two years before Jeanne Paquin established a branch of her own business there). The character of Lucile was, in reality, not French at all, but the invention of Lucy Sutherland (1863–1935), an Englishwoman who divorced her first husband and later became Lady Duff Gordon. In *Theater and Fashion: Oscar Wilde to the Suffragettes* (1994), Joel H. Kaplan and Sheila Stowell speak admiringly of her "calculated impudence" in sending out into the world in 1891 "an exuberant collection of 'personality gowns,' provocative creations in light fabric" that were colored "in a bold palette of scarlet, jade, viridian, and tyrian purple" and that "formed the outer limit of what was permissible to wear in good society" (39). For the stage, too, she created costumes "informed by the same flamboyant eroticism that had characterized her off-stage garments" (40). But she had competitors in the theater world. Among them were Alice Comyns Carr

FIGURE 6.1: Ellen Terry as Lady Macbeth, 1889, John Singer
Sargent (1856–1925). © *Tate, London 2014.* (Plate 12.)

Figure 6.2: Aubrey Beardsley, *Portrait of Mrs. Patrick Campbell*, reproduced from *The Yellow Book* 1 (April 1894). *By permission of the Mark Samuels Lasner Collection, on loan to the University of Delaware Library.*

and Adeline (Ada) Nettleship, who designed and executed many of the gowns that Ellen Terry wore onstage (fig. 6.1), and especially the firm of "Mesdames Savage and Purdue," which supplied costumes for Wilde's *Lady Windermere's Fan* (1892), as well as for Pinero's *The Second Mrs. Tanqueray* (1893), including the flower-like artistic dress depicted in 1894 by Aubrey Beardsley in his notorious *Portrait of Mrs. Patrick Campbell* (55–56). In Beardsley's drawing of "Mrs. Pat" as Paula Tanqueray (fig. 6.2), for the first number of the *Yellow Book* magazine, the final stiff point of the gown's layered lace jabot, seen in profile, stands out from the actress's bosom like an erect nipple, which was surely not the effect that the "Mesdames Savage and Purdue" would have wished to convey.

Women dress designers, it seemed, might earn a living and build reputations by creating their own versions of Aesthetic display, but they could not always control the uses made of their work in masculine representations. Neither could they always succeed in convincing the public that their creations were their own and not attributable to men. Franny Moyle, the most recent biographer of Oscar Wilde's wife, Constance Lloyd Wilde (1859–1898), reports that Oscar's friend, the writer Robert Sherard, assumed that "Oscar himself designed Constance's wedding dress," given its Aesthetic form and "saffron" color. But as Moyle reminds readers, with "her art schooling and her natural interest in fashion and embroidery, it is far more likely that Constance designed her own outfit, in conjunction with . . . [Ada] Nettleship" (85).

If women of the late nineteenth century were active in shaping modes of Aesthetic self-presentation, onstage and off, so too did they play equally crucial roles as professional fashion journalists and as authors of books on Aesthetic style, writing both about what women did wear and what they ought to wear. The Aesthetic movement gave them a chance to be paid for articulating their views on matters such as dress and interior decoration that had traditionally been the province of the domestic sphere inhabited by middle- and upper-middle-class women—ladies' drawing rooms, where talents and opinions, however brilliant, received no financial compensation. Indeed, new access to the professional and public world of taste making became one of the main sources of conflict between Aesthetic women and their male counterparts, for it generated a rivalry that defined and sometimes poisoned relations between these two otherwise interdependent groups.

As Talia Schaffer notes in *The Forgotten Female Aesthetes*,

> [the] men's and women's activities were, in a sense, complementary. While men told educated male readers to start appreciating beauty, women told beauty-loving female readers to get educated. Female aesthetes, in particular, wrote for an audience of women whose instinctive knowledge of beauty was 'the feminine equivalent' to real art and urged them to higher, more informed tastes. These female aesthetes stood at the junction of aesthetic beauty-consciousness and New Woman co-educational ferment. (2000, 21–22)

But as Schaffer also observes in the introduction, co-written with Kathy Alexis Psomiades, to their 1999 volume *Women and British Aestheticism*, "Aestheticism both empowered and erased women writers." Its effects were double sided: "On the one hand . . . aestheticism's emphasis on beautiful descriptions chimed in well with Victorian critics' requirement that women confine themselves to attractive writing styles. On the other hand, the aesthetes' valorization of professional artistic training often made women writers' domestic experiences seem glaringly amateurish" (1).

Charlotte Gere reminds readers, in *Artistic Circles: Design and Decoration in the Aesthetic Movement* (2010), that in the popular imagination "too great an interest" in matters of "decoration and beautification" labeled a man as "effeminate" and potentially opened him up to "mockery and satire" (67). Yet male aesthetes looking to prosper in the world of journalism deliberately positioned themselves to elbow out female competitors, as they took on work in what had been a feminine preserve. The protagonist of Ella Hepworth Dixon's "New Woman" novel of 1894, *The Story of a Modern Woman*, gets an education in these changed realities of London's Grub Street when, having fallen on hard times, she goes in search of commissions from publishers and editors. At the offices of a periodical titled *The Fan*, she encounters "a well-dressed, supercilious" man with "a rather affected voice" who, while treating her with scant courtesy, explains the ways of the paper he edits:

> "I dare say," replied Mary a little stiffly, "that you are dreadfully busy."
>
> "Oh, as to that, of course, we're frightfully 'rushed'—especially just now, at the middle of the month. We come out, you see, on the 23rd. I'm most anxious, you see, to make *The Fan* a success. I want it to be quite the smartest thing out, and a real authority on dress and fashion. As to the dress part, I'm not afraid of that. I do it all myself."
>
> "Indeed!" said Mary, to whom the young man who spends his life describing petticoats was as yet an unknown entity. She felt vaguely uncomfortable as the supercilious editor's eye dwelt upon her, not feeling sure that he would approve of the shape of her sleeves, and being morally certain that he was by this time aware that her gown was not lined with silk. (111)

Competition of a different sort disfigured the relationship between the poet and critic Arthur Symons and Violet Paget, who wrote essays and fiction as "Vernon Lee." Stefano Evangelista details a correspondence in the 1880s pervaded by Symons's "resentment" of her intrusions on what was supposedly his aesthetic territory, and Symons's unjust portrait of her in letters to others "as an intellectual vulture feeding on his ideas" (99).

Nevertheless, middle-class women who either needed or wished to make their way in the literary world took every possible advantage of opportunities to exercise influence over the formation and the application of Aesthetic principles, whether through periodicals or through books. Often these women served as more than mere popularizers of Aestheticism, for they were also innovators themselves in theory and practice. In *Graham R.*, her 2005 biography of Rosamund Marriott Watson, the late Victorian "Woman of Letters" who sometimes published as "Graham R. Tomson," Linda K. Hughes describes how the author went about "recording impressions of London in her fashion column" in W. E. Henley's paper, the *Scots Observer*, which became the *National Observer* in 1890 (116). Hughes classes her among those fashion writers who, "in keeping with the overlapping of aestheticism and commodity culture, the decorative arts and high art," breached the boundary "between humdrum journalism and literature with their wit, literary allusions, and prose style." "Graham R." turned her columns on dress into autobiographical occasions, while defying the notion of women as purely ornamental objects and portraying them instead as active "agents and connoisseurs" (117).

No one did more to bridge the divide between Aestheticism and a mass audience, especially of women readers, than Mary Eliza Haweis (1848–1898), the daughter of an artist and the wife of a clergyman. With her early advocacy of William Morris, she may be better remembered now for her pronouncements on the House Beautiful—on how women could select appropriate colors and types of furniture to suit Aesthetic interiors. She was just as interesting and important a commentator on how women might achieve, in accord with Aesthetic precepts, the body beautiful (while also being a more than competent visual artist, who illustrated her own work). Over one hundred years later, in a 1981 book titled *The Language of Clothes*, the Pulitzer Prize–winning American novelist and critic Alison Lurie would speak of "clothing as a sign system," explaining that "today, as semiotics becomes fashionable, sociologists tell us that fashion too is a language of signs, a nonverbal system of communication" (3); thus, "To choose clothes, either in a store or at home, is to define and describe ourselves," for "just as with spoken language, such choices usually give us some information" (5). Mary Eliza Haweis, publishing as "Mrs. H. R. Haweis," had already advanced much the same argument, and in terms just as sophisticated, in her 1878 volume *The Art of Beauty*, a collection of articles originally written in the early 1870s for *St. Paul's Magazine*, which was edited by Anthony Trollope. In chapter 2 of Haweis's book, titled "The Importance of Dress," she made clear the premise with which she began: "In nothing are character and perception so insensibly but inevitably displayed, as in dress, and taste in dress. Dress is the second self, a dumb self, yet a most eloquent expositor of the person" (11); moreover, "Dress bears the same relation to the body as speech does to the brain; and therefore dress may be called the speech of the body" (2004, 17).

At the same time, however, Haweis's chief concern was with discovering a way to speak through the body that was not merely expressive but also aesthetically pleasing. The Victorian Age was, after all, a period when fashion had become so extravagant in its details that "a dress now claims to be considered as a work of art":

> Now if dress be worth all this elaboration, if it intends to reach, as it evidently aspires to do, the platform of a picture, or a poem, or a fine building, the art it adopts must be either good or bad art. I believe the melancholy truth to be that we can hardly find a modern dress which is not throughout in the worst taste and opposed to the principles of good art. . . .
>
> If everybody who could hold a pencil were suddenly called upon to paint a picture, there would be only a few out of every score at least who would betray any sense of grace, perspective, colour, or design. Would it not be wise for those unpossessed of the sacred fire to receive instruction of some wholesome kind before they wasted time and good material to so little purpose?
>
> But what is true of painting is true also of dress. We need not all paint, but we have all got to dress, and the sooner dress is recognized by our women as an art-product the better. . . .
>
> Yet dress and a proper care for it ought not to minister merely to vanity. . . . A woman ought to care what she wears for her own sake and for the sake of those about her. (13–14)

Although these words may have sounded like the prelude to a set of inflexible rules, albeit ones that reflected the dictates of the Aesthetic painters and makers of decorative objects whom Haweis admired, they were not. They led, on the contrary, to a declaration of individual liberty as the first condition for women's artistic self-fashioning:

But how difficult it is for a woman to be really well dressed, under the existing prejudice that everybody must be dressed like everybody else!. . . . [The] majority have succeeded in suffocating the aesthetic minority, many of whom are now forced to suppress really good taste for fear of being called "affected." We shall never have any school of art in England, either in dress or decoration of any kind, until the fundamental principle of good art is recognised, that *people may do as they like* in the matter, and until women cease to be afraid of being laughed at for doing what they feel to be wise and right. (15; emphasis original)

Talia Schaffer has suggested that the difference between the female aesthetes of the 1880s and 1890s and their rebellious feminist contemporaries, the "New Women" writers, turned on their political attitudes. These two groups were "intimately connected and strongly allied," for both "constituted the vanguard of radical change" (2000, 18); yet the "female aesthetes chose to participate in a high-art tradition rather than a political movement," using their public platform "not to bear witness to the desperate need to expand women's lives but to . . . question the value and the limits of that expansion of female identity" (25). Such a distinction, however, between the "New Woman" as progressive, and the Aesthetic woman as conservative, will not account for Haweis's radical pronouncements of the 1870s, made in the service of the pursuit of beauty. In aligning even so-called ordinary women, engaged in the seemingly mundane task of dressing, with avant-garde English artists, while arguing not merely for women's right to experiment and innovate, but for a change in modern women's temperament and conduct—for a new boldness, fearlessness, and imperviousness to the censure of others—Mary Eliza Haweis certainly blurred the line between conservative and progressive thought. In volumes such as *The Art of Decoration* (1881), she also displayed her own talents as a visual artist, illustrating Aesthetic modes of dress, not merely as a theorist and advocate (fig. 6.3).

By the 1890s there were many "New Women" who were also Aesthetic women. Some were apt to locate the sort of charm associated with artful dressing in unusual and unexpected places. In the eyes of the Irish short story writer "George Egerton" (1859–1945), born Mary Chavelita Dunne and known for her Bodley Head volumes with bindings and title pages by Aubrey Beardsley, a woman's naked flesh could be just as artistic a sight as any drapery.

" *Yet Nature is made better by no mean,*
But Nature makes that mean; so o'er that art
Which, you say, adds to Nature, is an art
That Nature makes."—SHAKESPEARE.

FIGURE 6.3: Mary Eliza Joy Haweis, frontispiece from *The Art of Decoration* (London: Chatto and Windus, 1881). *By permission of the Mark Samuels Lasner Collection, on loan to the University of Delaware Library.* (Plate 13.)

In her short story "At the Heart of the Apple" from *Symphonies* (1897), Egerton celebrated the "perfect nude figures" of a mother and child bathing together, while concentrating on the "supple strength" of the body of the young woman, with her "beautiful glistening shoulders," "white arms cleaving the water," and hair that "fell like a glorious mantle below her waist" (212–13). Egerton could, however, also conjure up more conventionally attired Aesthetic forms and replicate more conventional Aesthetic prose in describing them, especially when her purpose was to critique images dear to her Aesthetic and Decadent male contemporaries, as she demonstrated in a story titled "The Mandrake Venus" from *Fantasias* (1898). There she pilloried the romanticized and exoticized visions of prostitution that circulated among the Aesthetes, through her delineation of a "great Harlot mother" (69) who is the personification of syphilis but who looks like Oscar Wilde's Salome, had Sarah Bernhardt ever played her onstage (as Wilde had hoped):

> She lay supinely, darting keen though languid glances through her heavy lids, from eyes that burnt with sombre fire, and lured as a serpent . . . her hair—strange hair, black yet gold in its lights, so that no man knew its real colour—was crowned with scarlet flowers; a long scarf or mantle of the thinnest tissue, saffron in hue, shot with carmine, richly broidered with gold, hung from her shoulders; it was caught at the hollow of her throat by a clasp of a myriad shining gems. (64)

This diseased creature, with a "leprous, white body" beneath her robes (67), is accompanied by what can only be described as a troupe of mini-Salomes, or perhaps "Salomettes," as "from each aisle women advanced, clad in garments of cobweb tissue that clung to their swaying limbs, and parted airily to the rhythm of their steps—fluttering, trembling into ever-changing hues. They swept on in sinuous lines . . . scattering scarlet blossoms as they danced, until their little white feet seemed to dip into a sea of blood" (65).

If "New Woman" writing was sometimes indistinguishable from Aesthetic prose, with its self-conscious melding of beauty and strangeness, so too, as Elizabeth Wilson notes in *Adorned in Dreams: Fashion and Modernity* (1985), "By the 1890s many features of aesthetic dress had been gradually incorporated into the fashionable dress of the day" (216). Christopher Breward places the time of that melding a decade earlier, asserting, "[By] 1881 a taste for Aesthetic dressing had permeated fully through the more arty fringes of metropolitan society" (197). Regardless of how universal the shift may or may not have been in the 1880s, there is certainly no doubt that by the nineties—spurred in part by the influence of the Rational Dress movement, in which women such as Constance Lloyd Wilde were active—"Bustles as well as crinolines had at last ceded to the long, slender skirt" (Wilson, 216). By the turn of the century, society women such as Maud Sambourne Messel (1875–1960), daughter of the *Punch* cartoonist Linley Sambourne, had absorbed and incorporated orientalist Aesthetic elements into their personal style, in garments like Messel's "grey silk crepon bolero-styled jacket and skirt" ornamented with "great swirls of . . . Chinese-styled embroidered silk braid," designed by "Mme. Hayward of New Bond Street" (Taylor 2002, 119). The effects of this evolutionary development and assimilation were felt, moreover, across the ocean. "Even the American Gibson girl," according to Elizabeth Wilson, "whom many feminists believed at the time to be a prototype for the 'new woman' of the 1890s and 1900s, may claim her descent from the pre-Raphaelites" and from the impact upon Charles Dana Gibson, the Gibson girl's creator, of the drawings of George du Maurier, chief satirist of the Aesthetes for *Punch* magazine (fig. 6.4) in the 1880s (216).

As we move toward the end of the nineteenth century, in other words, the Aesthetic woman increasingly merges with other avant-garde constructions and simultaneously goes mainstream, across the arts and across the ocean. Thus we find her, for instance, assuming a dominant role in turn-of-the-century works produced by the New York–based portrait photographer, Zaida Ben-Yusuf (1869–1933). Images such as Ben-Yusuf's 1898 *The Peacock's Plumage*, which featured two "peacocks"—a haughtily beautiful model in a flowing tea gown, posed beside a mirror, and a parasol-like object fashioned out of a sheaf of feathers—combined multiple Aesthetic tropes to produce what Frank H. Goodyear III calls "photographs that are more than mere likenesses," as the photographer "aspires to transcend the recording nature of the medium to realize an image that is not only technically competent but also invested with beauty and artistic refinement" (57). At the same time, the reproduction and circulation of such an image—in this case, in the June 1898 issue of the magazine *Photo-Era*—demonstrated what Kathy Psomiades, in *Beauty's Body: Femininity and Representation in British Aestheticism* (1997), refers to as "the commodity nature of artistic products" (95). The spectacle of both the beautiful woman and the feathered decorative object was "gratifying the material tastes of an audience," as "high aestheticist art became more widely known and more highly valued" (95)—valued in the economic, as well as the intellectual, sense.

Many Aesthetic women themselves had hurried along this process of public acceptance and even of commodification wherever possible, for their lives (or at least their livelihoods) depended upon it. Kate Greenaway (1846–1901), a protégée of John Ruskin and a disciple of his high-minded philosophy

FIGURE 6.4: George du Maurier, illustration reproduced from
Max Beerbohm, *A Note on "Patience"* (London: Miles, 1919). *By
permission of the Mark Samuels Lasner Collection, on loan to the University of
Delaware Library.*

of beauty, relied nonetheless on the sales of her illustrated books and rejoiced
when the profits came rolling in (fig. 6.5). Like other middle-class women
artists of the Aesthetic movement, Greenaway could not survive on lilies
alone. She was not distressed by the popularity of her art as an inspiration for
"children's clothes and greeting cards" but by the pirating of it, when countless manufacturers imitated her work and did not pay her royalties (Engen,
78). *Yellow Book* artists such as Katherine Cameron (1874–1965), Nellie Syrett
(1872?–1971?), and Mabel Dearmer (1872–1915), who followed Greenaway's lead in depicting women or young girls in languid, pre-Raphaelite
poses, wearing Regency-inspired costumes or Aesthetic pinafores (fig. 6.6),

FIGURE 6.5 (LEFT): Kate Greenaway, *Young Girl Waving a Rose Branch*, pencil and watercolor, 1886. *By permission of the Mark Samuels Lasner Collection, on loan to the University of Delaware Library.* (Plate 14.)

FIGURE 6.6 (RIGHT): Katherine Cameron, *The Black Cockade*, reproduced from *The Yellow Book* 13 (April 1897). *By permission of the Mark Samuels Lasner Collection, on loan to the University of Delaware Library.*

also followed her into the lucrative field of children's book publishing, where women illustrators received a warmer reception than they did in exhibitions and galleries. Their *fin-de-siècle* drawings of prettily dressed or half-dressed, flower-like prepubescent girls satisfied the demands of middle-class adults who wished to elevate children's tastes, even as they catered to the pedophilic desires that underlay Victorian visual culture in general.

As the image of the artistically garbed Aesthetic woman or girl became widely marketable, Aestheticism itself remained a paradox. It was at once the refuge of outsiders—of those born on the margins and of those who adopted Bohemian identities as an antibourgeois protest—and a vehicle through which outsiders could exert cultural influence, regardless of whether they were otherwise accepted. Writing of the literary salon maintained by Oscar Wilde's friend and "Sphinx," the Jewish novelist Ada Leverson (1862–1933), Emily D. Bilski and Emily Braun describe its "habitués, whatever their success," as embodiments, in social terms, of "deviance," for they were "Anglo-Irish among the British . . . Catholics and Jews in Anglican England, and . . . homosexuals" (54). Yet many of these so-called deviants, especially women, were also drawn into mainstream discourse through their participation in the rhetoric of dress, which was shared across the margins and the center of female communities. Many, too, helped to shape that discourse.

Some women Aesthetes reveled in an alien and self-consciously unfeminine identity, defining it as a precondition for serious art. In one of the poems for *Long Ago*, their 1889 volume inspired by fragments from Sappho, the aunt and niece who wrote together as "Michael Field" depicted the initiation into Apollo's chosen band of artists as a brutal transformative process involving a sexual violation—a rape by the Greek god (who presented himself first in the form of a tortoise, then of a powerful snake) that turned maidens into fallen women and outcasts, before rewarding them with admission to the company of the elect. "Michael Field"—that is, Katharine Bradley (1846–1914) and Edith Cooper (1862–1913)—could scarcely have been a more transgressive pair themselves, as an incestuous lesbian couple allied in close friendship with another Aesthetic same-sex pair, the designer Charles Ricketts (1866–1931) and the painter Charles Shannon (1863–1937). When, however, they wrote in their private journals of social occasions with other Aesthetic women, their descriptions moved from the high-minded and spiritual to the frankly material—to appreciations of details of dress as precise and also as breathlessly enthusiastic as anything in a fashion column: "At this point callers entered— Mrs. M. Drummond, Burne-Jones' famous sitter and model. . . . Every wonder of the type was there . . . the uplifted growth of hair, the colourless blur about the mouth, the pure lines of brow and cheek. She wore a cloak of dark peacock green and fawn boa; round her bonnet, like the cloak in shade, little peacock feathers of softest hue and shimmer mingled with the hair" (Sturge Moore, 116–17).

The particular tropes of women's Aesthetic self-fashioning may have represented, at least at first, opposition to bourgeois norms. But these new conventions of dress also gave outsiders admission to an alternative community, based on shared tastes, where they enjoyed positions as style leaders. And as the mainstream gradually embraced their avant-garde principles, so these 'exotic' women grew into admired figures. Doubly alien as both Anglo-Irish and Jewish, the Davis sisters—Eliza and Julia, who later became, respectively, the journalist and dress historian "Mrs. Aria," and the novelist Julia Frankau, aka "Frank Danby"—dealt regularly with anti-Semitism, a fact recorded in Eliza's 1922 memoir, *My Sentimental Self.* Jews were regarded as a so-called oriental race that could never be fully assimilated. Julia Davis Frankau, however, used the perception of Jews as un-English to reframe her identity as modishly oriental—indeed as Asian. Eliza's description of her sister's self-presentation is like something straight out of a production of Gilbert and Sullivan's *The Mikado* (1885), combined with J. M. Whistler's painting, *The Princess from the Land of Porcelain* (1863–1865). Remembering Julia's fin-de-siècle drawing-room, with its "pots and jars of all shapes . . . jade green walls and . . . the little Japanese trees which held for her a great fascination," Eliza Davis Aria paints an Aesthetic word-picture of Julia herself: "I can see her now clad in a black Japanese gown, invaded by golden dragons, seated in a deep chair; at her back an enormous cushion embroidered with . . . scarlet flowers . . . her hands holding a piece of cambric, her eyes looking up from this to fix themselves in dreamy adoration on a little stunted dark green tree rooted in sand planted in blue and white china" (63). If the Aesthetic movement had made it desirable for Englishwomen to appear Japanese, then who better to show them how to do it than another "Oriental"?

Throughout the latter part of the nineteenth century, the Aesthetic movement blurred the lines between outsiders and insiders, as it created new standards for defining these identities and generated new opportunities, particularly through its emphasis on fashion, for women who defied convention. It also blurred the boundaries that separated cultures and nations. Aesthetic style in dress was an international phenomenon that—like the women who modeled, wore, designed, sold, photographed, painted, or wrote about it—moved easily from one cosmopolitan center to another. The firm of Liberty, for instance, which became the best-known purveyor of Aesthetic fashion in general and of Japanese-influenced tea gowns in particular to the women of London, also made itself a fixture in Paris, first displaying Aesthetic costumes in the Exposition Universelle of 1889 and then establishing the "Maison Liberty" in 1890. As Alison Adburgham reports, "Already in France *any* softly draping silk was being called *soie Liberty*, and now the fashionable ladies of Paris flocked to buy the genuine fabrics and order aesthetic gowns" (40). They could, therefore, dress themselves like the Englishwomen who frequented artists' colonies such as the ones that sprang up in the summer resort of Dieppe, where in the early 1890s they might have encountered Mabel Beardsley (1871–1916), the actress sister of Aubrey Beardsley, who distinguished herself by wearing elaborate clothes that "recalled a lady of the Italian Renaissance," and who used her Aesthetic appearance to further her career on the stage (Syrett, 79).

Participating in the world of Aesthetic fashion at the turn of the century proved a route by which women of varying backgrounds and talents, from diverse locations, could advance themselves in the public sphere. It heightened their visibility and their mobility, in many senses. The very breadth and fluidity of what Aestheticism encompassed in terms of visual style—everything from Rational Dress to Pre-Raphaelitism to Orientalism to Medievalism to Regency-inspired pinafores—made it a movement open to individual shaping, whether by those who defined it through fashion writing and fiction writing, by those who posed onstage or offstage for a living in Aesthetic garments, or by those who sewed and sold their own visions in fabric.

We can, therefore, safely imagine that the ultimate outsider—Adriana, Woody Allen's fictional alien from the 1920s—would have found a way both to exercise her dressmaking skills and to satisfy her creative and theatrical ambitions in the Belle Epoque, drawn into the transnational world of Aestheticism. Yet, so long as we are fantasizing, we might as well go further. Let us picture this time traveler's ultimate fate—one that probably would have led to more conventional forms of travel, across the English Channel. For there is every reason to believe that, in Paris or Dieppe, the heroine of *Midnight in Paris* would have met her British counterparts and been lured to London, where—like the real-life dress-designer known as Lucile—she would have costumed the actresses, the models, the writers, and the society women whom the Aesthetes, male and female alike, drew, sculpted, photographed, or painted. And since we are breaking the boundaries anyway between reality and fiction, may we not assume that, in an exhibition such as the Victoria and Albert Museum's *The Cult of Beauty: The Aesthetic Movement 1860–1900*, there was at least one portrait of an Aesthetic woman wearing a creation from the Maison Adriana?

Clothing and Colonialism in Conrad's *Heart of Darkness*

Pouneh Saeedi

> When a series of missionary photographs arrived in England in the late nineteenth century, they caused outrage. The mutilations had been strategically photographed against white for maximum impact. The children came from the Congo but the man accused of their suffering was white, European and royal.
>
> —From the documentary *Congo: White King,*
> *Red Rubber, Black Death* (2003)

The history of the colonization of the Congo, as manifested in the above passage, is interwoven with strands of black and white, with whiteness being presented, initially, as a signifier for spirituality and civilization and blackness as a symbol of the darkness of the heart and mind. Similar chromatic and contextual designations color Joseph Conrad's *Heart of Darkness* (1899). Here white and black are carried over to the more abstract realms of light and darkness, and the fabric of European colonization of the African continent is laid bare as the narrator of the story within the story, Charlie Marlow, delineates his journey to the Congo and his pursuit of the monomaniacal colonizer, Kurtz. Much ink has been spilled on the racial aspects of colonialism in Conrad's text, with Chinua Achebe's groundbreaking article, "An Image of Africa: Racism in Conrad's 'Heart of Darkness'" (1975), being perhaps the most provocative of them all in that it uncovers racial elements that had remained hidden to Western eyes. There has, however, not been much mention of the symbolic strands of the text that go slightly beyond dermal boundaries to clothe the bodies of both the "civilized" white and the "savage" black. As this essay will seek to demonstrate, the fabric of Conrad's novella constitutes coverings of various kinds and the characters wear textual layers that enhance the mysteries lying latent in *Heart of Darkness*, a tale centered on a colonialist expedition that, ultimately, brings Marlow closer to an understanding of the darkest recesses of his own psyche. Marlow's soul-searching journey would have been in vain, were it not for his keen observation of exterior details that are in direct correlation with the hidden interiors they adorn. In short, clothing, in its multitudinous aspects, has a major role in a series of un-coverings that transpire in the warp and woof of Conrad's rich text, including a disrobing of the colonialist core of some of its European characters.

Clothing is a dominant trope in *Heart of Darkness*, as is evident in the various allusions to weaving in the text, including Conrad's reference to Marlow's narrative as "spinning yarns." Further, the two white women at the Brussels office in charge of the so-called *mission civilisatrice* are said to be knitting with black cotton. Marlow is believed to be the atypical seaman, "his propensity to spin yarns be excepted," and it is this predilection of his that lends him such a keen insight for *integumenta*, the exterior coverings of an interior truth. Conrad portrays the protagonist's fascination for the exterior covering in the following metaphorical terms:

> The yarns of seamen have a direct simplicity, the whole meaning of which lies within the shell of a cracked nut. But Marlow was not typical (if his propensity to spin yarns be excepted), and to him the meaning of an episode was not inside like a kernel but outside, enveloping the tale which brought it out only as a glow brings out a haze, in the likeness of one of these misty halos that sometimes are made visible by the spectral illumination of moonshine. (9)

One could attribute Marlow's delight with the chief accountant's impeccable appearance later on in the story to his keen observation of the exterior, a trait he shares with his creator, Joseph Conrad himself, whose meticulous delineation of the main occupants of *Nellie*, a boat anchored on the Thames where the passengers, and on a metanarrative level, the readers, hear Marlow's tale, as well as his graphic description of the natural surroundings that sets the tone for the novella's focus on outward details. Upon describing Marlow's facial features and postures, Conrad paints a clear picture of the landscape in terms that highlight both his proclivity for graphic delineation and his predilection to visualize the world as analogous to an expansive piece of fabric: "The water shone pacifically; the sky, without a speck, was a benign immensity of unstained light; the very mist on the Essex marsh was like a gauzy and radiant fabric, hung from the wooded rises inland, and draping the low shores in diaphanous folds. Only the gloom to the west, brooding over the upper reaches, became more somber every minute, as if angered by the approach of the sun" (8). As will become clear throughout this essay, the contrapuntal correlation of darkness and light in the novella, which is hinted at in the above passage, is carried over to characters whose opposing qualities unfold deep-seated truths that become further manifest in clothing.

There is a slight hint of contrast and comparison within the context of clothing from the very beginning of the story, in Conrad's allusion to the toga donned by the imaginary ancient Roman explorer in the London of yore, which would have been akin to the perceived wilderness that Marlow sets foot in. The toga constitutes part of a cluster of symbols highlighting this contrast:

> Sandbanks, marshes, forests, savages,—precious little to eat fit for a civilized man, nothing but Thames water to drink. No Falernian wine here, no going ashore. Here and there a military camp lost in a wilderness, like a needle in a bundle of hay—cold, fog, tempests, disease, exile, and death,—death skulking in the air, in the water, in the bush. . . . Or think of a decent young citizen in a toga—perhaps too much dice, you know—coming out here in the train of some prefect, or tax-gatherer, or trader even, to mend his fortunes. Land in a swamp, march through the woods, and in some inland post feel the savagery, the utter savagery, had closed round him—all that mysterious life of the wilderness that stirs in the forest, in the jungles, in the hearts of wild men. (9–10)

Upon closer scrutiny of the passage, being "civilized," drinking "Falernian wine" and donning a "toga," in their association with culture, begin to form a cluster that stands in contrast to "utter savagery" and "the wilderness." At the root of "culture," which is closely linked with "civilization," lies natural and mental growth, in that the term stems from the Latin *colere*, with its wide range of meanings, including "to cultivate," as is evident in Cicero's phrase *cultura animi*, and growth and cultivation imply maturity in time (Williams, 87). The "Falernian wine" is said to have been "required to be kept a great number of years before it was sufficiently mellow" (Adam, 322), and the "toga," taking its name from the Latin *tegere* (to cover), could be crafted only in the course of time, indicating the passage of a considerable amount of time, which has allowed for civilization to set in and, along with it, its many manifestations including various clothing, among which is the toga. The temporal difference that separates the so-called civilized from the uncivilized is further heightened when Marlow refers to the temporal discrepancy existing between himself and the "savages" of Africa in the following lines: "They had been engaged for six months (I don't think a single one of them had any clear idea of time, as we at the end of countless ages have" and "The *prehistoric* man was cursing us, praying to us, welcoming us—who could tell?" (37; emphasis added). Only in the passage of centuries, might the nakedness and diet of hippo and human meat of the savages be replaced with tokens of civilization, including clothing and possibly cultured wine. Time, along with space, is part of a cosmic machine imagined in the metaphor of "knitting" in one of Conrad's surviving letters:

> There is a—let us say—a machine. It evolved itself . . . out of a chaos of scraps of iron and behold!—it knits. I am horrified at the horrible work and stand appalled. I feel it ought to embroider—but it goes on knitting. You come and say: "this is all right: it's only a question of the right kind of oil. Let us use this—for instance—celestial oil and the machine shall embroider a most beautiful design in purple and gold." Will it? Alas no. You cannot by any special lubrication make embroidery with a knitting machine. And the most withering thought is that the infamous thing has made itself without thought, without conscience, without foresight, without eyes, without heart. It is a tragic accident—and it has happened. . . . It knits us in and it knits us out. It has knitted time, space, pain, death, corruption, despair and all the illusions—and nothing matters. (*Joseph*, 56–57)

Tangible threads of the above citation run through Conrad's text as diversified metaphors of knitting and clothing are woven into his tale. A prime example is the description of the two knitting women at the Brussels office where Marlow is to undergo a thorough physical examination before he sets off to the "dark continent." At this point, it is as if Conrad has set his narrative in messianic times, "a simultaneity of past and future in an instantaneous present" (Benjamin 1969, 24). Knitting, as in the above citation, constitutes a metaphor for temporal transcendence in *Heart of Darkness* and a means of getting at the unfathomable kernel of life. The two women replicate the archetypal figures of the Fates as they engage in knitting while most men who pass through their door are bound to either meet their deaths or undergo the most traumatic experience of their lives. The three Fates (the spinner, Clotho;

the allotter, Lachesis; and the cutter of the thread of life, Atropos) are evoked despite the difference in their number, as has been pointed out by Johanna M. Smith, a comparison further reinforced in Conrad's use of the phrase "uncanny and fateful" in the description of the older one of the two (187). There is a touch of comic relief when the reader is introduced to them for the first time, brought to the fore in the contrast of the two—one being slim, young, and active; the other, fat, old, and immobile, though brimming with wisdom. When later in the story Marlow is reminded of the latter of the two as "the most improper person to be sitting at the other end of such an affair" (64) as he is chasing an incapacitated Kurtz, one cannot but empathize with him and feel a chill run down one's spine. The actual encounter between Marlow and the knitting women is an *Erlebnis*, a term used in association with the conscious mind and the senses, hence fleeting in nature, while his later remembrance of those women in the midst of the African wilderness is an *Erfahrung*, which signifies an incorporated wisdom, therefore lasting (see Benjamin 163). Such a clear distinction in the types of experiences that the narrator undergoes from a cognitive perspective will be useful in better understanding why certain scholars, as shall be shortly observed, see two Marlows in the novella and not one.

What strikes Marlow in his fateful encounter with the knitting women is not only their nonchalance, which brings to mind the impassibility of the likes of Madame Defarge in Charles Dickens's *Tale of Two Cities* (1859), but also the use of "black" wool by two white women in a cryptic art that becomes closely associated with the fatal experiences of white men in the heart of darkness.[1] The chromatic contrast of white women knitting black wool becomes reversed in Marlow's sighting of "a bit of white worsted" around the black neck of a native whom he observes in the midst of what he calls "black shadows of disease and starvation." Marlow's subsequent comments suggest that were it not for the "white worsted," the reclining native would hardly have caught his attention, for it is this bit of cloth that gives rise to an entire array of questions in the seasoned seaman's mind: "Why? Where did he get it? Was it a badge—an ornament—a charm—a propitiatory act? Was there any idea at all connected with it? It looked startling round his black neck, this bit of white thread from beyond the seas" (20–21). As magical and extraordinary as this "bit of white thread" appears to Marlow, the "black rags" wound round the loins of a batch of native African prisoners, seemingly charged with violating laws enforced by the white colonizers, on the contrary, give them a dehumanizing air in the white seaman's mind as he goes on to describe how the "short ends [of the black rags] behind waggled to and fro like tails" (19).

In the figure of the European-installed native guarding over these prisoners, it is his "uniform jacket with one button off" that draws Marlow's attention in particular. Missing a button or being unbuttoned, as is the case of a seemingly drunk white man he runs into shortly after, becomes a signifier for sloppiness and lack of zeal for work, which takes on highly negative connotations in the novella. Similar negative sentiments are expressed by Marlow in his description of a white "pilgrim," a term he uses in reference to the colonizers who are "strolling aimlessly about," dressed in pink pajamas, who does a horrible job upon taking over from the narrator's black helmsman after the latter is slain in an onslaught launched by Kurtz as the white colonizers get close to his headquarters in the heart of the jungle: "Besides, I was anxious to take the wheel, the man in pink pyjamas showing himself a hopeless duffer at the business."[2] The "pilgrim" donning "pink pyjamas" is a prime specimen of idle colonizers, who despite carrying staves, "symbols of authority which white men generally were wont to carry in the colonies" (Watt, 222), lack the work ethic required for the expansion of a European empire. Ian Watt in his in-depth analysis of *Heart of Darkness* highlights the importance of "work" in the text as a "moral positive" (221), an instance of which appears in the presentation of "work" as a prophylactic against madness. As pointed out by Watt, "the reason [as to why Marlow didn't go ashore for a howl and a dance] was just that he was too busy navigating the steamboat and keeping an eye on the fireman: these duties, he says, provided enough 'surface-truth . . . to save a wiser man'" (226).

One of the more prominent representations of work in clothing comes to the fore in the impeccable image projected of the chief accountant he encounters upon arriving at the company station in the Congo. Marlow is fascinated by the accountant, whose impeccability in the midst of the African wilderness prompts him to initially mistake the figure of the accountant for a vision: "I respected the fellow. Yes; I respected his collars, his vast cuffs, his brushed hair. His appearance was certainly that of a hairdresser's dummy; but in the great demoralization of the land he kept up his appearance. That's backbone. His starched collars and got-up shirtfronts were achievements of character" (Conrad, *Heart*, 21).

The accountant is praised even more as we are told how he was "devoted to his books, which were in apple-pie order." Clothing and colonialism become linked in this part of the narrative as we learn that it is his attempts at instilling a work ethic in an African woman to take care of his appearance that allows the accountant to maintain such an immaculate appearance. "I've been teaching one of the native women about the station," the accountant says, adding: "It was "difficult. She had a distaste for work." Instead of feeling pity for the African woman, Marlow, however, expresses inner admiration for the white accountant, saying: "Thus, this man had verily accomplished something" (21).

The technique of delayed decoding dominant in Conrad's narrative, which is "based on the pretence that the reader's understanding is limited to the consciousness of the fictional observer [who, in the case of *Heart of Darkness*, would be Marlow]" (Watt, 270; explanation added), does not allow us to gain access to the African woman in any sense, neither to her appearance, nor to her consciousness—the two of which are, incidentally, interdependent, as observed in the novella. Nonetheless, the appearance of another native woman in the story, which constitutes a climax in the narrative, sheds some light on the pristine, albeit resistant, form of exterior an African native woman would be in a position to project were she given some scope for action. The African mistress of the villainous Kurtz is described in some length, in the course of which Marlow's audience on the *Nellie* could not have helped but vicariously feel as spellbound by the image she conjures in the mind as the narrator had been, upon actually laying eyes on her:

> She walked with measured steps, draped in striped and fringed cloths, treading the earth proudly, with a slight jingle and flash of barbarous ornaments. She carried her head high; her hair was done in the shape of a helmet; she had brass leggings to the knee, brass wire gauntlets to the elbow, a crimson spot on her tawny cheek, innumerable necklaces of glass beads on her neck; bizarre things, charms, gifts of witch-men, that hung about her, glittered and trembled at every step. She must have had the value of several elephant tusks upon her. She was savage and superb, wild-eyed and magnificent; there was something ominous and stately in her deliberate progress. And in the hush that had fallen suddenly upon the

whole sorrowful land, the immense wilderness, the colossal body
of the fecund and mysterious life seemed to look at her, pensive, as
though it had been looking at the image of its own tenebrous and
passionate soul. (Conrad, *Heart*, 60)

One's fascination with Kurtz's mistress can be attributed to a variety of
factors, not the least of which is her embodiment of an enigma that goes beyond her scant apparel. She is both "ominous" and "stately" and "savage" and
"magnificent" as she exudes a fecundity imbued with an air of mystery. In addition to her perplexing appearance, her oneness with Mother Earth makes
her coextensive with the tangled terrain she treads, making her a master of
an indomitable territory that has become taboo to the European colonizer
on grounds of the incurable diseases and impenetrable darkness that it har-
bors. More than the "innumerable necklaces of glass beads on her neck; bizarre things, charms, gifts of witch-men that hung about her," the key to her
dazzling appearance lies in "the value of elephant tusks upon her."

The ivory that adorns her is significant for a number of reasons. First, it
signifies her seeming nonchalance toward the killing of so many living creatures for the sake of adorning her already glittering body; second, it links her
to the ivory-obsessed Kurtz, who has the posts of his own house—one's house,
in a way, represents an extension of one's body—in the heart of the jungle
ornamented, as it initially seems to Marlow, with the cut-off heads of native
Africans; and third, her use of ivory, the desired object of European colonizers in Africa, to further enthrall them, associates her with a concept labeled
by Homi Bhabha as "sly civility," a veiled method of resistance, potentially in
the language of the colonizer (see 93–101). In addition, she is, unwittingly,
involved in a form of masquerade as she pretends to become an extension of
Kurtz's object of desire, ivory, although in actuality it is she who commands
respect in her otherworldly poise and gait. In her figure, we see the modulation between disposal-as-bestowal in Bhabhian terms and disposition-as-
inclination (see 156), meaning that along the boundaries of the authority inscribed on the surface of her skin, she demonstrates a disposition of her own
as she takes in the colonial presence around her on her own constitutional
terms (fig. 7.1).[3]

In her vitality and fecundity, she stands in stark contrast to Kurtz's white
European fiancée, who is referred to in the novella as the "Intended." As an
"intended," the Intended lacks every intention and finds more meaning in

A BAKONGO GIRL.

FIGURE 7.1: Herbert Ward, *Five Years with the Congo Cannibals* (1890).

dedicating herself to an embodiment of masculine power—for that matter, a dead one (after all, Kurtz has been dead for a year when Marlow meets her)—than to having a will of her own. Her lack of *joie de vivre* and the desire to remain in the past rather than move ahead come to the fore in the detailed description of the Intended set a year after Kurtz's death in the African jungle:

> She came forward, all in black, with a pale head, floating towards me in the dusk. She was in mourning. It was more than a year since his death, more than a year since the news came; she seemed as though she would remember and mourn forever. She took both my hands in hers and murmured, "I had heard you were coming." I noticed she was not very young—I mean not girlish. She had a mature capacity for fidelity, for belief, for suffering. The room seemed to

have grown darker, as if all the sad light of the cloudy evening had taken refuge on her forehead. This fair hair, this pale visage, this pure brow, seemed surrounded by an ashy halo from which the dark eyes looked out at me. Their glance was guileless, profound, confident, and trustful.

She carried her sorrowful head as though she were proud of that sorrow, as though she would say, "I—I alone know how to mourn for him as he deserves." But while we were still shaking hands, such a look of awful desolation came upon her face that I perceived she was one of those creatures that are not the playthings of Time. For her he had died only yesterday. (72–73)

Upon a closer comparison of Kurtz's white Intended with his black mistress, it becomes apparent that a connotative transvaluation of black and white has taken place, which is similar to the description of a European city (most likely, Brussels) he arrives in, described in terms of the Biblical phrase "whited sepulcher": "I arrived in a city that always makes me think of a whited sepulcher. Prejudice no doubt. I had no difficulty in finding the Company's offices. It was the biggest thing in the town, and everybody I met was full of it. They were going to run an over-sea empire, and make no end of coin by trade" (13). "Whited sepulcher" signifies that which is beautiful on the outside but evil and deadly in the inside, and an observation from the Book of Matthew from the (Douay-Rheims) Bible will shed further light on the implied inversion inherent in the phrase and Conrad's reference: "Woe to you scribes and Pharisees, hypocrites; because you are like to whited sepulchers, which outwardly appear to men beautiful, but within are full of dead men's bones, and of all filthiness" (23:27). Similarly, the Intended, notwithstanding the whiteness of her skin, takes on dark characteristics, and Kurtz's black mistress manifests features that link her to light and life; the only major difference between the chromatic and constitutional inversion that takes place in these two characters and the metaphor of the "whited sepulcher" is that in the latter the exterior is imagined as purely white versus its black interior, while in the earlier comparisons there is an indication of the inner white/light and/or black/darkness on the exterior.[4] Herein lies one of the beauties of the text that needs to be tackled closely, for unlike, for example, Charles Baudelaire's poem *Le Cygne*, which appears in the French poet's masterpiece *Les Fleurs du Mal* (1857), and *Ulu: An African Romance* (1888), a story by the less known writer-explorer

Joseph Thompson, blackness is not to be read as darkness (of the spirit) and, vice versa, whiteness is not to be interpreted as (intrinsic) brightness.[5] The white complexion of the Intended and the dark skin of the African mistress are not to be aligned with their connotative significations of good and evil; on the contrary, Conrad's novella encourages an interpretative inversion of those signs.

The atmosphere that surrounds the mahogany door to the Intended's apartment is akin to the one experienced by Marlow at the door that opened to the two knitting women at the Company prior to his departure to Africa; back then, the thought of the Unknown reigns supreme, and at this moment "horror"—an almost onomatopoeic term for the dark and deadly experiences of the colonizers in the heart of Africa—echoes through the air as he waits for the Intended. Once she steps out, it is as if the black clothes she has donned have been woven by those archetypal guardians of the "door of Darkness" (14).[6]

As we see in the above passage, Conrad allows the interior to seep onto the exterior beyond bodily boundaries: Not only is the white Intended dressed in black, but the darkness of her attire oozes into her surroundings so much so that she embodies doom and gloom; vice versa, the black mistress is ivory-studded and glitters with light and life at her every step. True that Chinua Achebe condemns "the author's bestowal of human expression to the one and the withholding of it from the other," adding that "it is clearly not a part of Conrad's purpose to confer language on the 'rudimentary souls' of Africa" (255); yet, even he concedes that "the Amazon" has won Conrad's "special brand of approval" in being "in her place" (earlier, Achebe gives a series of examples in line with the author's admiration for things being in their place). Despite Achebe's insistence on Conrad's colonialist tendencies, there are moments in the narrative, including the above perspective on the two contrary female figures, which leave us wondering as to how much of a staunch colonialist Conrad actually was. After all, as subaltern as "the Amazon" might be, she does manifest an ability for expression, albeit through extralinguistic means facilitated by the ornamentations that adorn her skin. In brimming with sensuality and sexuality and simultaneously resisting integration into the symbolic order of law and language, she becomes akin to what Jacques Lacan has referred to as a "stain" in being an embodiment of the narrator's decentered self-consciousness and a blot that is interpreted based on his inner desires.[7] The reason why I am suggesting such an interpretation of her is in line with how she commands attention in a way that is sensual, yet reminiscent of death; how she is domineering, yet cannot be contained in words. She emerges against a backdrop of shadows and is shrouded in silence, and as ineffable as she is, she mesmerizes those around her, especially in her association with the mysterious Kurtz. In being stained (both in its literal and Lacanian senses), she imbues those around her with desire and embodies the opposite of the plain, unstained Intended of Kurtz, who only knows how to surrender herself to the symbolic order, as is clear in her donning of black attire for months upon Kurtz's death. On the other hand, the so-called Amazonian woman, while adorning herself with what appears to be Kurtz's gifts to her, has made all those trappings of "brass leggings," "brass wire gauntlets," "innumerable necklaces of glass beads," including the "value of several elephant tusks," her own in combining them with "charms," "gifts of witch-men" and "bizarre things" so as to have them bespeak her own bodily and local language. In fact, the short but powerful excerpt from Conrad's novella on Kurtz's mistress reiterates how his depictions of corporeal ornamentation and clothing go beyond dermal boundaries to unveil a deeper truth lying at the heart of the characters' souls.

In order to better understand the chromatic shifting that takes place in Marlow's narrative and the interpenetration of exterior outfit with interior psyche, one should take note of how the exterior layers of the body, clothing included, mirror the inner transformations of the narrator. Within this context, Miriam B. Mandel's observation on there being two Marlows in the novella rather than one is worth noting:

> There are two Marlows in the story: One is the older, wiser Marlow who tells the story, who is concerned with philosophical and moral issues (presented in traditional black, white, and gray), and who strives for intellectual understanding (light-dark, bright-dim imagery); the other is the younger, adventure-seeking Marlow who experiences the story, who looks outward, not inward, for understanding, who is interested in the specific fact, and not the philosophical generalization. (310)

As mentioned earlier, the Marlow that emerges from the "heart of darkness" is experienced—*erfahren*—unlike his earlier self or the Russian devotee of Kurtz whose garish clothing hints at inexperience. In fact, one of the most colorful representations of clothing and character in *Heart of Darkness* takes place in the delineation of this young Russian man, whose "be-patched" appearance, in addition to youth and inexperience, betokens an essential hybridity and a hovering within the between-and-betwixt zone of liminality:

> His aspect reminded me of something I had seen—something funny I had seen somewhere. As I maneuvered to get alongside, I was asking myself, "What does this fellow look like?" Suddenly I got it. He looked like a harlequin. His clothes had been made of some stuff that was brown holland probably, but it was covered with patches all over, with bright patches, blue, red, and yellow—patches on the back, patches on the front, patches on elbows, on knees; colored binding round his jacket, scarlet edging at the bottom of his trousers; and the sunshine made him look extremely gay and wonderfully neat withal, because you could see how beautifully all this patching had been done. A beardless, boyish face, very fair, no features to speak of, nose peeling, little blue eyes, smiles and frowns chasing each other over that open countenance like sunshine and shadow on a wind-swept plain. (53)

The delineation in such glaring colors of the Russian places him in between the black and white zones, a realm of ambivalence that can be ascribed to a set of different factors. First, he is Russian, which makes him neither a pure European nor a pure Asian or African Other; second, he is neither really young nor mature enough in years as his "beardless, boyish face" indicates, and, thirdly, he is neither a colonialist exploiter nor a colonized exploited and is so malleable that he hangs on Kurtz's every word like Gospel. The garish colors used in his apparel and all the patches on it hint at an indecisiveness of character that is also reflected in the comparison made between his countenance and "sunshine and shadow on a wind-swept plain." In being of a composite essence—a trait that comes to the fore in his outward appearance, not to mention clothing—the Russian devotee of Kurtz takes on marvelous characteristics; however, his guru, himself a prime hybrid, in being the offspring of a half-English mother and a half-French father, ends up assuming monstrous features.

Marlow's initial observation of Kurtz's European origins bears no indication of contempt; quite on the contrary, in his mind the more shadings of the white European blood are involved in one's making, the better the outcome, as he goes on, admiringly, to say: "All Europe contributed to the making of Kurtz;

and by and by I learned that, most appropriately, the International Society for the Suppression of Savage Customs had entrusted him with the making of a report, for its future guidance" (50). Marlow goes on to recount some of the specifics of the report, including its horrid ending, which calls for the eradication of the native African subjects in the following terms: "Exterminate all the brutes!" (51). However, Conrad's novella revolves around Kurtz having incorporated the darkness he had sought to illuminate and the "brutish" characteristics he had been intent on eliminating. Homi Bhabha's comment that "what is disavowed is not repressed but repeated as something *different*—a mutation, a hybrid" (111) comes to the fore in the case of Kurtz.

In the cases of both Kurtz and the Russian, who, in addition to Kurtz's Intended, form part of a triad, described by Ian Watt as the "only three people from whose intelligence and disinterestedness Marlow might expect more," but who also "share one linguistic trait: they are addicted to the idealizing abstractions of public discourse, to a language that has very little connection with the realities either of the external world or of their inner selves" (245), there exists the "dialogic" characteristic that is an inherent feature of hybridity. As Caroline Walker Bynum has posited, there is a "dialogic" in hybridity, "because [it is] inherently two. Its contraries are simultaneous and in conversation with each other. . . . Hybrids both destabilize and reveal the world" (160). In fact, the dialogic has very much to do with an inner split that, based on the above observations, denies the hybrids access to the deep truth within and the realities without; as much as this becomes evident in the apparel worn by the Intended (her wearing black despite the lapse of a year since Kurtz's demise) and the Russian (his garishly colorful and "be-patched" appearance, which makes him akin to a "harlequin" in Marlow's eyes), it manifests itself in the physiognomy of Kurtz, who, despite mostly being delineated as being a disembodied voice, is said to have a "lofty frontal bone" and being "impressively bald" (Conrad, *Heart*, 49). The emphasis laid on Kurtz's head harkens back to the beginning of the novella, where an old doctor—whose own "threadbare coat," on a semiotic level, bespeaks experience—is measuring Marlow's head so that he can later on diagnose any of the changes that might take place in the narrator's cranium should he ever return from his journey to the "heart of darkness," especially in light of the following observations: "The wilderness had patted him on the head, and, behold, it was like a ball—an ivory ball; it had caressed him, and—lo!—he had withered; it had taken him, loved him, embraced him, got into his veins, consumed his flesh, and sealed his soul to its own by the inconceivable ceremonies of some devilish initiation" (49).

According to Marlow's comments, Kurtz had fallen victim to the very darkness he had intended to illuminate, and his obsession with ivory, a symbol of the African wealth and charm, had ended up making him one with his object of desire. In other words, in a nonmystical sense we no longer "know the dancer from the dance." As ironic as that may sound, there is a prefiguring of the inevitability of Kurtz's fate in a sketch drawn by him a year earlier, which Marlow comes across in the outer station prior to his close encounter with the "villain": "Then I noticed a small sketch in oils, on a panel, representing a woman, draped and blindfolded, carrying a lighted torch. The background was somber—almost black. The movement of the woman was stately, and the effect of the torchlight on the face was sinister. It arrested me . . ." (27–28).

The impact of the painting is arresting for a variety of reasons. First, the bearer of the torch is a woman, and women have not been sketched in favorable colors, so to speak, throughout the novella, especially in terms of their living in a world "too beautiful altogether," which "if they were to set it up it would go to pieces before sunset" (16).[8] Second, the woman is "draped and blindfolded," a clothing reference denoting her own lack of knowledge and insight; and, third, "the background [remains] somber" despite the "lighted torch." The only noticeable change that the lighted torch seems to bring about is to endow the woman's face with a "sinister" look. The woman charged with enlightening her surroundings not only fails in her task but also has the means of the *mission civilisatrice*, the torch in her hand—after all, the sketch can be interpreted as a pictorial allegory of the whole novella—turn into an object of self-destruction. The fact that the one other time the term "stately" is used in the text is in the portrayal of Kurtz's African mistress in tandem with the word "ominous," leads us to attach a negative connotation to "stately," one that evokes a deathlike quality, as is indicated in the phrase "to lie in state" and the term "stateroom."

An explication of "habitus," a concept that falls within the same cultural paradigm as clothing in being associated with a form of (an exterior) performance that sheds light on the interior of the mind, can further clarify the significance of Conrad's use of "stately" and some of the other adjectival and adverbial descriptions that run through the text within the context of character delineation. Pierre Bourdieu defines habitus as "an acquired system of generative schemes objectively adjusted to the particular conditions in which it is constituted" (95). Habitus manifests itself in corporeal terms, as it has a direct affinity with the performance of identity. As posited by Richard Jenkins, "In Bourdieu's work [habitus] is used to signify deportment, the manner and style in which actors 'carry themselves': stance, gait, gesture, etc. . . . It is in bodily hexis [a Greek term with a meaning not dissimilar to the Latin *habitus*] that the idiosyncratic (the personal) combines with the systematic (the social)" (74; explanation added).

The "stately" habitus of Kurtz's African mistress and the "draped and blindfolded" evoke wonder, as is respectively indicated by "the hush that had fallen suddenly upon the whole sorrowful land" and in how "it arrested" Marlow. What distinguishes wonder from other passions is that "unlike the other passions that have good or evil as their objects and hence involve the heart, wonder has only knowledge as its object and thus occurs strictly in the brain. . . . The object that arouses wonder is so new that for a moment at least it is alone, unsystematized, an utterly detached object of rapt attention" (Greenblatt, 19–20).

The Charlie Marlow that is delineated at the beginning of the novella in the figure of a seasoned seaman has experienced many a wonder and is beyond good and evil. While the traumatic sojourn in the wilderness seems to have left its marks on the outside of Kurtz's body, appearing on his "lofty frontal bone," the changes wrought on Marlow have taken place inside, as had been suggested by the Company's old doctor (Conrad, *Heart*, 15). For one thing, the Buddha-like habitus that he assumes is an indication of Marlow's transcendental state of mind, one that is beyond the domineering dichotomies of good/evil, white/black, light/darkness, etc. While he is initially described as being atypical, for "to him the meaning of an episode was not inside like a kernel but outside," in the passage of time, he becomes an embodiment of all those experiences he has come to acquire in the course of his exposure to social fields other than his European one (5). His habitus that comes to the fore in "the pose of a Buddha preaching in European clothes and without a lotus-flower," manifests a reconciliation of seemingly contravening cultural aspects of his own European world and that of the Other (6). Whereas his original goal in traveling to the "heart of darkness" was to conquer it and illuminate it with "light," Marlow seems to have reached the realization that "darkness has an autonomy of its own" (Said, 30) and should thus be embraced on an equal footing with "light," and so it is that the threads of white and black, manifest in the form of light and darkness, initially set against each other, end up coming together not only in the narrator's embodiment of yin and yang but also, in Conrad's metanarrative, in the texture of "an immense darkness" spread across the heart of the European sky.

Notes

The White European royal accused of so many atrocities in the Congo in the late nineteenth century was the Belgian King Leopold II (1835–1909), and the fact that the Berlin Conference (1884–1885) recognized his rule in the territory gave him a free hand in the exploitation of the native Congolese. That Joseph Conrad's *Heart of Darkness* was embedded in the colonialist *Zeitgeist* of the late nineteenth century, is, for example, meticulously explored in Patrick Brantlinger's highly informative article "Victorians and Africans: The Genealogy of the Myth of the Dark Continent." Brantlinger highlights parallels between particular events in the novella and the ongoing colonialist expeditions, an example of which comes to the fore in the similarity between Leopold II's goals in the Congo and the Eldorado Exploring Expedition in *Heart of Darkness*: "To tear treasure out of the bowels of the land was their desire, with no moral purpose at the back of it than there is in burglars breaking into a safe" (32–33) (see Brantlinger, 178). As shown in the documentary *White King, Red Rubber, Black Death* (directed by Peter Bate and broadcast on *BBC Four*), one need only replace Kurtz's madness over ivory in *Heart of Darkness* with Leopold II's obsession with extracting more and more rubber from the native Congolese to get a sense of the actual exploitation of the Africans subjected to the Belgian emperor's rule. In the novella, Kurtz is engaged in chopping off the natives' heads, while as shown in the documentary, European colonizers operating under Leopold II would have the hands of the natives cut off to enforce their draconian rules.

1. Initially, Madame Defarge appears to be simply knitting, and only later does it become clear that she has been stitching the names of those who are to meet their deaths. The editor of the text has kindly reminded me of the parallel existing between the depiction of knitting women in both Conrad's and Dickens's stories and the *trictoteuses* ("the knitting women") of the French Revolution, who would sit beside the guillotine during public executions and knit in between the beheadings.

2. Ian Watt views the labeling of the colonizers as "pilgrims" within a nexus of literary analogies that make ironic usage of symbols, tropes, and classical mythology in line with highlighting the emptiness of the contemporary world. Watt draws on James Joyce's use of Homer's *Odyssey* in his *Ulysses* and T. S. Eliot's allusion to the legend of the Holy Grail in *The Waste Land*. Similarly, the colonizers are said to have "wandered here and there [. . .] like a lot of faithless pilgrims bewitched inside a rotten fence. The word 'ivory' rang in the air, was whispered, was sighed. You would think they were praying to

it" (222). Also, interestingly, Conrad seems to have had the feminine (or, in this case, the effeminate) connotation of "pink" in mind in this context, at a time when color coding babies with pink and blue ribbons had not become quite customary. According to Lynn Peril, one of the earliest examples of this color coding in literature takes place in 1868, when Louisa May Alcott included a scene in her *Little Women* wherein Amy March "puts a blue ribbon on the boy and a pink on the girl, French fashion" (4).

3. I am using "masquerade" in a sense close to that postulated by Luce Irigaray, in that it "has to be understood as what women do in order to recuperate some element of desire, to participate in man's desire" (133). In the native African woman's case, however, I am hesitant to say that her masquerade comes at the cost of "renouncing [her own] desire," which is what Irigaray suggests in her definition of the term.

4. Bruce R. Stark has pointed out how closely the Intended has been associated with death and deathlike images: "[The Intended's house] is within a city called 'sepulchural'; it is on a street that looks like a boulevard in a cemetery; its front door resembles the entrance of a mausoleum; its cold fireplace looks like a monument; and its piano shines like a sarcophagus" (540).

5. For a better understanding of the contrast between the representative figure of white femininity, Andromache, and the *negresse* in Baudelaire's poem, "Le Cygne," Gayatri Chakravorty Spivak's article, "Imperialism and Sexual Difference" is extremely useful. Spivak posits that "indeed, if Andromache is the over-specified condition of emergence of the title-image (the swan), the only possible function of the negress would be to mark the indeterminate moment when specificity is dissolved towards the poem's end." See Koelb and Lokke, "Imperialism and Sexual Difference," 323.

6. Johanna M. Smith draws a parallel between the two knitting ladies and Sin, half woman and half serpent as a character in John Milton's *Paradise Lost*, who is the "portress of hell gate" (187); yet, one can also compare these two women with the figure of Error in Edmund Spenser's *Fairie Queene*: "Halfe like a serpent horribly displaide,/ But th'other halfe did woman's shape retaine,/ Most lothsom, filthie, foule, and full of vile disdaine" (I.i.xiv). While the association of the knitting women with Sin is significant in that Sin's offspring from her father, Satan, is Death (the most common experience to befall the men who pass through the "frame of darkness" in Conrad's tale); likening these women to Error brings to mind, not only the "mistake" made by men imbued with a sense of hypermasculinity in their quest for gaining mastery over otherness, but also the many "wanderings" (going back to the original sense of "error") it takes to reach their goal, if at all. Although those venturing out in the Dark Continent are, unlike Redcrosse in *Fairie Queene*, no knight, yet, like him, they are *errant*, both erring and wandering, Interestingly, Conrad alludes to "Knights" in the first example he gives of an ancient adventurer in a foreign land (see 8).

7. The stain is a blot that is void in meaning unless interpreted by the subject's desire

in a certain way. As Slavoj Žižek asserts, a "stain" translates into a self-consciousness that is decentered (66). A good example of the Lacanian stain in painting is the *momento mori* that appears in Holbein's *The Ambassadors*, which is a blot until, upon carefully scrutiny, it appears like a skull. The image of the African woman, similarly, concretizes the decentered self-consciousness of the narrator in *Heart of Darkness*.

8. It is worth noting that the word "beautiful" has been used disparagingly throughout the text. The resignation the manager manifests in their immediate failure in tracking down Kurtz is "beautiful," so is Kurtz's seventeen-page report to the International Society for the Suppression of Savage Customs, whose postscriptum is so horrid that Marlow decides to get rid of it before handing it over to the official who approaches him for Kurtz's documents; moreover, the patches on the Russian's clothes are said to have been done "beautifully"; and last but not least, the term is used in the description of Kurtz's Intended three times.

8

The Midwife's Clothing

Jessie Fauset In and Out of Fashion

Kimberly Lamm

*A*consumer product almost inextricably linked to the assumed super-ficialities of self-display, it is easy to dismiss fashionable clothing as symptom-atic of women's unreflective participation in the visual cultures of capitalism. Because of deep-seated ideas about women's affinity with the superficialities of the image, and the work this affinity performs confirming women's insig-nificance, there is a pervasive suspicion of fashion and "finery" within both feminist and antifeminist thought.[1] Though obviously men wear clothing and participate in fashion, their strong associations with the instability of color, and the frivolity of prettiness, make fashionable clothing a cultural practice most readily associated with women.[2] We could say that fashionable clothing attaches to the assumption that women are inclined to be narcissistic and su-perficial, distracted by imaginary surfaces and slumbering through political realities. The role fashionable clothing plays in the literary fiction produced by the New Negro Women of the Harlem Renaissance tells a different and far more complicated story.

Until recently, scholarship on the American New Woman as a visual and sartorial production had almost uniformly assumed that this figure was white.[3] However, since 2000, an important body of scholarship has emerged that performs the crucial work of allowing the New Negro Woman to come into view. Attending to the possibilities of play in material and popular culture, reading bodies categorized through race and gender in the nuanced interstices between force and defiance, this work calls attention to the multiple ways the construction of racial difference inflected the constellation of modernity, visuality, and femininity.[4] To render this complexity, new scholarship on the New Negro Woman places black women's self-productions within the dia-lectics of capitalist modernity and relinquishes the impulse to decide whether New Negro Women are "dupes or resistors" (Barlow et al., 22). Instead, the authors see the material objects of their self-presentation as part of a complex and desirous negotiation with the visual economies of racism and sexism in the United States.

Carla Peterson's essay "Eccentric Bodies," a foreword to the 2001 collection *Recovering the Black Female Body*, encapsulates the primary impetus of this work and demonstrates the foundations black feminist literary criticism set into place for the study of the New Negro Women's contributions to popular and material culture. "Eccentric Bodies" captures the transformative energy with which black women entered American modernity, while still attesting to the originary impact of the transatlantic slave trade, the long span of its unfolding, and the sedimentation of its legacies. For Peterson, eccentricity is a "notion of off-centeredness to suggest freedom of movement stemming from the lack of central control," and she traces the transformation from "the sentimental strategies of decorporealization and normalization" that characterized the Black Women's Club movement of the nineteenth century into modern black women's propensity to "flaunt the eccentric black female body" and put it on celebratory display without shame (2001, xiii). Peterson argues that the heroines crafted by writer Emma Dunham Kelley-Hawkins represent a transitional moment in which black women were "freed from the yoke of racial oppression and the duties of racial uplift" and therefore "able to explore the pleasures offered to the modern world" (xiv).[5] These pleasures include "high culture, fashionable dress, household ornamentation, and fine foods" (xiv).

The idea of femininity implicitly moving through this list can be considered a response to what Peterson describes as the "simultaneous masculinization and feminization of the black female body, which was consequently perceived as grotesque" (xi). Indeed, in the Darwinian discourse of "civilization," which determined so many beliefs about race and gender in the nineteenth and twentieth centuries, the blurring of gender differences was a sign of savagery. Moreover, the campaigns of extrinsic and intrinsic violence that forced black women to embody the extremities of both genders justified multiple forms of work—sex work, as well as physical and reproductive labor—and reinforced their exclusion from femininity as well as their subservience to the white women who could claim femininity as their natural right.[6] The proliferation of visual images that characterized early twentieth-century visual culture underscored this exclusion and subservience. In her 1925 essay "The Task of Negro Womanhood," the writer Elise Johnson McDougald describes a black woman's encounter with her own image in American visual culture and the assignment to work implicit within it: "She realizes that the ideals of beauty, built up in the fine arts, have excluded her almost entirely. Instead, the grotesque Aunt Jemimas of the street-car advertisements proclaim only an ability to serve, without grace or loveliness" (103). The appearances of fashionable dress in the cultural productions of African-American women from the early twentieth century suggest that clothing was a fabrication—a material act of recreation, an aesthetic reproduction, a truthful fiction of "grace" and "loveliness"—that translated the black female body from the lie of definitive servitude to the truth of multiple and unpredictable desires.

The fictional world of Harlem Renaissance writer Jessie Fauset (1882–1961) exemplifies New Negro Women's deployment of the imaginary textuality of fashion to recalibrate perceptions of black female bodies into twentieth-century modernity. Almost every piece of writing Fauset authored includes descriptions of clothing's forms, textures, and colors that covertly bring sensuality into the textual weave of her literary compositions. Both surface embellishment and subtext, clothing is a thematic accompaniment to Fauset's literary exploration of black women's desires to become visible and valuable parts of the American cultural fabric. The young women at the center of her narratives consistently touch, try on, and design beautiful, flattering clothing. These acts register their desires to be seen in a perceptual field where dark skin is not assumed to be an assignment to undervalued forms of physical and reproductive labor or an impediment to the pleasures attributed to femininity. In the 1920 text "The Sleeper Wakes: A Novelette in Three Installments," Fauset describes her protagonist Amy gazing at a dainty Parisian dress: "It was not the lines or even the texture that fascinated Amy so much, it was the grouping of colors and shades" (91). Fauset's character Laurentine from the 1931 novel *The Chinaberry Tree* is a talented clothing designer and possesses "lovely fingers" that "flash in and out of lengths of gorgeous shades of silk, georgette, and velvet" (29).

These depictions reflect the characters' artistic inclinations and talents, while also indirectly representing Fauset's own literary artistry and its subtle engagement with twentieth-century material and visual culture. Through her character Melissa in *The Chinaberry Tree*, Fauset highlights the connections among language, writing, and fabric: "She would dress and go for a walk. As she opened the closet door, she remembered her diary carefully tucked away between the inside wall and an old heavy suitcase filled with odds and ends of sewing no one had ever disturbed. Involuntarily her hand closed on the purple bound book, into which so many of her revelations had gone" (93). A passage like this suggests that Fauset foresaw the argument Roland Barthes makes in *The Fashion System* (1983), namely, that fashion is more than the visual materiality of clothes, but transforms into "written garment[s]" (3). Fauset's subtle deployment of the relationship between word and image is particularly well suited for rendering the "written garments" of the Harlem Renaissance.[7] Her literary descriptions of the textures, colors, folds, and shapes of clothing are not only crucial to the embroidery of her work's visual surface but covertly "write" the black female body with black women's self-reflective claims to their sensuous desires. By ribboning these claims through her texts, Fauset's work testifies to the challenges of creating living forms of black femininity untethered from the exploitation attendant upon the histories of enslavement as well as the assertions of purity and propriety marshaled to defend against those histories. Perhaps the most wide-ranging and entrenched consequence of slavery and black women's defenses against it is the assumption that they should naturally give themselves to others' pleasures and care. Complicating her iconic status as the "midwife" of the Harlem Renaissance, Fauset created literary texts that portrayed black women who imagined themselves outside the imperatives to care for others. Her depictions of clothing are central to that imagining, but also contributed to her unstable place in the fashioning of American literary history.

The sartorial themes in Fauset's work, the stories they tell, and the aspirations they manifest have not been analyzed in detail.[8] This line of inquiry has been foreclosed by the criticism that Fauset's work only consists of melodramatic plotlines in which light-skinned black women attempt to pass into the American middle class. Fauset's attention to clothing informs but also disappears into these assessments, strongly suggesting that the pervasive assumption that fashionable clothing is frivolous takes on added meaning for black women. For Fauset's characters, their attraction to fashionable clothing has been read as a complicit and unreflective desire for whiteness. This assessment is the flipside of a perception that her characters frequently come up against: namely, that black women engaged in self-adornment and display are putting themselves on the sexual market without shame, thereby justifying forms of sexual commodification and indignity that insidiously continue histories of enslavement.

The long-entrenched bias against femininity is another significant but largely unnoted impediment, both for Fauset's work and her characters. It is

Hortense Spillers, the literary critic who theorized the history of the transatlantic slave trade as the inscription of a radical "ungender[ing]" of black bodies who has most eloquently pinpointed femininity as the gender identity easiest to devalue (1987, 207). In her essay on Gwendolyn Brooks's *Maud Martha* (1953)—another literary text by an African-American woman writer decorated with images of clothes—Spillers discusses, with characteristic wit, the difficulty of allowing femininity into a form of discursive visibility since it is considered, for the most part, useless and obsolete: "Trapped between the Scylla of feminist mandates on the one hand and the Charybdis of dominative and patriarchal modes of power on the other, the subject of 'feminine attributes' is apparently abandoned to a useless set of traits, not unlike a sixth toe or finger in some phase of human evolution" (1985, 132). Despite this mutually reinforcing disdain, Spillers attempts to bring "feminine attributes" into relief by turning to the work of Friedrich Schiller and his characterization of femininity as "maximum changeability" and "maximum extensivity" (134). Spillers draws upon this definition to illuminate Maud Martha's "highly developed powers to *play* and to play well within the framework of possibilities to which she has access" (137). Fauset's characters possess similar capacities for the imaginative malleability of play.

Until scholars like Spillers, Deborah McDowell, and Anne duCille made Fauset's work a serious object of black feminist literary criticism, the assessments outlined above created significant impasses to understanding the complexities of her literary production. Drawing upon the tradition the work of these scholars exemplify, I analyze three texts that represent the span of Fauset's career and begin to suggest the various and interrelated roles fashionable clothing play in her fictional designs: the short stories "Emmy" (1912–1913) and "The Sleeper Wakes: A Novelette" (1920), and her well-known novel *Plum Bun* (1928). Highlighting the relationship between these texts and the aspects of New Negro visual culture they engage with and allude to, I argue that through fashionable clothing, Fauset's characters arrange images of themselves that mediate between their bodies and the world. Building upon Anne Hollander's famous insight that "dress is a form of visual art, a creation of images with the visible self as its medium," I contend that Fauset's depiction of fashion works as a form of self portraiture that allowed for the possibility of fictionalizing versions of the self. Fauset's literary portraits quietly resist the assumption that black women's bodies manifest race, gender, and sexuality as immediately visible essences that can be contorted into icons vulnerable to other people's needs and desires (1993, 311). With their deceptively simple prettiness, their love of color and play, Fauset's depictions of clothing undermine the histories and assumptions that inform black women's iconicity. Articulating an emergent form of black feminism, Fauset's "written garments" attempt to address other black women and participate in a collective wish to artfully arrange their images and not simply accept those passed down from and circulating through dominant American culture.[9]

"EMMY"

Fauset's attention to clothing as a claim to femininity, and the political import of this claim, has been obscured by the perception that fashionable clothing and the real work of racial politics are incommensurate (which is reasonable in many respects). Much of Fauset's writing was published in *The Crisis: A Record of the Darker Races*, the official journal of the National Association of the Advancement of Colored People, which had a steadfast political purpose. As W. E. B. Du Bois explains in the journal's inaugural issue: "The object of this publication is to set forth those facts and arguments which show the danger of race prejudice" (10). To that end, Du Bois declares that *The Crisis* "will first and foremost be a newspaper: it will record happenings and movements in the world which bear on the great problem of inter-racial relation, and especially those which affect the Negro-American" (10). Fauset was the literary editor of *The Crisis* from 1919 to 1926. Her shrewd literary eye turned the magazine into one of the central forums for the development of the Harlem Renaissance. She published and promoted the rich, prismatic work of Langston Hughes, Jean Toomer, Claude McKay, and Nella Larsen in its pages. These artists produced literary texts that made *The Crisis* much more than a newspaper; they helped open apertures for seeing how "the great problem of inter-racial relation" affected people on the other side of the veil. Their literary artistry crystallizes the imaginative resources African-Americans developed and deployed to counter racism's insidious effects.

Fauset's literary depictions of fashionable clothing are one of those imaginative resources. They also function as a crucial pivot between *The Crisis*'s necessarily sober focus on reporting the racial mapping of the world and the journals and magazines addressing African-American women such as *Ringwood's Afro-American Journal of Fashion* (1891–1894) and *Half-Century Magazine for the Colored Home and Homemaker* (1916–1925). Implicitly, these periodicals were devoted to the project of combating the particular ways women encounter racism. As Noliwe M. Rooks documents in her study *Ladies' Pages*, such magazines, run by and addressed to African-American women, functioned as handbooks for fashioning selves capable of renouncing the sexual degradation of enslavement and its reverberations in service work. They responded to the needs of African American women who were, in Rooks's words, "overwhelmingly concerned with addressing their veracity and fashioning a counter representation that showed them in a more culturally acceptable light" (15). In multiple ways, these magazines sold the idea that consuming fashion and beauty products was a sure path for women to place themselves in arenas of acceptable visibility. In her analysis of *Ringwood's Journal*, Rooks writes, "Fashion's relevance was consistently invoked by those desirous of donning the mantle of 'ladyhood,' and fashionable display was described as a crucial prerequisite for inhabiting public spaces such as churches, political meanings, and social events" (65). As Rooks notes, many of the models in advertisements meant to appeal to African-American women were often depicted as white, thereby underscoring the equation between feminine beauty and whiteness (22).

Fauset's short story "Emmy" is about a young woman's indoctrination into the rules that governed the idea that beauty belongs to whiteness. Less obvious is the story's portrayal of how a woman's desires to adorn herself in fashionable clothing are read within that perceptual field. Published in two installments in *The Crisis*, "Emmy" is accompanied by two images that carefully modulate the critique animating the story. The story opens with the title character reciting a lesson about racial typologies: "'There are five races,' said Emmy confidently, 'The white or Caucasian, the yellow or Mongolian, the red or Indian, the brown or Malay, and the black or Negro'" (23). This schematic account of racial categories and their accompanying skin colors comes at the bequest of her teacher, Miss Wenzel, who has made it her mission not only to indoctrinate Emmy into racial hierarchies but to situate herself within it: "Now to which of the five do you belong?" (23). Before answering the question, Fauset follows Emmy as she moves through the aesthetic qualities of typological portraits, finally placing herself within its narrow spectrum of physical features: "And yet the Hottentot, chosen with careful nicety to represent the entire Negro race, had on the whole a better appearance. 'I belong,' she began tentatively, 'to the black or Negro race'" (23). Oblivious, it seems, to the Hottentot's historically construed link to disease and denigration, Emmy focuses on the "careful nicety" with which this Hottentot was depicted and sees a "better appearance."[10] For Emmy, identifying with the "Negro race" is an act of aesthetic affiliation.

Though Emmy gives the "right answer" to the question of what race she belongs to, Fauset makes it clear that her protagonist did not internalize the implications of Miss Wenzel's lesson. A conversation with her friend Mary shows that Emmy has yet to discern her place in the racial order of things. After asking Emmy if she "minded" what happened in class—a question Emmy does not understand—Mary tries to explain by calling attention to the problem Emmy poses: "Everybody in Plainville says all the time that you're too nice and smart to be a—er I mean, to be colored. And your dresses are so pretty, and your hair isn't funny either" (52). Emmy's elegant clothing manifests her resistance to the derelict submission racial epithets are meant to produce. This resistance is made clear in a later conversation between the teacher, Miss Wenzel, and her sister: "Of course it doesn't cost too much to live here, but Emmy's clothes! White frocks all last winter, and a long red coat—broadcloth it was, Hannah. And big bows in her hair—she has got pretty hair, I must say!" (25). Miss Wenzel's exclamation of mild outrage tempers when she moves through the details of Emmy's adornment; it is as though their details seduce Miss Wenzel into reluctantly admitting to the black girl's beauty.

Emmy's beauty, which her clothes and accessories magnify, interrupts the racist alignments among black skin, poverty, and ugliness. Her link to French culture makes this interruption all the more disorienting. Emmy's mother speaks and translates French, and employs a French maid named Céleste. Her teacher, Miss Wenzel, comments: "She's got to have some of the wind taken out of her sails, some day, anyhow. Look how her mother dresses her. I suppose she does make pretty good money—I've heard that translating pays well. Seems so funny for a colored woman to be able to speak and write a foreign language" (25). This incredulity expresses a presumption that African-Americans are—or should be—tethered to national domesticity and therefore embody the ground of racial origins. Emmy's beautiful clothes defy this presumption. They connect her to France, a foreign language, translation, and a cosmopolitan affluence. Together these subjects suggest that fashion "translates" the black female body away from habitual perceptions of its domesticated and denigrated state.

The allusions to France in "Emmy" indirectly testify to the rich range of Fauset's intellectual pursuits and her participation in black international writing. She was fluent in French, traveled to France and North Africa, participated in Pan-African conferences, and published her travel reports in the pages of *The Crisis*. In *The Practice of Diaspora*, Brent Hayes Edwards analyzes Fauset's travel essays, stressing their "persistent and pervasive internationalist outlook" (135). He argues that when reading her travel writing, "it is evident that Fauset cannot be easily pigeonholed as solely an apologist for the urban U.S. black bourgeoisie" (135). A critical version of Miss Wenzel's surprise that Emmy's mother speaks French, these older arguments domesticate Fauset and her work. Edwards's reading of Fauset's journalism is part of his argument that in the transnational literature of the 1920s, "black" is perpetually in translation, without originals or stable referents. The idea of wearing fashionable clothing produced in other countries contributes to this productive instability. It fosters the idea that the body can willfully move through, and is therefore not subjected to, the commodity flows that extend beyond the domestic borders of the nation and the purportedly stable meanings kept there. That is, clothing translates the black female body into an unstable site without an original essence that justifies black women's fixed placement in the American national imaginary. Fauset stated in an interview that she liked France because it allowed her "to live among people and surroundings where I am not always conscious of 'thou shall not'" (quoted in Edwards, 140).

"Emmy" exemplifies how Fauset's fiction maps the subtle mechanisms by which black women receive the message "thou shall not": a moralizing injunction that thwarts the possibility of translating racial difference into less punitive forms. Because of Miss Wenzel's failure to "show Emmy kindly—oh, very kindly—her proper place" (25), she gives Emmy a gift: a poem by Robert Louis Stevenson called "A Task" ("To be honest, to be kind, to earn a little and spend a little less . . .") inscribed in calligraphic lettering and placed in an oblong frame. As Fauset describes it, "The phrase [was] picked out in blue and gold, under glass and framed in a passé-partout" (25). This dubious gift daintily inscribes the connections among femininity, goodness, and modesty, but also highlights Fauset's astute understanding of the ways in which words inscribe themselves at the ideological edges of vision, particularly in the effort to make inequalities natural. When Emmy attempts to read and understand the poem, Fauset puts a particular stress on the word "capitulation," with its connotations of humility, submission, and defeat (26). As Fauset will later explain, "Afterward Emmy always connected the motto with the beginning of her own realization of what color might mean" (26).

Fauset's character Emmy does not capitulate, but her childhood sweetheart, Archie, does. Archie advocates for passing because racism will bar him from a career (a reality of which Fauset was acutely aware). In an argument Archie says to Emmy, "Just being Emilie Carrel seems to be enough for you. But you just wait until color keeps you from the thing you want the most, and you'll see" (28). Archie takes an engineering job in Philadelphia and is able to do so because he passes for white. In a letter he sends to Emmy he describes an incident in which he almost gets caught. He happened upon some old friends—the Higgins family—whom he describes as "all sorts of colors from black with 'good' hair to yellow with the red, kinky kind" (30). When he escorts Maude Higgins to the train station, he accidentally encounters the son of his boss. Maude's propensity for stylish attire, an attribute Emmy shares, diverts attention away from the fact that she is black, which leads Archie to reflect upon style and sophistication: "You know, it's a queer thing, Emmy; some girls are just naturally born stylish. Now there are both you and Maude Higgins, brought up from little things in a tiny inland town, and both of you are able to give any of these city girls all sorts of odds in the matter of dressing" (30). Rendering the process of figuring out what "made her grow so cold" upon reading this letter, Fauset describes Emmy looking into the mirror: "She turned and looked in the glass to be confronted by a charming vision, slender—and dusky" (30). From her mirrored image, she translates the implications of Archie's story: "I am black . . . but comely" (30). That is, when looked at through the eyes of those who capitulate to racism's terms, her "comeliness" distracts from or compensates for her black skin. Turning away from this insight, she assures herself with the exclamation, "Archie loves you, girl!"

The photogravure image meant to illustrate this turn in Fauset's story portrays a black girl sitting at a vanity table, looking at herself in the mirror, holding a letter in her hand (fig. 8.1). The rendition of the girl's face in the oval mirror appears in complete three-dimensional detail and focuses attention on her hair and skin, as well as her warm, intent expression. The girl's white sailor dress and the table she sits in front of have been printed so they appear only in sketched outline, which allows the clarity of the girl's portrait image to become all the more prominent. The caption represents Emmy's reassurance that Archie loves her—"'Archie loves you, girl,' she said to the face in the glass"—as though she needs to reiterate these words to see herself in the frame of beauty. However, the casual comments in Archie's letter, the feelings it provokes, and the events that unfold from this point forward in the story seem

FIGURE 8.1: Illustration from *The Crisis: A Record of the Darker Races.* December 1912. Pg. 80. *The Modernist Journals Project (searchable database). Brown and Tulsa Universities, ongoing. http://www.modjourn.org.*

to encapsulate Fauset's most crucial point about the presumed disjunction between blackness and beauty.

When Mr. Fields, Archie's boss, sees him in Philadelphia with Emmy, Archie confronts the fact that passing is an unreliable solution, and the "comeliness" of a young black woman's fashionable style can be flipped with a cruel ease into evidence of her presumed lasciviousness. Once Mr. Fields notes that Emmy is black, she is no longer a lady in his eyes, but a conniving "colored woman" Archie has adorned with clothing: "'If it isn't young Ferrers, with a lady, too! Hello, why it's a colored woman! Ain't he a rip? Always thought he seemed too proper. Got her dressed to death, too: so that's how his money goes!'" The next day at work, Mr. Fields asks him: "Where'd you get your black Venus, my boy?" He also continues to stress her monetary appetites, her excessive and unjustifiable demands: "I'll be you don't have one cent to rub against at the end of the month. Oh you needn't get red; boys will be boys" (32).

Promoted to be Mr. Fields's second-in-command, Archie decides to postpone his engagement with Emmy and arranges a visit to confirm the wisdom of this decision. Emmy assumes he wants to set up a definite date for their wedding and puts on a red dress for the occasion: "'Being in love is just— dandy,' she decided. 'I guess I'll wear my red dress'" (35). This dress becomes a significant feature of a pleasurable tableau that augurs a favorable future: "The gray mist outside the somber garden, the fire cracking on the hearth and casting ruddy shadows on Archie's hair, the very red of her dress, Archie himself—all this was making for her a picture, which she saw repeated on endless future Sunday afternoons in Philadelphia" (35). Emmy's picture of an "endless future" does not materialize; it is abruptly halted by Mr. Fields's picture of black women, his perception of their worth, intentions, and ravenous appetites, all of which fuel Archie's fear that his success and security will be impeded.[11] When Emmy hears him admit that her dark skin is the reason he is postponing their wedding, she is terribly hurt but decides, quite strategically, to reject him. Here Fauset describes Emmy's stance before announcing that in fact she is breaking their engagement: "She turned and faced him, her beautiful silhouette distinctly outlined against the gray blur of the window" (138). After Archie's departure, she opens the window and hears a song "wretchedly" played by a neighbor. Emphasizing Emmy's sadness and frustration, Fauset writes: "She crossed heavily to the armchair and flung herself into it" (139).

The image that accompanies this installment of "Emmy" is a full-length portrait of a girl who wears not a red dress but, quite crucially, a white one, decorated with dainty flowers (fig. 8.2). Nor does the image evoke Emmy's shock or frustrated sadness, but illustrates instead Archie's image of her as the "whitest angel ever lived, purity incarnate" (134–136). In this portrait taken by the famous Scurlock portrait studio in Washington DC, the young woman's head rests on her palm as she looks sweetly and wistfully into the distance. She has adorned herself in a decidedly ladylike dress and arranged herself in a pose that suggests dainty passivity, not the cool calculation Emmy demonstrates while wearing her red dress. Such modulation is understandable, as Fauset's work emerged from and circulated through a world dense with ready-made perceptions about black women's sexuality. When Mr. Fields finds Archie miserable over his breakup, he snatches up the photograph of Emmy (an interesting textual iteration of the images that accompany the story) and exclaims: "It's your colored lady friend again. Won't she let you go? That's the way with these black women, once they get a hold of a white man—bleed 'em to death" (37).

FIGURE 8.2: Illustration from *The Crisis: A Record of the Darker Races.*
January 1913. Vol. 5. No. 3 Pg. 135. *The Modernist Journals Project (searchable
database). Brown and Tulsa Universities, ongoing. http://www.modjourn.org.*

The portrait of the girl in the white dress accompanying "Emmy" represents two intertwined aspects of New Negro visual culture: the centrality of portraiture and the anxious scrutiny brought to images of black women. It is well known that with the increased availability of photographic technologies at the onset of the twentieth century, the portrait's history of honorable presentation became a crucial tool for those who were fighting against a denigrating visual hegemony that prized whiteness. Du Bois was the most prominent of those who advocated for the rhetorical impact of portrait photography.[12] For African-American women, portraiture documented their access to the cosmetic industry as well as dressmakers and beauty salons, and advertisements for these services often drew upon the visual language of portraiture in their illustrations. And yet, portraits were also sites in which black women were disciplined for their purity. In the portrait photographs Du Bois displayed in *Exhibit of American Negros* for the Paris Exposition of 1900, women exemplify proper and respectable femininity, which radically circumscribes femininity's potential for eccentricity and play and rests on the exclusion of anything that hints of sexual flamboyance. Such portraits were evidence of African-American men's capacities to marshal black women's sexualities— presumed to be capricious—and put their bodies to work for the project of producing a civilized race. In her analysis of the portrait photographs linked to Du Bois, Shawn Michelle Smith insightfully notes that "Du Bois' African American women are honored foremost as reformed subjects of patriarchal discipline, as sexually errant beings reined in by patriarchal control" (373).

The impulse to discipline the images black women produce with their bodies attests to how saturated American visual culture was with Darwinian ideas about race, femininity, and display. While Emmy sees her red dress as the visual center of the tableau that represents a future life of fulfilled wishes, what this character does not seem to understand—though Fauset clearly did—is how her red dress is easily subsumed by arguments prominent in nineteenth- and early twentieth-century thought that equated colorful, ostentatious display with primitive savagery. Many intellectuals—including architectural theorist Adolf Loos, feminist Charlotte Perkins Gilman, and cultural critic Thorstein Veblen—adopted Charles Darwin's treatise on sexual selection and the ideas about racial inferiority that subtended it—cast in the language of "sub species"—to stress that excessive ornamentation indicates one's low and feminized place on the evolutionary ladder.[13] These ideas informed perceptions that black women who participate in modern visual culture by adorning their bodies with brightly colored clothing—red dresses, for example—were primitive, outside the bounds of taste and respectability, which confirmed their denigrated place the national imaginary. It isn't as though Emmy's clothing makes or breaks Mr. Fields's perception of her as a "black Venus," but by focusing on the iconography of the red dress, Fauset depicts how the assumed frivolity of clothing is easily transformed into damning evidence that justifies racist and sexist assumptions.

Fauset's work registers a shrewd understanding of both evolutionary arguments regarding visual display and their consequences for black women living in the early twentieth century, particularly those who sought to see themselves within the frame of feminine beauty. These arguments are consistently thematized in her fiction and gained more depth and specificity as her work developed. In *The Chinaberry Tree*, Fauset writes about young black women who fashioned themselves in colorful, dynamic, eye-catching clothes and makes a point to show that this choice signaled a willingness to be consumed, sexually and indiscriminately. Building upon and complicating the dense iconography of the red dress, Fauset describes the bright and dynamic image her character Melissa creates with her clothing. She wears "a dark blue velvet suit" designed in "gay, almost too wild spirits" (41). The rest of her ensemble also expresses a wild dynamism: "Her skirt was circular, her shapely legs and feet were incased in the nattiest possible tan leggings and shoes; her velvet beret assumed of its own volition the jauntiest possible angle" (41). A drunk and angry young man will try and force her to ice skate with him. When Melissa refuses him, he calls her "anybody's girl" (44).

Though "Emmy" ends too neatly, with all conflicts resolved—Archie admits his race to Mr. Fields, returns to Emmy for forgiveness, and even gets his job back—the red dress serves as a remnant of Archie's intentions to hide their relationship, and therefore represents the black female body's precarious status within the American visual economy: "Afterward the sight of that red dress always caused Emmy a pang of actual physical anguish. She never saw it without seeing too, every detail of that disastrous Sunday afternoon" (137). In "Emmy," and in Fauset's fiction more generally, clothing is without a doubt a practice of bodily self-fashioning that brings her characters forms of pleasure that resist the subservience black women in the United States are expected to embody. What Fauset's work is equally committed to, and what the accompanying photogravures belie, is a literary exploration of how the display of those sartorial pleasures register and transform in a cultural field dominated by white patriarchal authority.

ADVERTISING BEAUTY AND BLACK FEMINISM

It would be easy to dismiss the images that accompany "Emmy" as forms of the capitulation Fauset's story thematizes. While the photogravures certainly draw attention to the less trenchant dimensions of the story, and keep Emmy's

When Our Soldier Boys "Come Marching Home"
How Must the Girls Greet Them?

"THE KASHMIR WAY"

With smooth, clear skin and soft, pretty hair.
Our guarantee: *Your money back if you are not pleased.*
Agents wanted.

KASHMIR SKIN PREPARATION
Marvelous—it does the work.
KASHMIR HAIR BEAUTIFIER

50c EACH
8c POSTAGE

Free! Free! *The Kashmir Beauty Book*
tells you how to be beautiful.

KASHMIR CHEMICAL COMPANY
Dept. K, 312 South Clark St.   CHICAGO, ILL.

FIGURE 8.3: Advertisement from *The Crisis: A Record of the Darker Races.* February 1919. Vol. 17. No. 4 N.P. *The Modernist Journals Project (searchable database). Brown and Tulsa Universities, ongoing. http://www .modjourn.org.*

red dress and its dense set of associations in the less visible visuality of Fauset's literary text, the images do not overtly temper the protagonist's connection to blackness, nor do they shy away from highlighting the connection between the girl's skin color and her feminine beauty. What images do and don't do in Fauset's work becomes even more compelling when we think about them in relationship to the proliferation of advertisements for beauty products newly made for and marketed to African-American women in the early decades of the twentieth century. As was the case with "Emmy," Fauset's writings were often initially published in the serial publications of the black press like *The Crisis*, and were therefore read, looked at, and subtly experienced in proximity to the advertising images and slogans that addressed New Negro Women.

The advertising for consumer products that proliferated in New Negro Modernity promised black women the privilege of creating their self-images on terms of their own choosing. However, as many scholars have made clear, the terms of feminine beauty were more often than not implicitly white.[14] This was particularly true in the advertising images for the cosmetics industry. Images soliciting customers for Madame C. J. Walker's and Kashmir Chemical Company's whitening creams and hair straighteners, which appeared often in the back pages of *The Crisis*, make the connection between light skin and feminine beauty pretty clear. In a full-page advertisement for the Kashmir Chemical Company's "skin preparation and hair beautifiers," published in the January 1919 edition of *The Crisis*, there are two women, quite fashionably dressed, posing before and flirting with two returning soldiers (fig. 8.3). The women are wearing sporty and decorative daywear—complete with skirts composed of frilly tiers and pleats and intricately designed Art Deco accessories—that typified fashion during World War I. The fact that the advertisement's focus is on the women's clothing rather than skin cream or hair lotion suggests that Kashmir Chemical Company is selling an idea of beauty and a type of woman who would buy their products. Since the illustrator composed the figures with a thickly drawn outline against the white page, and has used only the faintest dots to suggest skin color, the women in this ad appear to have white or light skin. Such images exemplify an aspect of early twentieth-century visual culture in which, as Caroline Goeser explains, "African American women received widespread and conflicting messages of race pride mixed with racial erasure" (197).

Fauset's own work was situated within this contradiction. An advertisement for Fauset's 1929 novel *Plum Bun* that appeared in *The Crisis* features the

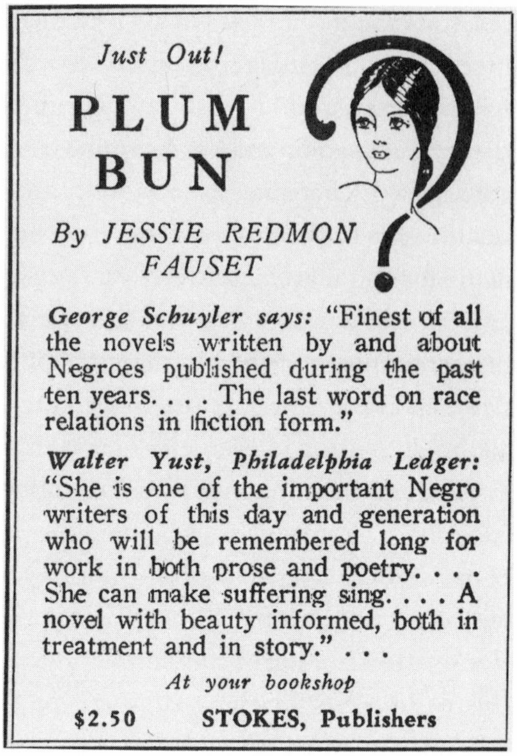

FIGURE 8.4: Advertisement from
The Crisis: A Record of the Darker Races.
April 1929. Vol. 36. No. 4 Pg. 139.
*The Modernist Journals Project (searchable
database). Brown and Tulsa Universities,
ongoing. http://www.modjourn.org.*

profile of a pretty woman in the upper right hand corner (fig. 8.4). Again, the
illustrator utilizes the white page to suggest phenotypically white skin, which
is further emphasized by her inky dark hair. The profile sketch of her dainty
visage is encircled by a black question mark to suggest—not so subtly—that
figuring out the woman's racial identification motivates the plot, and is the
reason, along with her dainty and light-skinned feminine prettiness, to buy
the book .[15] This advertisement for *Plum Bun* demonstrates that Fauset's work
tipped over into the world of advertisements and beauty products, which
makes analyzing her work in the context of print journalism all the more
pressing and interesting.[16]

Reading Fauset's work in relation to the image world of magazine advertising encourages readers to see the material conditions pressing upon
Fauset's writing life.[17] Fauset was never able to realize her dream of writing
full time, and she taught high school French in order to make a living. In the
hopes of writing a story that would sell big and support her literary ambitions,
Fauset studied the writing that appeared in popular magazines. In an interview that appeared in the *Boston Evening Transcript*, she admitted to "analyzing
whole issues of *The Saturday Evening Post* to discover what makes popular read-

ing" (quoted in T. Davis, xvi). The images of clothing and commodities that appear throughout Fauset's fiction attest to her desire for a popular audience. As Davis explains, "Her attention to the latest fashions in clothing and housewares, from lounging pajamas and thin cotton dresses for women to blue dustpans and yellow kitchenware, suggests that she was making an effort to appeal to the segment of modern women who more typically read magazines rather than novels for amusement" (xvi). By weaving descriptions of these objects into her work and drawing upon their familiarity to women who read magazines, Fauset covertly addresses other women and the desires they express through acts of visual consumption. There is more to this address than soliciting women to buy Fauset's books. Shopping for clothes and consumer objects intended for the pleasures of adornment, whether in department stores, in magazine advertisements, or in the pages of Fauset's fiction, were expressions of freedom for those shaped by histories in which black women's bodies and sexualities had been commodified. Shopping for and adorning clothes was a way to claim the terms through which one participated in commodity flows and consumption.

The scholarship of McDowell and DuCille has drawn out the proto-black feminisms at work in Fauset's literary attention to clothing.[18] In *The Coupling Convention*, DuCille offers a compelling interpretation of the sartorial themes in Fauset's work and that of Nella Larsen, with whom she is often paired. DuCille links the appearance of clothing in their narratives to the songs and performances of female blues singers to argue that these writers' attention to clothing is a bourgeois version of the blues. The pleasure Fauset's characters take trying on, designing, and imagining themselves with clothing is, according to DuCille, "the literary equivalent of the woman-proud blues lyric" (93). Developing this comparison, DuCille writes: "Silks and satins, capes and coats, dressing and lounging pajamas are as central to the bourgeois brand of 'somebody done somebody wrong' songs that these texts sing as were paints and powders to the classic blues performance. Not only is tremendous attention paid in these novels to what women put on their bodies but the characters are finely aware of how their bodies look in what they put on them as well" (94).

Engaging directly with the critiques of Larsen's and Fauset's work as too bourgeois—and in the case of Fauset, too prim, white, and straitlaced— DuCille argues that these writers' attention to clothing "is not merely the frivolous fluff of which novels of manners are made" (93). Linking clothing to music is significant, as music has been a legitimate form of African-American cultural and aesthetic production that attests to blackness not as a set of biological or genetic traits but, as Alys Weinbaum writes, "a structure of feeling produced in reaction to the particular forms of racism that structure racial formation in the United States" (2004, 223). As an expression of that structure of feeling, music turns those forms of racism on their heads by "creat[ing] continuit[ies] of connection and racial solidarity" (223).

By bringing the blues and clothing together, DuCille opens the possibility that Fauset's work can be read as an emergent form of black feminism attentive to the particular forms of sexism and racism black women experience. This feminism does not announce itself explicitly but is, as McDowell notes, "oblique" and "ambivalent" (1985, 88). In *Blues Legacies and Black Feminism*, Angela Davis argues that the songs and performances produced by early twentieth-century blues singers are "quotidian expressions of feminist consciousness" (xvii). Depictions of sexuality are crucial to these songs of black women's everyday lives, because in the context of emancipation "sexual love was experienced as physical and spiritual evidence—and the blues aesthetic evidence—of freedom" (45). Davis shows that Gertrude "Ma" Rainey, Bessie Smith, and Billie Holiday articulate a feminist consciousness that had yet to be identified as such. Davis seeks to reveal the "hints of feminist attitudes [that] emerge from their music through the fissures of patriarchal discourses" (xi). In so doing, she charts the work of women in the midst of fabricating— as in crafting, making, and creating—insurgent forms of black feminism that sustain "sexuality as tangible expression of freedom" and covertly challenge white male control over black female sexuality (8). An important part of this challenge is creating narratives that other women can identify with and make part of public discourse. In her analysis of songs that represent sexual abuse, Davis writes, "Hearing this song, women who were victims of such abuse consequently could perceive it as a shared and thus a social position" (28). Similarly, through fashionable clothing, women could create a visual discourse that attested to their individual and collective abilities to overcome public and private expectations that their primary aspiration should be to care for others.

The prominent male intellectuals of the Harlem Renaissance were not sympathetically attuned to the black feminism animating Fauset's work. In *The Big Sea* (1940), when Langston Hughes details the beginning of his career and his initial encounters with the artists, writers, and intellectuals who created the Harlem Renaissance, he states: "Jessie Fauset at the *Crisis*, Charles Johnson at *Opportunity*, and Alain Locke in Washington were the three people who midwifed the so-called New Negro into being" (73). The figure of the midwife in Hughes's statement puts reproductive labor at the imaginary forefront of Harlem Renaissance literary culture. It is not surprising that the figure of the midwife did not attach to Charles Johnson and Alain Locke with the same definitive tenacity.[19] Midwifery is more closely aligned with essentialized connections between women of color and reproductive labor. Representing Fauset's contribution to the Harlem Renaissance through the figure of the midwife seems, at first glance, to be harmless enough, but describing her work through an image of a woman who helps give birth became ground of permission that allowed Hughes and others to dismiss Fauset's persona, just as black women's reproductive work is undervalued in the cultural marketplace. That is, naming Fauset a "midwife" represents an idea about black women that made it difficult for Fauset to become a consistently well-regarded part of the Harlem Renaissance canon.

The first black woman to graduate from Cornell University and become a member of Phi Beta Kappa, an accomplished writer, editor, translator, and teacher, Fauset did not, to my knowledge, work in the realms of reproductive labor and domestic service traditionally assigned to black women.[20] But as the iconic description of Fauset as a midwife suggests, neither was she entirely free from the expectation that black women perform work in the name of reproducing the race. In New Negro Modernity, elite African-American women were expected to reproduce a new race of people who could properly represent a black civilization's past and future glories. This mandate for perfected forms of biological reproduction extended to aesthetic reproduction of their bodies and selves, and women were expected to compose stable image-repertoires through which new ideas about blackness could be received and recognized.[21] For the women affiliated with the Harlem Renaissance, the idea that women should craft images of their bodies pleasing enough to solidify communities and symbolically cohere New Negro culture was particularly strong. Nella Larsen's *Quicksand* (1928) elegantly exposes the burdens of this dubious honor. The advertisement for cosmetics produced by the Kashmir Chemical Company analyzed above illustrates the idea that women beautifully embody "home," as do the portraits that accompany "Emmy," but less explicitly. British scholar Lola Young astutely outlines how women's capacity for

biological reproduction translates into expectations that they carry and uplift the symbolic weight of culture and community. Young writes that women
"hold a key symbolic position as actual and potential reproducers/bearers of
the 'race'; they demarcate the boundaries of racial/national groups; they are
deemed responsible for preserving and handing down culture through being
primarily responsible for child-rearing. Notions of beauty and sexual attraction are intimately linked to these gendered functions, and turn on women's
symbolic representativeness and their attraction to men" (416–17).

Young describes what amounted to a trap for African American women
living in the early twentieth century. They inhabited a visual world in which,
to recall McDougald's "The Task of Negro Womanhood," the "ideals of
beauty" are based upon black women's exclusion, and the images of them that
do proliferate "proclaim only an ability to serve" (103). If black women's primary purpose is to serve, then their difficulties producing images that cohere
an idea of community make them all the more vulnerable to becoming con-
tainers for people's hostilities and disappointments.

Indeed, we see the inverse of Hughes's emblematic description of Fauset
as a midwife in his 1926 manifesto "The Negro Artist and the Racial Mountain." Reacting against Du Bois's imperative for the black artist to present an
image of upper-middle-class respectability and prioritize the work's rhetorical message of uplift over the individual artist's expression, Hughes argues
against the imperative for black artists to adopt the imperatives of dominant
white culture. He celebrates instead "the so-called common element," which
he describes as "the people who have their hip of gin on Saturday nights and
are not too important to themselves and the community, or too well-fed, or
too learned to watch the lazy world go round" (41). While Hughes makes a
compelling argument for resisting the "urge within the race toward whiteness,
the desire to pour racial individuality into the mold of American standardization," he uses a gendered typology—"a Philadelphia club woman"—to make
his point about white criteria of taste and choice (40). A thinly disguised car-
icature of Fauset, who grew up and worked in Philadelphia, this "Philadelphia
club woman" is ashamed of her race and its distinctive cultural productions.
She does not like jazz, and her taste in portraits reveals the depth of her internalized racism and self-hatred. Creating an emphatic rhythm by repeating the
pronoun "she" at the beginning of each sentence, Hughes writes: "She doesn't
care for the Winold Reiss portraits of Negroes because they are 'too Negro.'
She doesn't want a true picture of herself from anybody. She wants the artist

to flatter her, to make the white world believe that all Negroes are as smug and as near white in soul as she wants to be" (43).[22] Hughes relies on the typology of the prim and repressed middle-class black woman to make his point about the internalized racism of the black middle class, but also ignoring the fact that for black women, the persona of the urban primitive invited accusations of prostitution.

With the emergence of African-American literary criticism of the 1960s, critiques of Fauset's work became sharper, and the dismissal of the femininity associated with fashion and decor, much more explicit. David Littlejohn describes Fauset's novels as "vapidly genteel lace-curtain romances" with a "stuffy tiny-minded circulating library norm" (49–50). In *The Negro Novel in America* (1965), Robert Bone first characterizes *The Chinaberry Tree* as "uniformly sophomoric, trivial, and dull," and then goes on to facetiously announce that this novel is "about the first colored woman in New Jersey to wear lounging pajamas" (108). Bone's assessment is packed with assumptions about the relationships among femininity, clothing, leisure, and bourgeois visibility. His emblematic depiction registers shock that a black woman would willingly participate in such tableaus of leisure and expresses hostility that a woman's claims to pleasure have interrupted reliable icons of black women toiling and suffering. No doubt Fauset's characters have aspirations to participate in the pleasures afforded to those unburdened by poverty, but Bone ignores the limitations Fauset's characters come up against, and the punishment they receive, when expressing these desires.[23]

"THE SLEEPER WAKES"

Published in *The Crisis* eight years after "Emmy," Fauset's short story "The Sleeper Wakes" demonstrates that clothing is not a mere bourgeois trifle in Fauset's work, but a means to claiming blackness as an aesthetic affiliation. "The Sleeper Wakes" centers upon a protagonist named Amy, a biracial character orphaned, the story implies, by the shame of miscegenation and adopted by a noble and caring black family. Amy is another of Fauset's young female protagonists enticed by fashionable clothing's potential to make their bodies into "sites" of "deeply felt pleasure" (Peterson 2001, xiv). As the title of the story suggests, Amy "wakes up" to the overlapping histories of racism and sexism that impinge upon her claims to that pleasure. Accompanied by nuanced illustrations provided by Fauset's friend, the Harlem Renaissance painter and illustrator Laura Wheeler, what is most compelling about this awakening is that Fauset's character does not renounce the desires articulated by fashionable clothing, but instead she refashions them into a conscious choice to identify with blackness.

The story's opening mise-en-scène takes place in a Marshall's department store. Amy is in the midst of admiring a "lovely little sample dress, which was not from Paris, but quite as dainty as anything that Paris could produce" (91). The saleslady puts the dress on Amy, and Fauset makes this act into an occasion to create a layered portrayal of colors, shapes, textures, and skin. Highlighting the proximity of Amy's skin to whiteness, the colors of the dress, substantiate the connection between whiteness and the feminine beauty in commodity culture. "The saleswoman slipped the dress over the girl's pink blouse, and tucked the linen collar under so as to bring the edge of the dress next to her pretty neck. The dress was apricot-color shading into a shell pink and the shell pink shaded off again into the pearl and pink whiteness of Amy's skin" (91). While looking at herself in the mirror, Amy then notices that two men have been admiring her from across the space of the department store. She is thrilled and confused by their gazes. Underscoring the connections among fashionable clothing, twentieth-century visual culture, and consumption, Amy's most immediate frame of reference is the movies: "She wanted to get home and think, think to herself about that look. She had seen it before in men's eyes, it had been in the eyes of the men in the moving-pictures which she had seen that afternoon. But she had not thought *she* could cause it" (91).

There is a strong suggestion within "The Sleeper Wakes" that Amy's deep, and even indulgent, investment in fantasy and fabrication is propelled by uncertainty about her racial origins. Her biological parents never make an appearance in the story, and Amy is troubled by the question of whether she is white or black: "'Mrs. Boldin, tell me, am I white or colored?' And Mrs. Boldin told her that truly she did not know" (92). The story suggests that since she does not fit easily into racial categories, Amy finds a place for herself in a fantasy life that is shaped by popular and consumer culture, in particular, movies: the twentieth-century version of fairy tales, which as a child she would "pore over . . . her face flushed, her eyes eager" (92). Describing the plot of the movie she saw that afternoon to her adoptive parents and younger brother, Amy exclaims: "it was the most wonderful picture a girl such a pretty one and she was poor, awfully. And somehow she met the most wonderful people and

they were kind so kind to her. And she married a man who was just tremen-
dously rich and gave her everything" (93). This plot summary describes not
only a movie Amy just saw but the story of the life she wants to lead. It also
aptly characterizes the plots of Fauset's own fiction—if her critiques of their
racial limitations go unnoticed—and prefigures her efforts to transform her
last two novels into screenplays. Fauset's dreams to write screenplays were
not realized, but the desire for transformation—textual, visual, and bodily—is
expressed in her literary texts like "The Sleeper Wakes" through clothing.

Though Amy is unreflectively steeped in the promises of consumption,
the story is accompanied by illustrations that are compelling intermediaries
between the text of Fauset's fiction and the visual appeals of advertising.
Composed with a loose but delicate precision by Wheeler, the illustrations
for "The Sleeper Wakes" complicate any simplistic notion that her work only
mimics the white ideals proposed by consumer culture. In her illustrations,
Wheeler creates patterns with delicate and thin crosshatched lines that blur
into shadows and the blank white spaces of the page. The simultaneously
dense and light texture of these drawings seems to be an extension of the
loose and diaphanous layers of the clothing Fauset's protagonist Amy wears.
In the story's first illustration (fig. 8.5), Wheeler creates a family portrait with
Amy at its center; her adoptive mother, father, and brother form a triangle of
adoring eyes. Her dress is sketched to call attention to the cut of her bodice
and the pleats of her skirt, which fall gracefully from the waist. The angle of
her head highlights her dark bob, the stylistic signature of the New Woman,
and like the profile of the young women in the advertisement for *Plum Bun*,
Wheeler takes advantage of the white page to suggest Amy's light skin. The
light, almost ethereal qualities of this drawing may be attempts to visually render Amy's character, for she is described as a "beautiful, inconsequent creature
with her airy, irresponsible ways" (92). And yet, its unabashed indulgence in
feminine detail also reflects Amy's capacity to sense beauty's multiple and unpredictable manifestations. Though her parents can barely stand her brother's
attempts to play the cornet, Amy finds it "lovely" and encourages him to keep
playing (93). Connected to her attentive eye for clothing, Amy's sympathetic
ear for her adopted brother's efforts suggests that fashion can also become a
structure of feeling that creates blackness as a form of aesthetic affiliation.

In the privacy of her bedroom, Amy creates a self-portrait with herself
clearly posed at the center. This self-portrait exhibits the wish that wearing

FIGURE 8.5: Illustration by Laura Wheeler from *The Crisis: A Record of the Darker Races.* August 1920. Vol. 20. No. 4 Pg. 169. *The Modernist Journals Project (searchable database). Brown and Tulsa Universities, ongoing.* http://www.modjourn.org.

beautiful clothing—and the compositional talents this act reveals—will allow her body to pass into a white American fairy tale. Alluding, through pink and yellow, to the story's opening scene in the department store, Fauset writes:

> She lit one gas-jet and pulled down the shades. Then she stuffed tissue paper in the keyhole and under the doors, and lit the remaining gas-jets. The light thus thrown on the mirror of the ugly oak dresser was perfect. She slipped off the pink blouse and found two scarfs, a soft yellow and a soft pink,—she had them in a scarf dance for a school entertainment. She wound them and draped them about her pretty shoulders and loosened her hair. In the mirror she apostrophized the beautiful, glowing vision of herself. (93)

Amy creates an idealized representation of herself: a glowing portrait of her own making to which she calls out in hope. This imaginative version of herself cannot find its full expression in the domestic comforts the Boldins provide. After sewing "steadily after school for two months," Amy runs away to live in Greenwich Village (94). There she meets Zora Harrison (perhaps an allusion to Zora Neale Hurston) whose exotic, deep and richly colored clothing appeals to Amy: "Purple, dark and regal, enveloped in velvets and heavy silks, and the strange marine blues she wore, and thus made Amy absolutely happy" (94). Daring and experienced, capable of wielding her homoerotic appeals in a protofeminist direction, Zora Harrison initiates Amy into representation as deception, encourages her to become instrumental, present herself as white, and marry a wealthy man who will encourage and support her artistic leanings.[24] Following the script Zora sets out for her, Amy marries the rich Stuart James Wynne, thereby placing herself in a fantasy made real: "There were two weeks of delirious, blissful shopping. . . . Amy was absolute mistress" (97). The primary appeal of Amy's marriage—"blissful shopping"—and the fact that it is short lived—"two weeks"—suggests how strongly fashion and consumption has shaped this character's vision of romantic happiness and love.

While the feminine beauty associated with racial indeterminacy was thought to sell novels, in "The Sleeper Wakes," as in so much of Fauset's fiction, the passing that racial indeterminacy makes possible results in shame and punishment. Amy gradually becomes aware of Wynne's virulent racism and sees the weakness of her beauty to defend against it. To intervene in Wynne's violent threats to lynch Stephen, the new valet, Amy not only admits to her own blackness but calls it into being: "'I *am* colored. . . . I feel it inside me'" (99). She claims Stephen is her brother and threatens to expose her husband's marriage to a colored woman. Amy's decision to claim blackness to protect Stephen from lynching makes it clear that blackness is not an unquestioned, a priori identity but one chosen in response to racist violence.

Marriage to a black woman is unacceptable to Mr. Wynne, and he divorces Amy. As a salve to her misery, Amy returns to her love for sewing and begins to work as a dressmaker. The following passage suggests that clothing continues to be a practice for fantasizing and fictionalizing other versions of the self. In so doing, Fauset shows that fashion traverses individualized desires and connects to other women whose bodies also do not neatly align with the racial designations of white and black:

There was a sewing room off to the side from which Peter used to wheel into the room waxen figures of all colorings and contours so that she could drape the various fabrics about them to be sure of the best results. But today she was working out a scheme for one of Madame's customers, who was of her own color and size and she was her own lay-figure. She sat in front of the huge pier glass, a wonderful soft yellow draped about her radiant loveliness. (102)

From this mirrored image that includes herself and the idea of another woman—"who was of her own color and size"—Amy begins to fantasize about working as a designer: "'I could do some serious work in Paris,' she said out loud to herself" (102). As with "Emmy," this allusion to French fashion underscores Fauset's connection to French culture and the idea of blackness that productively troubles and exceeds the domestic borders of the nation. Mr. Wynne calls to reclaim Amy, but not in marriage. Once inside her home, Wynne offers her a ring, "a heavy dull gold band, with an immense sapphire in an oval setting" (103). This ring does not represent his desires for marriage, but to have Amy as his mistress: "A white man like me doesn't marry a colored woman" (104). Amy is now confronted with the underside of the pleasant fantasies she attached to the male gaze: "She saw life leering mercilessly in her face" (104). She slaps Wynne "in a sudden rush of savagery" and he slaps her back, making her fall to the floor. Wynne inscribes her humiliation with a string of racial epithets.

In Wheeler's illustration depicting this scene (fig. 8.6), Amy lies on the floor face down; the only part of her head made visible is the dark and detailed rendition of her hair. Her alignment with the horizontality of the ground contrasts sharply with the prior image that highlights her proud and upright place in the spotlight of her adopted parents' admiring love. Amy's dress is deliberately sketchy and incomplete; the mantel and fireplace are drawn only in part, which creates a large blank space above Amy's body. The incompleteness of Wheeler's drawing suggests a desire to avoid fully inscribing this violent scene into three-dimensional form and its presumed connection to a complete and final picture. Indeed, the conclusion of "The Sleeper Wakes" moves into other possibilities. Amy resolves to identify as black, returns to the Boldins and declares that she will become a "citizen of the world" (107). This is Amy's awakening that has yet to be realized in visual form. She decides to set up a dressmaking business on her own, "in a rich suburb, where white women would

FIGURE 8.6: Illustration by Laura Wheeler from *The Crisis: A Record of the Darker Races.* October 1920. Vol. 20. No. 6 Pg. 271. *The Modernist Journals Project (searchable database). Brown and Tulsa Universities, ongoing. http://www.modjourn.org.*

pay for her expertness, caring nothing for realities, only for externals" (107). This business will allow her to work with and help "colored people"—"the only ones who have really cared for and wanted me" (107). Amy will work on the surface of white consumer culture, but she also finds a resonant depth for herself within it, which could be considered analogous to black women's partial and differentiated identification with advertisements for beauty products that rely upon a connection between whiteness and feminine beauty. The fact that such a scene is left unaccompanied by an illustration suggests that while the defeat of a black woman is visually familiar, black women's desires for the transformations that will take them beyond the familiar historical scripts are not. Fauset keeps them within the "written garments" of her literary text.

While packing to leave, Amy wonders if her brother Cornelius "still plays on that cornet?" (107).

Amy's talent for designing fashionable clothing and the memory of her brother's cornet are charged remnants of earlier aesthetic investments that can now shape her conscious place as a black woman in a predominantly white world. Such negotiations would be difficult to maintain in isolation, which makes it important that Fauset's friend Wheeler provided the illustrations for "The Sleeper Wakes." Rather than simplify Amy's story, Wheeler's images add to its density and are faithful to the complexity of Fauset's literary imagination. Her illustrations highlight the fact that Amy's attention to clothing can be considered a glimpse into the subtle politics of black women's sartorial innovations and is not a self-evident cultural practice that should be condemned in embarrassment or glossed over as incidental.[25]

FASHION, WORK, AND PASSING IN *PLUM BUN*

Though there has been substantial scholarly attention to *Plum Bun* (1929), I revisit the novel here because it so elegantly develops the sartorial themes of Fauset's work. In *Plum Bun,* Fauset creates a narrative that explores relationships among fashionable clothing, femininity, race, visual art, consumption, and passing. Placed in proximity to "Emmy" and "The Sleeper Wakes," it is clear that Fauset honed her attention to how these themes and practices inflect and reinforce each other. She drew upon the novel's temporal layers to show how her light-skinned heroine, a member of the black middle class and steeped in the promises of early twentieth-century American consumer culture, has been shaped by a past in which racism and sexism narrowed black women's lives with more punitive severity. Connected to this inheritance is the link *Plum Bun* makes between the desire to buy and adorn clothing and the work assigned to black women that revolves around it, particularly the domestic labor of laundering and mending clothing.

Plum Bun tells the story of Angela Murray, a character who "like[s] the luxuriousness of being 'dressed up' " and has dreams that extend beyond the stories of struggle contained within the small spaces of her parents' modest home (21). In the following passage, Fauset depicts Angela's and her parents' perceptions of their home, suggesting that the differences between them are the result of their connection: "To Junius and Mattie Murray, who had known poverty and homelessness, the little house on Opal Street represented the *ne plus ultra* of ambition; to their daughter Angela it seemed the dingiest, drabbest chrysalis that has ever fettered the wings of a brilliant butterfly" (12). Rejecting her parents' stories of "difficulties overcome, of arduous learning of trades, of the pitiful scraping together of infinitesimal savings," Angela hopes that "[s]omewhere in the world were paths which led to broad thoroughfares, large, bright houses, delicate niceties of existence" (12). These desires are intimately connected to Angela's talents for drawing and painting: "Her eye for line and for expression was already good and she had a nice feeling for color" (13). For Angela, artistic practice is a passage to a life free from dingy sacrifice. As Fauset's narrator explains, Angela's "gift was not for the end of existence; rather it was an adjunct to a life which was to know light, pleasure, gaiety and freedom" (13).

Fashionable clothing is the link between Angela's artistic talents and her desire for a life of bourgeois pleasures. Images associated with clothing, shopping, and art are often clustered together in the scenes that compose her story. Angela spends her Saturdays "in search of a new frock or intent on the exploration of a picture gallery" (56). Describing Angela's Sundays, Fauset writes, "she would turn over her wardrobe, sorting and discarding; read the week's forecast of theatres, concerts, and exhibits" (65). As the layering of verbs, objects, and activities in this passage begins to suggest, fashion and clothing are not just pretty accessories in *Plum Bun*, they are an important part of its dense literary texture and intricate narrative form.[26] By making Angela a visual artist who sees clothing as an expression of her artistic leanings, the analogies between Fauset's attention to clothing and her work as an African-American woman writer becomes more prominent.

In *Plum Bun*, clothing, shopping, and visual art form a set of pleasurable practices that are intimately bound up with passing for white. As Miriam Thaggert insightfully argues, there is an affinity with passing and fashion, as both rely upon the "subtleties of vision" and "strategically confuse the spectator of the black female body" (70). By producing this confusion, fashionable clothing becomes a site through which Fauset's characters articulate their aspirations for bodies that cannot be easily read or placed. Angela inherits the connections between fashion and passing from her mother: "It was from her mother that Angela learned the possibilities for joy and freedom which seemed to her inherent in mere whiteness" (14). Angela spends afternoons with her mother in Philadelphia's department stores; they are able to frequent such spaces because of their light skin. "Mrs. Murray loved pretty clothes, she liked shops devoted to the service of women; she enjoyed being even on the fringe of fashionable gathering. A satisfaction that was almost ecstatic seized her when she drank tea in the midst of modishly gowned women in a stylish tea room" (15). Passing does not so much express a desire for white skin as such, but the privileges and pleasures bestowed upon it. Of Mrs. Murray's passing, Fauset writes: "She had no desire to be of these people, but she liked to look on; it amused and thrilled and kept alive some unquenchable instinct for life which thrived within her" (15). The feelings evoked by her outings lift and enliven the daily grind of taking care of her family's clothing: "to stand in the lobby of the St. James' fitting on immaculate gloves; [an] innocent, childish pleasure pursued without malice or envy contrived to cast a glamour over Monday's washing and Tuesday's ironing, the scrubbing of kitchen and bathroom and the fashioning of children's clothes" (16). Because passing provides access to pretty and luxurious clothes, it allows Mrs. Murray to claim and enjoy the surplus value of her daily labors, or at least "cast a glamour" over them.[27]

Against scenes of department store passing, Fauset delineates the arc of Mrs. Murray's work life. The third chapter of *Plum Bun* opens with Mattie beginning the domestic work that maintains her Opal Street home: "Monday morning brought the return of the busy, happy week. It meant wash-day for Mattie, for she and Junius had never been able to raise their ménage to the status of either a maid or putting out the wash" (27). Mattie does not consider this work onerous, because she performs it for her own family and not another's. For Mattie

> had known what it meant to rise at five o'clock, start the laundry work for a patronizing indifferent family of people who spoke of her in her hearing as "the girl." . . . For this family she had prepared breakfast, gone back to her washing, served lunch, had taken down the clothes, sprinkled and folded them, had gone upstairs and made three beds, not including her own and then had returned to the kitchen to prepare dinner. (28)

Notice how the care and maintenance of clothing are consistent parts of her daily work cycle. Working as a seamstress was just a little less arduous, but more precarious. The families that hired seamstresses "had a disconcerting habit of closing their households and departing for months at a time, and there was Mattie stranded and perilously trying to make ends meet by taking in sewing" (28).

When Mattie begins working for a well-known actress named Madame Sylvio, she encounters a precarity of another kind. Because of the actress's commitment to luxury, Mattie was "seeing something of the world and learning of its amenities" (30). At the same time, Mattie is allowed this access because of the presumed link between blackness and sexual availability and the idea that she embodies both beneath the sheen of her light skin. This actress employs black women because "hers was a carelessly conducted household, and she felt dimly that all coloured people were thickly streaked with immorality" (29). It is because of this dim feeling that the actress hired the woman who would become Angela's mother: "She knew that in spite of Mattie's white skin there was black blood in her veins; in fact she would not have taken the girl on had she not been coloured" (29). When Mattie complains to her employer that "Haynes Brokinaw, politician and well-known man about town" expects sexual dalliances to be delivered along with messages, Madame Sylvio makes it clear that sexual availability is part of the work that comes with her race, "streaked," as she assumes, "with immorality." Brokinaw shares the actress's assumptions that Mattie embodies a licentious sexuality that is readily available. He assumed that she has been left unprotected by patriarchal authority: "'Sit here and tell me about your mother,—and your father. Do you remember him?' His whole bearing reeked with intention" (29). Junius Murray, who works as a coachman and will become Angela's father, saves Mattie from subjecting herself again to Haynes Brokinaw.

Angela inherits aspects of her mother's work life but is not fully cognizant of how it has been inflected by the burden of black women's sexual vulnerability. However, Brokinaw's proprietary claim to Mattie's body, and the racist link between blackness and lasciviousness that subtends it, insidiously repeats itself when Angela moves to New York City and attempts to pass for white. After a long courtship, Angela is stunned that her lover, Roger Fielding (his last name echoing Mr. Fields of "Emmy"), wants her to become, not his wife, but his well-kept mistress. This repeats her mother's vulnerability at the hands of Brokinaw and the larger history of exploitation for which it figures. In her introduction to *Plum Bun*, Deborah McDowell discusses Angela's fantasies of accessing power through marriage, and writes: "What she will actually encounter in her relationship with Roger Fielding, the wealthy white man, is a replay of the racial prehistory of concubinage and sexual exploitation" (1990, xix). McDowell brings her shrewd insights to the economic dimension of Angela's desires and their cruel reversals. She explains that Angela's and Roger's market ventures "are for two radically different commodities. For her, the plum is power and influence attainable only through marriage to a wealthy white man. For him, the plum is sex, to be bought and consumed. Angela's game for marriage is Roger's foreplay for sex. Finally and ironically, Angela tries to 'buy' in a society that only allows her to 'sell'" (xix). This formulation provides a way to understand Angela's and her mother's attraction to fashionable clothing. It is a means by which they have asserted their capacities to buy things for themselves rather than sell themselves as things, an attempt, whether conscious or not, to reverse the position of black women during enslavement and its reverberations in twentieth-century American culture.[28]

Seeing herself in Roger Fielding's eyes while wearing attractive, eye-catching clothing is an important aspect of Fauset's portrayal of Angela and Roger's relationship. Fauset seems to take just as much pleasure rendering Angela's sartorial ensembles as Angela takes wearing them. Describing Angela's appearance for her first dinner date with Roger, Fauset indulges in the details that together compose her image, as though she herself is a portrait artist: "She touched up her mouth a little, not so much to redden it as to give a hint of the mondaine to her appearance. Her dress was flame-colour . . . of a plain, rather heavy beautiful glowing silk. The neck was high in the back and girlishly modest in front. She had a string of good artificial pearls and two heavy silver bracelets. Thus she gave the effect of a flame herself" (122).

Though clothing is intimately caught up in Angela's desire for Roger, her compositional talents extend far beyond the repetitions and failures of their relationship. Her drawing and painting consistently inform the visual language through which Fauset creates Angela's observations and perceptions. And as *Plum Bun* turns to its conclusion, Angela forges a career as a fashion illustrator and is on her way to becoming a talented portrait painter. McDowell argues that the convergence of these talents is the point at which Angela's "self-development begins in earnest" (xxi).

A significant aspect of Angela's self-development is her increased sensitivity to the cruelties of racism that her acts of passing indirectly support. Angela spurns her sister Virginia to save face in front of Roger, a mistake she bitterly regrets. However, when a young woman named "Miss Powell," a fellow student from her drawing class, is denied a scholarship to study at the

Fountainbleau School of Fine Arts, Angela takes a reflective turn toward racial affiliation: "After all, this girl was one of her own. A whim of fate had set their paths apart but just the same they were more than 'sisters under the skin'" (340). Angela seeks out Miss Powell, and upon arriving at her Harlem apartment, is pleasantly stunned by her silk dress: "plainly made but of a flaming red from which the satin blackness of her neck rose," clearly a visual echo of the flame-colored dress Angela first adorned to see herself in Roger's eyes (342). This sartorial and visual correspondence could be said to suggest an emergent form of black feminism, an aesthetic affiliation that attests to women's particular desires to overcome the racist and sexist writing of their bodies. When Angela witnesses reporters aggressively questioning Miss Powell, she publicly admits that she too is black. Her history of passing is labeled a "hoax" in the slander-hungry press, and she loses her job as a fashion illustrator. Angela is still able to satisfy her dream to travel to France, however. She immerses herself in learning from the Old Masters housed at the Louvre and the galleries of the Luxembourg, reaffirming "that her aim, her one ambition, was to become an acknowledged, a significant painter of portraits" (375). Angela's aspirations to become a portrait painter represents New Negro Women's desires to become more than appealing images within portraits, but also to fashion the perceptual frames through which black women are allowed to appear—a good way to describe Fauset's aspirations too.

FASHIONING A PORTRAIT OF THE AUTHOR

Taking up *Plum Bun*'s emphasis on portraiture and fashion, in conclusion I turn to a photographic portrait taken of Fauset at a Harlem photography studio, an image she submitted with her 1928 application for the Harmon Negro awards program (fig. 8.7). As I have argued throughout this essay, Fauset's elegant attention to clothing's forms and colors represents her characters' artistic inclinations, which in turn figures for the desire to fashion a self free from others' limited and punitive expectations of the black female body. Framed within the photographic portrait's language of visibility, recognition, and dignity, Fauset's attention to fashionable clothing becomes a material enactment of the possibility of portraying oneself to the gaze of a predominantly white world on one's own terms.

In this particular portrait, Fauset presents herself as stylish and fashionable, but also demure. Her posture is relaxed, but her face seems tentative and

FIGURE 8.7: Portrait photograph of Jessie Fauset. Century Art Studio, 112 W. 125th St., New York. *Library of Congress.* (Plate 15.)

slightly tense. Fauset's hair, sculpted carefully into a short bob, and her silk dress, loose fitting and with a drop waist, signals the writer's participation in the fashions of the 1920s and resembles Wheeler's depiction of her charac-ter Amy as a young flapper. Other aspects of the photograph accent Fauset's sense of arrangement and design. Fauset sits in a decorative chair made of dark wood that has been carved into a dense three-dimensional pattern that helps to highlight the sheen and clean, modern lines of her silk dress. She sits at a three-quarter angle, and the photographer's light, which seems to ema-nate from the painted and curtained backdrop behind her, creates a smooth pattern of shadows across her dress and skin. Her legs are crossed, which calls attention to the neatly pleated flounces of her dress, her knee-length hemline, and her bar-strapped shoes with their slightly boyish mid-size heel. These aspects of her attire register the emphasis in early twentieth-century fashion on women's freedom of bodily movement. (Bar-strapped shoes were designed to hold in a woman's feet while dancing.) Fauset also wears a long string of pearls, one of the flapper's signature accessories, but she holds them gingerly, almost nervously.

I focus on this photographic portrait, not to ground my analysis in Fauset's biography, but to stress that her depiction of clothing created unpredictable seams among Fauset's literary texts, the lived contours of her life, and the histories of ideas and assumptions about black women that occluded both from a full and generous view. The narratives I have analyzed here show that for Fauset, fashionable clothing was a fiction that revealed a truth: black women in early twentieth-century America were covertly resisting the assumption that their bodies, imaginations, and images should be put to work for others. Fauset's work allows us to read these sartorial productions as forms black feminism composed of everyday desires to fashion one's visible but ultimately unfixed place in the textures of cultural history.

NOTES

I would like to thank Michael Eng and Ann Holder for giving me helpful and generous feedback on this essay. Katherine Joslin and Daneen Wardrop deserve special thanks for their very thoughtful encouragement.

1. Tracing Western philosophy's denigration of the image, and the gendered inflections of this denigration in the build up toward modernity, Catherine Constable writes, "Women's association with appearance and adornment means that she too can be denigrated for being superficial and trivial" (192). Perhaps the strongest denunciation of clothing within the canon of feminist thought appears in Mary Wollstonecraft's *Vindication of the Rights of Woman* (1792). In chapter 13, Wollstonecraft argues that women's inclination for "finery" and their "immoderate fondness for dress" is symptomatic of their cultivated ignorance and demonstrates their proximity to black subjects:

> When the mind is not sufficiently opened to take pleasure in reflection, the body will be adorned with sedulous care; and ambition will appear in tattooing and painting it. So far is this first inclination carried, that even the hellish yoke of slavery cannot stile the savage desire of admiration which the black heroes inherit from both their parents, for all the hardly earned

savings of a slave are commonly expended in a little tawdry finery. And I have seldom known a good male or female servant that was not particularly fond of dress. (196–97)

See Wilson on modern feminism's condemnation of fashion. For a more recent example of the culturally pervasive idea that fashionable self-display is antithetical to feminist progress, see Faludi.

2. Silverman's well-known "Fragments of a Fashionable Discourse," which builds upon J. C. Flügel's "The Psychology of Clothes" (1930) and Quentin Bell's *On Human Finery* (1947), argues that fashion and display were masculine prerogatives until the eighteenth century, when "the male subject retreated from the limelight, handing on his mantle to the female subject" (139). For the conflation of capitalism, specularity, and women see Solomon-Godeau. In *Chromophobia*, a thorough analysis of the bias against color in Western aesthetics, David Batchelor writes that "colour is made out to be the property of some 'foreign' body—usually the feminine, the oriental, the primitive, the infantile, the vulgar, the queer or the pathological . . . [and] is relegated to the realm of the superficial, the supplementary, the inessential or the cosmetic" (23). See Galt for the denunciation of "pretty" in Western aesthetics, a foundational assessment that spills into film theory.

3. See Nancy F. Scott, Banta, Wilson, Smith-Rosenberg, and Banner.

4. See Thaggart, Sherrard-Johnson, Patterson, Jayna Brown, Rooks, Barlow et al., Baldwin, and both texts by Peterson.

5. See Peterson (2003) for a more extensive analysis of Kelley-Hawkins's work in relationship to modernity. In 2006 Katherine E. Flynn discovered that Kelley-Hawkins, who had long been considered one of the earliest African-American women novelists, was in fact white. P. Gabrielle Foreman insightfully argues that instead of expunging Kelley-Hawkins' novels from the canon of African-American literature, they should be read as "embedded in a cultural and iconographic archive that speaks to the multiple, conflicting, and multivalent investments in reading individual bodies and texts in relationship to sociocultural bodies of racial knowledge" (249).

6. See Bederman (25).

7. In *Enter the New Negro*, Martha Nadell argues that "interartistic" depictions— "publications that concretely mix word and image and foreground the relationship between two media"—were an important part of the Harlem Renaissance artistic practice (7). See also Goeser, Carroll, and Thaggart on the centrality of the word/image relationship in cultural production of the Harlem Renaissance.

8. See Sheehan's and Harrison-Kahan's work for a recent turn in Fauset scholarship attentive to the writer's focus on clothing.

9. See McDowell's "The Neglected Dimension of Jessie Redmon Fauset," which began the conversation about Fauset's negative and narrow treatment by her critics

and makes a strong argument for seeing the feminist dimensions of Fauset's work. As McDowell writes,

> Fauset explores the black woman's struggle for democratic ideals in a society whose sexist conventions assiduously work to thwart that struggle. Critics have usually ignored this important theme, which even a cursory reading of her novels reveals. This concern with exploring female consciousness and exposing the unduly limited possibilities for female development is, in a loose sense, feminist in impulse, placing Fauset squarely among the early black feminists in Afro-American literary history. (88)

10. See Gilman on the Hottentot.

11. For a great introduction to the sexual connotations of the "red dress" and its relationship to the black female body, see Holloway.

12. See Willis on the connections among the New Negro, photography, and clothing.

13. My understanding of Darwin's impact on these thinkers is indebted to Alys E. Weinbaum's chapter "Sexual Selection and the Birth of Psychoanalysis: Darwin, Freud, and the Universalization of Wayward Reproduction," in her study *Wayward Reproductions*.

14. See Barlow et al., Baldwin, Peiss, and White and White (their chapter "The Long-Veiled Beauty of Our Own World" in particular).

15. See Cherene Sherrard-Johnson's chapter, "Jessie Fauset's New Negro Woman Artist and the Passing Market," in *Portraits of the New Negro Woman*, 49–76. It is in reading Sherrard-Johnson's chapter that I first saw this advertisement for *Plum Bun*.

16. The idea of reading Fauset's work in relationship to the advertising that appears in the journals in which her work appeared was suggested to me by Jamie Harker during a panel session devoted to Fauset's work that took place at the Society for the Study of American Women Writers in the fall of 2009. I am also indebted to Harker's chapter on Fauset in *America the Middlebrow*.

17. In her introduction to *The Chinaberry Tree*, Thadious Davis explains that Fauset "was not a woman of leisure or means; she was not financially independent" (xvii).

18. In her 1985 essay, "New Directions for Black Feminist Criticism," McDowell began the work of analyzing black women writers' attention to clothes. Against the omission of race in feminist literary criticism and the blindness to gender in the establishment of the African-American literary canon, McDowell argues that the development of black feminist literary criticism depends upon highlighting the particularity of black women's writing (193–94). She outlines themes particular to the literary productions of African-American women, and, perhaps surprisingly, clothing—along with the thwarted female artist and the journey—is one of those themes. According to McDowell, clothing served as a way for writers Fauset, Zora Neale Hurston, and Alice Walker to represent their characters' desires to "shape perceptions of themselves" (194).

19. As Edwards notes, "One never sees this term applied in scholarship on the careers of Johnson or Locke, but it is a common descriptive in introductions to Fauset's work" (352).

20. For biographical information on Fauset, see Sylvander as well as Roses and Randolph (507–508).

21. In their introduction to *Double-Take*, Maureen Honey and Venetria K. Patton help to explain the shuttle between biological and artistic reproduction in the Harlem Renaissance: "Motherhood was a site of artistic reproduction because it encompassed the past rape of black women by white masters during slavery and because black mothers represented the anticipated better future of the race" (xxiii).

22. Like "The Negro Artist and the Racial Mountain," Wallace Thurman's review essay "Negro Artists and the Negro" (1927) exemplifies the tendency of second-generation Harlem Renaissance writers to rebel against the leadership of Du Bois and the "Talented Tenth," of whom Fauset was most definitely part. Thurman describes Fauset's work as "an ill-starred attempt to popularize the pleasing news that there were cultured Negroes, deserving of attention from artists, and of whose existence white folk should be apprised" (199).

23. With less venom and more subtlety, contemporary treatments of Fauset's work have often repeated such assessments. In *Reconstructing Womanhood*, Hazel Carby argues that Fauset's work reflects the writer's conservative ideology and is an extended argument for middle-class culture: "She represented in her fiction a middle-class code of morality and behavior that structured the existence of her characters and worked as a code of appropriate social behavior for her readers" (166–67). In a similar vein, Simone Weil Davis's discussion of Nella Larsen's *Quicksand* (1928) in *Living Up to the Ads* equates the attraction Larsen's protagonist Helga Crane feels for commodities as an objectification of herself. In "Shopping to Pass, Passing to Shop," Meredith Goldsmith equates Helga's love of objects with passing.

24. See Fuss for her classic essay on the homosociality at work in the visual culture of fashion.

25. Russ Castronovo places "The Sleeper Wakes" within the context of *The Crisis*'s "attempts to distill a political methodology from aesthetics" that could fight against widespread lynching (1456). He argues that Fauset's story represents beauty's political failures and marks a turning point in *The Crisis*'s and Du Bois's engagement with aesthetics: "Overvaluing beauty, specifically her own physical attractiveness, Fauset's heroine blunders in thinking that a white husband would prize physical attraction over deeply held racism" (1456). While Castronovo's reading is for the most part right, he does not question women as the embodiment of beauty, nor does he consider that the story's emphasis on beauty extends beyond Amy's physical features and into clothing.

26. McDowell (1990) describes *Plum Bun* as "a richly textured and ingeniously de-

signed narrative, containing plots within plots and texts within texts that comment on one another in intricate combinations" (xv).

27. This argument has been influenced by Xiomara Santamarina's *Belabored Professions*, particularly the chapter "Behind the Scenes of Black Labor: Elizabeth Keckley and the Scandal of Publicity," as well as Nan Enstad's *Ladies of Labor, Girls of Adventure*, in which she argues that the young immigrant women working in the garment factories at the turn of the twentieth century purchased clothing to "exercise their new entitlement as workers . . . [and] ma[k]e clothing a badge of their labor" (63–64).

28. In this sense, *Plum Bun* contests Carby's assessment that "Fauset did not consider the aftermath of slavery and the failure of Reconstruction as a sufficient source of echoes and foreshadowings for her representation of the emergent black middle class who needed a new relationship to history," an argument that encapsulates much of the criticism against Fauset's work (167).

9

Modeling for Men

The Early Jean Rhys

Hope Howell Hodgkins

Keep your head up steady and straight,
Though you're fainting under the weight!

All the boys that you meet
Will declare that you are sweet
Men will wait outside on the mat,
If you have that hat!
> —Ross and Greenbank, "Hats," from *Our Miss Gibbs*, 1909

Sur la robe, elle a un corps.   —Poet Blaise Cendrars, 1914

After all, for whom do women dress? Isn't it men that women wish
to please?   —Designer Jean Patou, 1920s

"I have been a mannequin. I have been . . . no, not what you
think. . . ."   —Jean Rhys, "Hunger," 1927

*N*ovelist Jean Rhys (1890–1979) may be read as champion of the colonialist victim, as the writer who gave a voice to the madwoman in the attic, or even as a quintessential Parisian *artiste* of the twenties, drifting from café to café. But it is useful to consider her hard road to modernist style. The peculiar convergence of literary modernism and *la mode* has become a truism. Nevertheless Rhys, who worked as a chorus girl, artist's model, and live mannequin for high-fashion shops before turning to fiction, brought an intimate perspective very different from that of the theorists of modernity and fashion. Rhys's youthful experiences, and especially the convergence of sex and literature in her relationship with the famous modernist writer Ford Madox Ford, taught her that both clothing and language offer means through which desires are mediated between men and women. Both the Gaiety musical shows she performed in and her literary apprenticeship contributed to an aesthetic of "modeling for men," in which Rhys dressed, acted, and wrote in order to please—but also to strike back at—the male sex.

This essay, then, examines the ways in which Jean Rhys developed her impressionist writing style, through which she described her life of modeling for men as an object for examination (while also divulging her own complicity in that life). For although she appears a classic example of the patronized female in literary modernism, Rhys also wrote about the mixture of resentment and longing in that life, which she located symbolically in beautiful clothing. That Ford was her writing master, and she his sexual mistress, is both a modernist inconsistency and a literary cliché, visible in the careers of other female moderns ranging from H.D. to Zelda Fitzgerald. But while Rhys came of age in a world that stripped literature and clothing of inessential details, modern Paris remained an environ in which women's clothing was presumed to be sexual: poet Blaise Cendrars observed admiringly of a futurist design by artist Sonia Delaunay, "She has a body on her dress" (64). Modern fashion also remained a field in which Jean Patou, *couturier* for the liberated flapper, could brag, "My gowns please men . . . [they] say to their wives, 'At last you are dressed according to my taste'" (Etherington-Smith, 72). Through her personal experiences, Rhys learned both to fear and to satirize those masculine tastes, and in her fiction she used her knowledge of what clothing means for women.

MANNEQUINS FOR MEN

Female modernists were particularly hard hit by modernism's anomalous combination of old and new. Rhys, like all women of the early twentieth century, matured amidst enormous fashion changes: pictures from when she was a little girl show her mother and aunts in the lacy, high-necked, full blouses and sleeves, above floor-length skirts, proper for the class and era. But Rhys never graduated into her mother's magnificence: by the time she was old enough to "let her skirts down," the expression was nearly passé. In two decades styles shifted from the tightly corseted S-shape of the 1890s and early Edwardian era, to loose Ragtime tunics and frocks, then to the shockingly short flapper styles that exposed the knees. Anne Hollander has described how the modern woman's silhouette was reduced even as she won more social freedom and respect (1978, 150–55). Thus Rhys learned to simplify the elements of dress style, from multiple layers to a few necessary items such as "a black dress and hat and very dark grey stockings" (*After Leaving*, 182). Likewise she developed a hard minimalist narrative style for her fiction, a "cold deliberation" in cutting excess from her stories (Ford "Preface," 26). Yet her rhetoric always evokes a sense of loss, and she maintained a sexual economics of dress learned in her chorus-girl days: "You look at your hideous underclothes and you think, 'All right, I'll do anything for good clothes. Anything—anything for clothes'" (*Voyage*, 22). How could this age-old relation to men, and to clothing, accompany the modernist "terrifying insight" and "singular instinct for form" that Ford praised in her stories ("Preface," 24, 25)?

The first answers lie in Rhys's early life, which like modernism itself combined twentieth-century freedom with premodern content. The perennial outsider, Ella Gwendolen Rees Williams was born a white colonial in West Indian Dominica, daughter of an increasingly impoverished Welsh doctor. At sixteen she was sent to school in England, where teachers and students mocked her Creole accent and she was miserable in the cold gray climate. A voracious reader but a bashful talker, she often appeared ignorant, with nothing but youth and beauty to recommend her. By age eighteen, the shy young Gwen Williams had quit her girls' school to study drama. Seemingly resourceless, told that she would never succeed in classical theater, she secretly signed a contract to perform in the chorus of a traveling musical. With news of her father's death in Dominica, the aunt serving as her guardian threw up her hands, and Gwen slipped into the demimonde.

The demimonde, a shadowy class of women who are neither fully prostitutes nor entirely respectable, provides the dominant mythology for Rhys's personal and literary worlds. And in fact it exemplifies the phenomenon of the patronized female in literary modernism—but "mythology" is here a key word. The demimonde itself was a fiction, of women for sale who were not sordid streetwalkers but glamorous performers, often actresses or dancers or singers; who exerted seductive power over the men maintaining them; who reaped rewards in the form of expensive clothing and jewelry. That a few such women existed does not historically validate the mythology, as identified by French novelist Alexandre Dumas *fils* and celebrated by avant-garde writers from Charles Baudelaire to Ernest Dowson to Marcel Proust. It is perhaps significant that the most famous half-worlds, *demimondaines*, and their praisers were French, and that Rhys loved Paris all her life; likewise that most writers romanticizing the demimonde were male, although the scandalous novelist Colette, with *Gigi* (1942), was a memorable exception. Rhys would learn first-hand the potential misery of the kept woman, yet she never quite relinquished her belief that another man or another dress might transform her existence.

Rhys, like her fellow chorus girls, was susceptible to the demimonde myths: as a girl she had poured over Filson Young's *Sands of Pleasure* (1905), about a young engineer's obsession with a Continental courtesan (Pizzichini, 39). And her *Voyage in the Dark* (1934) opens with its chorus-girl protagonist Anna reading *Nana*, Emile Zola's 1880 novel about a power-mongering prostitute. Anna's roommate Maudie advises her that it's "a dirty book," noting shrewdly, "I bet you a man writing a book about a tart tells a lot of lies" (9). But Maudie also helps Anna pick up the man who will become her first lover, for the girls share the romanticized hope of becoming one of those rare kept women who marries well and lives happily ever after. Anna recalls a headline trumpeting, "Chorus-Girl Marries Peer's Son" (64). The chorus girls' inconsistent worldliness characterizes the demimonde myth on both sides of the male-female gulf.

Moreover, in a second sense we can speak of the demimonde mythology of Rhys's life. As the above paragraph suggests, readers and scholars struggle to disentangle Rhys's actual biography from her autobiographical fictions. We do not know the details or the extent of her life as a prostitute, as a nude model, or in other temporary, marginalized jobs.[1] The issue becomes unusually fraught when we acknowledge that Rhys was not necessarily truthful in her personal reminiscences; that she did not always recall distant memories correctly; and that she was uninterested in logically successive histories. Consequently Carole Angier's biography moves constantly between the fiction, the evidence, and speculation about what we can know of this writer's life, especially in the space between 1909 and 1919, when the West Indian doctor's daughter married and moved to the Continent, where she eventually became the writer Jean Rhys.

In those ten speculative years, during a brutal Great War and large shifts in cultural mores, the girl who used various names—"Gwen Williams" at school, "Vivien," "Emma," "Ella" or "Olga Gray" on the stage and in her shadowy street life (Angier, 57)—learned the paradoxical use of modern dress and the female body. This unsentimental education began with her employment in the chorus lines of Gaiety shows, which were the forerunners of the twentieth-century musical comedy. We know that in 1909 and 1910 Rhys performed in traveling productions of the hit Gaiety musical *Our Miss Gibbs*, with a brief abortive sojourn in a music-hall revue called *Chanteclair*, a "Feathered Fantasy in Three Fits." Late in life, Rhys recalled *Chanteclair* as a barely rehearsed show that featured "a girl in tights walking across the stage, dropping an egg and clucking loudly" (*Smile*, 86). A contemporary reviewer commented that at least "the dresses should be the talk of London" (Angier, 57). The dress we see Rhys wearing, in a snapshot from the production, is a very short pantomime style, both little-girlish and—for 1910—sexually suggestive, with its display of long, stockinged legs. Two of the five girls are dressed as men, but with similar leg displays. If *Chanteclair*'s costumes made London buzz, they constituted pure spectacle for the ladies and gentleman of the audience.

Against the vulgar amusements of *Chanteclair* we may set the premier Gaiety show *Our Miss Gibbs*, with its coherent and almost perfectly decorous romantic story, adorned by clothing that wealthy stylish women aspired to wear themselves. Gaiety musicals presented two foci of desire: first, the ambition of marrying above one's station (a feat frequently enacted in the plots of such shows and occasionally in the actual lives of their stars); second, the goal of acquiring many beautiful, fashionable clothes and displaying them for admiration. Of course both these desires dominate women's demimonde myths; and we know that Rhys—who nearly stopped reading books during her chorus life, since the other chorus girls did not read—spent a year or more "reading" *Miss Gibbs*: daily, nightly, and in her dreams. In *Miss Gibbs*, the heroine Mary Gibbs is a beautiful and virtuous Yorkshire lass who has come to London to work in "Garrods" department store. Mary is in love with a young bank clerk who actually is the disguised heir to an earldom. When she discovers his deception, she breaks off their relationship; but after many comic plot twists and several spectacular song-and-dance numbers, all is resolved and they wed. This Cinderella plot was echoed in many musicals of the period, such as *The Shop Girl* (1894) and *The Earl and the Girl* (1903), and also *The Count of Luxembourg* (1911), which Rhys played in as well.

Equally compelling, for the girls in the choruses, was the fairy-tale sight of Gaiety performers who wed rich and titled men. The famous instance was that of Rosie Boote, an illegitimate child of vaudeville who had become a Gaiety star and then, in 1901, Marchioness of Headfort. In addition Gertie Millar, who starred in the London production of *Miss Gibbs*, would wind up as the Countess of Dudley; Gladys Cooper, with a smaller part in the same *Miss Gibbs* production, not only became a famous actress but married a baronet; and even out of the touring *Miss Gibbs* company, Rhys's friend Nancy Erwin became Lady Dalrymple-Champneys. Moreover the famed beauty Lily Elsie, star of *The Count of Luxembourg*, left the show mid-season to marry a wealthy man. For the watching Rhys, Cinderella lived; she did not discern the thin line between ladylike stars and the abyss of prostitution.

For that matter, even Gaiety shows walked a tightrope in terms of sexual enticement. Modern theater critic W. J. Macqueen-Pope praised the new decorum of the Gaiety Theatre, explaining that in 1893 founder George Edwardes did away with "lavish display of feminine limb. . . . Skirts replaced tights, and mystery, deep, alluring and irresistible, surrounded the female form" (11). Moreover, Macqueen-Pope recalled nostalgically, "To know a Gaiety Girl, to take her out to sup, that was a cachet about town" (392). As he noted, the performers, and the shows themselves, were considered perfectly ladylike—yet their desirability skirted the edge of suggestion. A knowing girl sings in *Miss Gibbs*,

> I am sure your education
> Is not complete at present, girls,
> Till you've met with one sensation
> That's really rather pleasant, girls,
> Get some man who's young and handsome
> To grasp you tightly. . . .
>
> It's rather nice—
> Take my advice
> And try it once or twice.
> Arms and the man,
> Arms and the man,
> Ev'ry man has two,
> That will surely do,
> Is it enough for you?
> You feel a thrill all through.
>
> —Caryll and Monckton, 158–161

Lady Betty's advice teeters between innocence and sexual knowledge, as did other Gaiety songs. In *The Sunshine Girl* (1912), heroine Delia specifically advises a balancing act between modest and seductive dress: "Just a little touch will often be enough . . . Just in case young Lord Tom Noddy comes to call!"

Rather than "display of feminine limb," a glimpse of lingerie is recommended: "Just a frilly frou-frou, / Not so very much; / What they see of you / Will 'frill' them 'frou and frou.' . . ." (Rubens, n.p.). Evidently the stylish costumes that fascinated the ladies in the audience served in other ways to catch the interest of men.

Certainly both Gaiety shows and early live-fashion displays were intimately connected; and the fashion shows were known to attract male viewers who did not care about the clothing. The use of live models may have begun with Charles Frederick Worth, promenading his pretty wife in his newly designed gowns; but mannequin shows as performances began in 1890s London, in the same era as Edwardes' Gaiety Theatre (Evans, 125ff). Dress designer Lucile claimed credit for the first runway parades, in which the models emerged from behind a curtain and walked a ramp, and which encouraged male attendance (Kaplan and Stowell, 116, 119). The women came to see the clothing, the men, rather overtly, to ogle the women inside the dresses. And while Lucile and French *couturier* Paul Poiret continued their private mannequin shows as the twentieth century began, they also staged and sold new fashions by means of public theatre (Rappaport, 185). Lucile dressed Gaiety stars such as Lily Elsie for *Count* and other shows (Kaplan and Stowell, 115); consequently reviewers often focused on the clothing, even helpfully identifying the designer and informing women which costumes were available ready-made from which department stores (Booth and Kaplan, 53). Accordingly, a review entitled "Frocks and Frills" termed *Count*'s opening a "brilliant success," supporting that claim merely by describing, scene by scene, the assorted "charming" costumes (Detmold, n.p.). Even the popular *Our Miss Gibbs* was especially known for several spectacular hats created by Maison Lewis (Macqueen-Pope, 424). "That's the last Parisian hat!" Garrods' *modiste* Madame Jeanne and the chorus sang. "Men will wait outside on the mat, / If you have that hat!" (Caryll and Monckton, 39–40). Publicity shots of the show's star Gertie Millar often included spectacular hats indeed (fig. 9.1). And men did wait outside for Gaiety girls, with varying intentions.

Undeniably, Gaiety musicals sold new clothing styles and (at least in fantasy) the girls inside them (Rappaport, 192). Most ominously for Rhys, the shows preached sexual attraction as a bankable possession and dress as the mutual means of exchange. While the shop-girl comedies presented sex as a commodity, albeit part of a decorous marital agreement, *Miss Gibbs* also taught young women that clothing was both the exorbitant price of, and the reward

FIGURE 9.1: "Gertie Millar as Mary Gibbs in 'Our Miss Gibbs,'" by Rita Martin, published by J. Beagles & Co.; bromide postcard print, 1909. © *National Portrait Gallery, London.* (Plate 16.)

for, seduction. For the real-life girls this suggested that—as hinted by some reviews—the fashionable dresses were the most valuable items on stage. In *Voyage in the Dark* Rhys would describe a businessman musing, "Have you ever thought that a girl's clothes cost more than the girl inside them? . . . You can get a very nice girl for five pounds, a very nice girl indeed. . . . But you can't get a very nice costume for her for five pounds. . . ." Obviously then, the chorus girl Maudie cheerfully concludes, "People are much cheaper than things" (40). In line with Gaiety song philosophy, Rhys's fictional alter egos cynically dress to entice men—but they wistfully suspect that stylish clothes really may add value to the woman who wears them.

Not surprisingly, the Gaiety chorus girl who would become the writer Rhys was drawn into an affair with a wealthy, well-connected Englishman. For about eighteen months she essentially lived a demimonde fantasy, spending most weeknights in Lancelot Grey Hugh Smith's mansion and her days shopping for dresses or taking singing lessons, while occasionally still performing in a show. Smith paid her rent and for her classes, took her to dinner, and bought her clothing. In fact it seems the first money her lover gave her was for new stockings (Angier, 66). The young Rhys hoped to marry him, and when he broke off the affair she was devastated: the fairy tale had failed her. For the next seven years, she existed in a shadowy true demimonde for which evidence is scanty. She lived with, and worked for, a woman who advertised herself as a Swedish masseuse; then she stayed with Shirley, a show-girl friend who had become a high-priced call girl. In each venue, Rhys probably sexually served men and gave a cut of her pay to her hostess. From Shirley she seems to have learned, as the protagonists of her first four novels attest, that the more expensive your clothes, the higher class of man you can pick up: "It Was All Due To An Old Fur Coat" (*Good Morning*, 184). Eventually Rhys became pregnant and in desperation contacted Lancelot Smith. In accordance with his first name, Smith "chivalrously" sent her money for an illegal abortion and thereafter paid her a small monthly stipend—from afar, through a lawyer. The glamorous demimonde life, the Cinderella Gaiety Girl conclusion: both turned, for Rhys, into lonely, often desperate circumstances.

"What was the difference between Nancy [Erwin] and me?" Rhys recalled asking herself when her first love affair ended. Erwin, the showgirl-turned-baroness, "was ruthless and I wasn't" (*Smile*, 94). But Rhys knew it was something further: "Some [chorus girls] were very ambitious, determined to make a good marriage . . . and if you imagine they ever did anything which might interfere with that you don't know the type" (88). Rhys herself had lacked that steely determination, and so she allowed herself to slip from Gaiety Girl to paid woman, a change that may permanently have altered her perspective on men. Many years later she mused, "It seems to me now that the whole business of money and sex is mixed up with something very primitive and deep. When you take money directly from someone you love it becomes not money but a symbol. The bond is now there. . . . It is at once humiliating and exciting" (97).

Her words might stand as epigraph for her first three novels; Lancelot Smith had unwittingly given her a major theme for her fiction: the humiliating excitement of modeling for men. Ironically Smith also, through his monthly stipend, enabled Rhys to buy notebooks and several brightly colored pens that attracted her in a shop window, along with the time and energy to record her pain and rage (*Smile*, 103–104). Yet that writing, as well as the anger, remained hidden for several years more. Rhys ceased performing in Gaiety shows, but she continued to experiment with jobs related to displaying one's self and one's clothing. She posed as a nude artist's model in London but refused—she claimed—to sleep with her employers. She seems also, with another girl, to have rented a corner of a Bond Street dress shop where they endeavored to sell hats (*Letters*, 294). In Paris of 1923–1924 she would gain the mannequin experience depicted in her stories and recalled by Julia in *After Leaving Mr Mac-kenzie* (26); in the later twenties she evidently worked as a receptionist "in a smart dress shop near the Avenue Marigny" (Angier, 125–27). These French jobs are vividly, repeatedly described in her fiction. And so are the more verifi-able next events in her life: marriage, to a man who chose her dresses; and then an affair, with a man who endeavored to direct her literary taste.

IMPRESSIONS FOR MEN

"He criticized her clothes with authority and this enchanted her," Rhys wrote in her first autobiographical novel. In *Quartet* (1928) the mysterious Stephan Zelli first promises to pay for Marya's dress and then critiques it: "It's not worth that. . . . Not that it is ugly, but it has no chic. I expect your dressmaker cheats you" (18, 19). He offers to support her financially; he critiques her mag-isterially. Zelli is very like Rhys's first husband Jean (John) Lenglet. Having turned down at least two chances for marriage in England from 1914 to 1917, Rhys agreed to marry a secretive Dutchman of whom she knew only that he did not demand sex without marriage; he would choose her clothing; and he would help her escape chilly London (Angier, 98–99). She trusted that Len-glet, a sometime journalist and *chansonnier* (also a spy and a thief) would pet her, patronize her, and buy her dresses. For in 1919, when Rhys embarked for the Continent to marry Lenglet, she needed clothing: her dressmaker retained her trunk of dresses, in lieu of unpaid bills (*Smile*, 114). She was moving from illicit relations with men to legal marriage, and from cold England to a warmer Europe; but she still had much of the dependent mentality of the kept woman, and that same mindset would, ironically, prepare Rhys to be inducted into modernism.

Her willingness, perhaps her desire, to be patronized showed in Rhys's dress. Western women's styles were becoming less layered and more unified than they had been for several centuries; and simplicity and easy movement were imperative for the footloose, cosmopolitan life Rhys increasingly led. But that simple unity also enabled women to try on certain famous types, such as Mary Pickford's childlike look, described by Hollander: "The vulnerable neck (now bare), the fluffy curls (now free), together with the short skirt, flat bust and high waist all lent themselves to a new look of attractive immaturity—not the attractions of a ripe young virgin but of a little girl" ("Women and Fashion," 115). Long before Vladimir Nabokov's *Lolita*, the Victorian sentimentalizing of childhood had engendered a peculiar penchant for child-women, a taste for which some women learned to cater. Accordingly Pickford (b. 1892) played little girls and ingénues until her career fizzled at the end of the twenties. Certainly the little-girl role appealed to Rhys, too: she appeared that way in *Chanteclair*, and she often had dressed that way for Lancelot Smith, who may have called her a baby, as Walter terms Anna in the novel based on that affair (Angier, 66; *Voyage*, 44). Moreover Rhys's fictional women sometimes speak in infantile diction, when recalling the good clothes and good times with men who supported them: "I'd darling muslin frocks covered with frills and floppy hats—or a little peasant dress and no hat," recalls the narrator of Rhys's early story "Vienne." This very thinly disguised alter ego uses nursery speech to evoke "the spending phase" of Rhys's life with Lenglet: "Nice to have lots of money—nice, nice. Goody to have a car, a big chauffeur, rings, and as many frocks as I liked" (*Left Bank*, 202, 221). As a woman whose beloved father died just when she needed help, Rhys seems to have played the child to certain father figures: Smith and Lenglet, who made love to her and dressed her; and then Ford Madox Ford, who made love to her and promoted her fiction. Even when married she acted the helpless small girl; and when Lenglet's money-making schemes collapsed, Rhys leaned elsewhere for support—specifically on Ford, then at the height of his influence as a practitioner of literary impressionism.

British literary impressionism, exemplified in Ford and his friend Joseph

Conrad, should not be confused with the earlier nineteenth-century Impressionism led by French painters. As French *modernité* predated British modernism, so the Impressionism of Claude Monet and Paul Cézanne predated Ford's theories by several decades; nor is it clear that he and Conrad used Impressionist painting as a model. "We accepted without much protest the stigma 'Impressionists' that was thrown at us," Ford recalled. "We saw that Life did not narrate, but made impressions on our brains. We in turn, if we wished to produce in you an effect of life, must not narrate but render impressions" (*Joseph Conrad*, 194–95). As Todd Bender summarized it, "Impressionist writers aim to record the way impressions impinge on consciousness to make that 'shimmering haze' which is life, and they try to control and manipulate the constructive activity of their audience" (46). In their evocations of light and mist, literary impressionists such as Virginia Woolf did resemble Impressionist painters; however these novelists also emphasized the chronology of perception, demonstrating that the often random order in which we perceive things differs from traditional narrative plotting (Berrong, 205; Peters, 24). Both the use of style, to influence perceptions, and the unsettling of artistic norms came naturally to Rhys, with her experience in dressing for men and in the failures of the traditional happily-ever-after storyline.

Of Rhys's apprenticeship and affair with Ford we have multiple accounts, all heavily biased. Ford's common-law wife, painter Stella Bowen, described the relationship grimly in her memoir *Drawn from Life* (1941); Ford portrayed it luridly in his 1932 novel *When the Wicked Man* (in which Rhys becomes the drunken Creole vamp Lola); even the cuckolded Lenglet provided his angry version in a 1933 novel called *Sous les Verrous* (surprisingly translated and edited by Rhys herself, and published as *Barred*). Each narrative contains verifiable elements of Rhys's *Quartet*, where a young impoverished couple in Paris sees the husband arrested and sentenced to prison for financial malfeasance. The pretty, needy wife meets an older, well-to-do artistic couple and is taken into their home—only to have an affair with the husband that destroys her marriage and embitters all four actors. In Rhys's novel, blame is freely passed around but surprisingly little attention is paid to literature as a factor. Yet both Ford and Rhys knew that she never would have been a writer without his urging and guidance. Nor would they ever have met, if not for her writing. In need of money, Rhys had taken some essays written by her husband to H. Pearl Adam, an influential English journalist working in Paris. Mrs. Adam was not interested in Jean Lenglet's articles but asked Lenglet's wife if she had written anything herself. Madame Lenglet produced her notebooks, with the accounts of her chorus-girl life, seduction, and downward spiral. Mrs. Adam cut, edited, and typed the fragmented scribbles; she showed them to the famous writer and magazine editor Ford Madox Ford, who subsequently trained, published, and renamed the author Jean Rhys.

Although much more attention has been paid to Rhys's sexual affair with Ford than to the literary training he gave her, the one cannot be understood without the other. Ford's literary impressionism, which affirmed the sensitive, passive consciousness (Kronegger, 14), dovetailed with Rhys's peculiar mixture of passivity and passion in response to masterful men. Rhys's writing would evoke modernist fascinations with the semiotic; because her fiction lacked traditional form and because it focused upon women's private lives it appeared naturalistic, even primitive, with her West Indian roots providing an additional exotic attraction. Likewise the jottings of her private diary, very little inhibited by formal punctuation or syntactical linkage, easily fit modernist ambitions of destroying convention, as did the diary's seamy references to a young woman's sexual education. Ford affirmed her writing and her self, since he believed that "all art must be the expression of an ego" ("On Impressionism," 167). But Ford also taught Rhys to shape and cut, translating her English stories into French (Angier, 134–35), in the service of artistic writing: "the whole of Art consists in selection" (*Joseph Conrad*, 195). More frankly than any other high modernist, Ford famously preached the paradox of artistic expression: "The Impressionist author is sedulous to avoid letting his personality appear in the course of his book. On the other hand, his whole book, his whole poem is merely an expression of his personality" ("On Impressionism: Second," 323). This enigma of disciplined self-expression especially amazes in Rhys's fiction, since she showed no inclinations for hard work or self-discipline in any other area of life.

Or perhaps she always had worked hard at one area, that of pleasing men. If Ford gave her his standard advice for young writers, she must have been eerily reminded of her earlier demimonde existence: "You will seek to capture [your reader's] interest; you will seek to hold his interest. You will do this by methods of surprise, of fatigue, by passages of sweetness in your language . . . you will alternate . . . you will seek to exasperate so that you may the better enchant. You will, in short, employ all the devices of the prostitute ("On Impressionism: Second," 333). These lines were written ten years before Ford met Rhys; yet they seem to evoke her understanding of the need to attract men's attention. And she may have undertaken, in her relations with Ford, the same sort of posing for men, in exchange for support, that she had practiced with Smith and with other, unknown lovers in her shadowy years: seeking at all costs, and by various devices, to hold his interest. Still, their relationship ultimately was more about writing than about sex; and in two surprising ways this affair differed from any other love affair, for Rhys.

First, Ford, unlike Rhys's previous lovers, does not seem to have cared about dressing her. Oddly enough that role was filled by Bowen, who recalled of their young protégée, "Ford gave her invaluable help with her writing, and I tried to help her with her clothes" (*Drawn from Life*, 166). In *Quartet*, Lois Heidler (based upon Bowen) constantly observes and critiques Marya's clothing, although she herself wears gaudy, tasteless outfits in contrast to the younger woman's fashionable simplicity (115). Lois buys Marya a lace collar, "to cheer your black dress up"; after the affair has begun, she begins publically proclaiming Marya's need for a new hat: "'She must be chic . . . She must do us credit.' She might have been discussing the dressing of a doll" (79, 85). Hugh Heidler's interest in Marya's clothes extends only to noting "the shape of her breasts under the thin silk dress she wore—a dark-coloured, closely fitting dress that suited her" (130). So Lois, just as she half-consciously acts as pro-curer for her husband, also dresses his mistress for him; in so doing she emphasizes the demeaning aspects of such an exchange. And indeed Rhys reveals in the fiction her own resentment at being so dressed—surprisingly, perhaps, since she accepted the patronage of men. But the Ford *ménage à trois* seems to have fanned a latent spark of liberty within her.

Perhaps a slippage in the term *chic*, as the story progresses, indicates Marya's (and Rhys's) growing cynicism about being dressed like a doll. In the first part of the novel, being chic means being stylishly dressed, as indicated in the speech of both Stephen and Lois (19, 85). But this standard usage slides into a more colloquial meaning, as Marya spirals downward: Too late, she thinks nostalgically of her husband, "He was kind to me. He was awfully chic with me" (125). If *chic* describes not style but kindness between individuals, not appearance but reality, it has acquired both communal and ethical significance. Yet the possibilities of this transformation—from aesthetic valuation to a moral trait—are swiftly undercut on the following page. When Marya tells the imprisoned Stephen that the Heidlers have lent her money, he comments, "They're chic" (126). We know that they are not kind, they merely put on an appearance of kindness, which is as important to them as a chic dress might be to others.

In any case, although Ford may have encouraged his protégée to "employ all the devices of a prostitute" in her writing, she did not. For a second striking aspect of Rhys's relationship with him was its independence where her writing was concerned. When men dressed her, Rhys accepted the support and the guidance; even late in life, she wrote, "I am not chic or elegant. I'm grotesque except somebody else dresses me and advises me. I was all right sometimes in Paris because Jean [Lenglet] bought all my clothes" (*Letters*, 77). Writing, however, was a different matter: "I was *dragged* into writing by a series of coincidences—Mrs Adam, Ford, Paris—need for money" (65). Although she originally worked at it partially to please her lover and father figure, the subsequent breakup meant that she ceased to model her writing after a man's stipulations. All her life she would remember the need for precision and discipline. Yet her fiction, even that written under Ford's tutelage, sometimes veered away from his recommendations. In his "Preface" to *The Left Bank*, Ford complained that when he tried to get Rhys to introduce "an atmosphere . . . some sort of topography" describing the Rive Gauche, she cut material instead (25–26). Over the years Rhys's novels steadfastly remained "the expression of an ego," and indeed the assertion of an ego, more than an effort to "hold his interest" at all costs. Even her early stories, written under Ford's guidance, show women modeling for men but stubbornly holding themselves apart.

In puzzling over what he saw as Rhys's refusal to include "descriptive passage[s]" in her *Left Bank* stories (1927), Ford had concluded, "Her business was with passion, hardship, emotions: the locality in which these things are endured is immaterial" ("Preface," 26). He seemed to miss Rhys's very material although minimalist evocation of Montparnasse, evinced in certain ironic parallels between high modernism and modern haute couture, between the pyrotechnic surfaces of aesthetic fiction and the rich fashions covering all-too-material bodies. This is the point at which clothing style and writing style coalesce, in Rhys's life and novels. In his rarefied fiction, Gustave Flaubert had boasted, subject does not matter: style may become "an absolute manner of seeing things" (154). But Rhys knew all too well the sexual economy in which both men and women value women more highly if their clothing—

their style—seems valuable. Hence she employs that Flaubertian aesthetic of high style ironically, to assert the primacy of the subject, the woman inside the clothing.

In two early stories in *The Left Bank*, "Mannequin" and "Illusion," Rhys shows women defining their relations to clothing, first in youth and then in age. "Mannequin" simply describes a day's work *chez* Jeanne Veron for a new young model. Anna is oppressed by cold rooms and "the cold eyes" of buyers, as well as the other mannequins, whose selves are encased in the archetypes they portray: the *jeune fille*, the *gamine*, the *femme fatale*, the *garçonne*, the *blonde enfant*—and the "frankly ugly" star with the "chic of the devil" (61, 64–65). The magisterial Madame Veron rules; her models must follow her aesthetic tastes. Consequently their day, like their job of wearing clothes not their own, is curiously static. "One asks oneself: Why? For what good? It is all *idiot*," Anna's friend remarks (69). It is only when Anna walks out into the Paris street at day's end that she feels "happy in her beautifully cut tailor made and a beret" (her own clothes); and all the models emerge, taking comfort in the epiphanic brief moment in which they are "gay and beautiful as beds of flowers" (69, 70). Although they resent the pressure to be automata for the *haute couture* system, the young women assume that the clothes they possess are inseparable from their selves, that their beautiful surfaces constitute an organic whole. The sketch offers no explanation or reconciliation for the mannequins' contradictions: it simply describes.

"Illusion," by contrast, presents a deliberate overanalysis, in this case of an older woman's relations to dress. The homely, "gentlemanly" spinster-painter Miss Bruce secretly collects a closetful of beautiful garments in which she claims a detached aesthetic interest. To the unnamed narrator, who discovers the contents of Miss Bruce's closet while its owner is in the hospital, the dresses constitute "everything that one did not expect" from an unobtrusive Englishwoman (*Left Bank*, 3). The friend first describes the gowns in sensuous detail: "a riot of soft silks . . . an evening gown of a very beautiful shade of old gold: near it another of flame colour: of two black dresses the one was touched with silver, the other with a jaunty embroidery of emerald and blue" (3). This collection shows, the speaker theorizes, Miss Bruce's "perpetual hunger to be beautiful and that thirst to be loved which is the real curse of Eve, well hidden under her neat dress" (4); that is, the middle-aged artist surely collects dresses because she has a secret desire to attract men. Soon we are immersed in speculative fantasy, about Miss Bruce's sad, illusory search for "the perfect Dress, beautiful, beautifying," and the dresses themselves are personified, shrugging their silken Gallic shoulders over the impossibility of making the spinster beautiful. The vignette swiftly concludes with Miss Bruce's own defensive response: "Why should I not collect frocks? They fascinate me. The colour and all that . . ." (5). But the damage is done: the reader cannot believe, any more than the spinster's friend believes, that she does not long to wear her dresses, and indeed to wear them for men. Whose is the titular illusion—Miss Bruce's or her friend's—Rhys never indicates. What is clear is that, while the young mannequins may be overidentified with their clothing, we indulge such illusions; but those women who claim a purely detached admiration for clothes are regarded with deep suspicion. Either one models for men (in the Patou cliché), or one refuses to "dress" at all. Thus Rhys's first stories used clothing to argue implicitly against both *haute couture* tradition and high-modern aestheticism.

Nevertheless the novels based on her affair with Ford, and her early life, demonstrate Rhys's continued affinities for modernism and fashion. As Ford inadvertently taught her, when he loved her, encouraged her writing, and then abandoned her, absence and obliquity merely show up the desires they cannot fulfill. Through a sort of *fort-da* strategy, the writer—like Freud's small grandson—endeavors to deal with loss by alternating presence and absence. In *Quartet* (originally *Postures*, 1928), both dress and literature are occluded by absence: all Marya's beautiful clothing is in the past, sponsored by her disgraced husband. When Stephan is arrested, Marya sells her dresses with the aid of her landlady, who accurately identifies the nature of her wardrobe: " 'This, for instance, this *robe de soirée* . . .' She pointed out the gem of the collection: 'Who would buy it? Nobody. Except a woman *qui fait la noce.*' " It is "not a practical dress," Madame Hautchamp explains, but "a fantasy" (37). The overglamorous evening gown is in fact an emblem of Marya's (and Rhys's) nature: the woman who dresses for men. And that the gown, in its turn, should be sold marks the end of Marya's fantasy world. Likewise her memories of lovely clothing haunt Marya near the novel's end, when—with both her affair and her marriage essentially over—she daydreams about "stupid things like a yellow dress that Stephan had bought her once at Ostend. . . . It had been fun to wear beautiful clothes and to feel fresh and young and like a flower" (164). Once, like the mannequins in Rhys's earlier story, she had felt an organic continuity with her beautiful garments, "like a flower"; but this passage makes clear that Marya feel the loss cruelly because she feels the absence of a man's love and financial security. Instead of beautiful clothing, she now has the Heidlers, whose obsession with saving conventional appearances mimics Rhys's style/substance dichotomy. "He went on to explain that one had to keep up appearances. That everybody had to. Everybody had for everybody's sake to keep up appearances." Heidler's banal language shows Rhys's Joycean ear for modernist style, while Marya's response cuts to the underlying substance. In explaining why she does not want to keep up appearances by coming to Lois's party, she says bluntly, "They'll tear me up and show you the bits" (113–14).

Just as stylish dress is largely gone from Marya's life, Rhys eliminated from *Quartet* any mention of literary gifts, whether hers or her lover's. Hugh Heidler is not a writer, let alone an influential literary spokesman. Rather he is an "English picture-dealer man," described vaguely as "a very important person in his way" (6, 9). He and his wife Lois (who paints) are constantly described in terms of middle-class conventionality rather than aesthetic interests. Ironically, the shady Stephan Zelli also deals in art, in his way: he first introduces himself to Marya as a "*commissionaire d'objets d'art*," telling her that he sells "pictures and other things" (17). The substitution of art dealing for writing makes Heidler a mere commodifier of art, scarcely better than Zelli, who fences stolen artifacts. Heidler also manipulates others' creative gifts: he has "made discoveries. He helped the young men," Marya is told (9). Clearly Rhys changed her lover's profession as an insult to Ford and in order to present him as parasitical. But the absence of literature also redounds upon her and may deeply impair the novel's quality.

For Marya, although a former chorus girl, is strikingly unskilled in any direction except making herself attractive. "She's a decorative little person— decorative but strangely pathetic," her friend Miss De Solla thinks (7). In fact, Marya always waits passively to be acted upon, never acting herself. She has been the "petted, cherished child" in her marriage, and when she moves into the Heidler household her youth, passivity, and dependence put her in the role of adopted child (22). No wonder then that Heidler's advances evoke the "fright of a child" in her and a queasiness in the reader, since he creeps into her bedroom like a father intent on molesting a daughter (90). And no wonder that Lois, the mother surrogate, not only attempts to dress her but displays a malevolent aggression, which manifests as jocular child abuse: "Let's go to Luna-park after dinner," she suggests. "We'll put Mado on the joy wheel, and watch her being banged about a bit" (85). Marya, and the reader, already have seen her image riding the merry-go-round to the strains of "*Je vous aime*": "a little frail, blond girl, who careered past, holding tightly on to the neck of her steed, her face tense and strained with delight" (57). Clearly a little girl cannot prevail over Heidler or his wife.

However, Marya's extreme passivity not only makes her vulnerable to the assertive, slightly predatory Heidlers, it degrades the novel. *Quartet* is noticeably less accomplished than Rhys's other novels, probably because the author's pain and anger were still too fresh for her to admit any guilt. In order to make her surrogate, Marya—who, like Rhys herself, sleeps with her hostess's husband and deserts her imprisoned spouse—perfectly innocent, she must make her perfectly helpless. Furthermore, Rhys's efforts to play with perspective fail, since they all hinge on the one point: Marya is like "L'Enfant Perdu or the Babe in the Wood," thinks her friend Cairn (92); Heidler himself observes that she cries touchingly, "quietly, all soft and quivering, her little breasts heaving up and down in painful, regular jerks" (129). The characterization may be all too true: Bowen recalled Rhys as "very pretty and gifted" but possessing "a complete absence of any desire for independence" (166). In any case, Marya becomes a vacuum that sucks life out of Rhys's narrative, and it is her own dependent nature that makes her a solitary woman at the novel's end.

STREETWALKING WOMEN AND INFANT RETURNS

In *After Leaving Mr Mackenzie* (1931), Rhys returned to her memories of the Ford affair; but this second novel is much less about the former lover and much more about clothes, aging, and female desperation. The narrative focuses entirely on the breakup's aftermath and ways of compensating for loss of love. In characterization, *Mackenzie* constitutes an extreme swing of the pendulum: where Marya was passive and vulnerable, Julia is active, aggressive, and even violent. While Marya lives first with her husband and then with the Heidlers, Julia is solitary, despite sporadic efforts to connect with her family or with a man. Where Marya was continually characterized by her youth, Julia's dominant—and only pathetic—trait is her aging appearance. And where Heidler of *Quartet* was masterful and egotistical, Mr. Mackenzie is passive, even when Julia makes a scene and strikes him in public. He is a shadowy and largely absent businessman, with only money to recommend him: it is "of new clothes" that Julia thinks "with passion, with voluptuousness" (20). With this alter ego, Rhys seems more willing to admit her own errors.

Certainly Julia's love affair with clothing may be read as a mistaking of style for substance. Repeatedly throughout the novel she endeavors to recreate herself through dress. Her first response to a need for cash is the thought "I must get some new clothes" (19). The narrative is book-ended by this value: it begins and ends with Julia, having received a little money from a grudging man, planning to spend it on dress (58, 182). And by the conclusion it seems that she equates clothing with love, or at least sees it as a means of purchasing love: "She began to imagine herself in a new black dress and a little black hat with a veil that just shadowed her eyes. After all, why give up hope when so many people had loved her?" (181–82). Yet the story, as it progresses, seems to validate that equation. Clothing and appearance indeed rule Julia's society: "People thought twice before they were rude to anybody wearing a good fur coat" (80). Style misleads the entire world, it seems.

Rhys used *Mackenzie* as a means of artistically shaping her own continuing anger: this novel in contrast to the free-flowing *Quartet* is stringently organized. It opens with Julia receiving a sort of severance check from her former lover, Mr. Mackenzie, through his lawyer; she watches Mackenzie's house and pursues him to a restaurant, where she makes a scene and slaps his face with her glove. A young Englishman, George Horsfield, observes her actions. He follows Julia, befriends her, and gives her enough money to travel to London. On her ten-day visit to London (the heart of the novel), Julia visits her unsympathetic relatives, her mother's deathbed, and the subsequent funeral. She contacts a wealthy former lover, who gives her money; she reencounters Horsfield, who gives her money and sleeps with her. Because she cannot believe that Horsfield truly cares for her, she returns to Paris, where she accidentally runs into Mr. Mackenzie again. He buys her a drink and gives her money once more, as the novel ends.

Julia is a conundrum: both Mackenzie and Horsfield puzzle over whether she is responsible for her own descent into the abyss. Her self-awareness unsettles Mackenzie:

> She had been an artist's model. At one time she had been a mannequin. But it was obvious that she had been principally living on the money given to her by various men. . . . One day she had said to him, "It's a very easy habit to acquire. . . ."
>
> He had not quite agreed with her. There would have been no end to the consequences of whole-hearted agreement. (26)

Mackenzie soon stops asking "intimate questions," being unwilling "to go too far or too deep" into Julia's point of view (27). The kindlier Horsfield, however, is "curious to speculate about the life of a woman like that and to wonder what she appeared to herself to be—when she looked in the glass, for instance . . . she must have some pretty pathetic illusions about herself or she would not be able to go on living" (91). Thus Rhys ironically, albeit somewhat heavily, summarizes male assumptions about fallen women: one does not quite want to see from the woman's perspective, in case his smug worldview is shaken; the other, while sympathizing, assumes that appearances must be all—at least for "a woman like that." In any case their alternating perspectives demonstrate Rhys's increased mastery of modernist style. She even uses a comical play on subject-object narrative to increase sympathy for Julia. Her public confrontation with her former lover, narrated from Mackenzie's perspective, alternates in short paragraphs between "She said" and his unspoken response:

> She said that Maître Legros had bullied her. . . .
>
> Well, he probably had. . . .
>
> She said that she had begun to cry. . . .
>
> Well, in all careers one must be prepared to take the rough with the smooth.
>
> She said that she had been determined never to accept the money. . . .
>
> "Well, well," thought Mr Mackenzie. "*Tiens, tiens.*" (31–32)

The more we see of Mackenzie's inner self, the less we like him (a narrative secret Rhys discovered between her first and second novels).

At the same time we are left with the question of Julia as active agent in her own fate. For she is a *flâneuse*, a female stroller of the Parisian and London boulevards. The original *flâneurs*, as Charles Baudelaire envisioned them, may have displayed themselves as dandies but they also posed as detached observers of the urban scene. For a woman, however, streetwalking implied prostitution, until modernity complicated the roles of men and of women. In the late nineteenth century window-shopping became respectable; by the twenties, as Hollander has theorized, shorter skirts had produced a "look of possible movement" important for liberated women (*Seeing*, 153). Independent streetwalking even may "be interpreted as an attempt to identify and place the self in the uncertain environment of modernity" (Parsons, 41).[2] Thus when Julia streetwalks, she is both displaying herself—and she is very aware of the possibilities of picking up men—and objectively observing her world, but she cannot tell how to combine the roles. Julia tells Horsfield that she left home "with just the same feeling a boy has when he wants to run away to sea. . . . Only, in my adventure, men were mixed up, because of course they had to be. . . . Do you understand that a girl might have that feeling?" (51). Horsfield pities her, but he cannot understand. Nor does Julia wholly reject traditional interpretations of her street wandering: men "had to be" mixed up in it. Early in the novel, a man follows Julia only to be repudiated; at the end, another man stops her and then, when he looks closely in her tired face, recoils: "*Ah, non, alors*" (187). Perhaps ultimately she is more weary streetwalker than free-spirited observer. As Deborah Parsons has pointed out, Rhys's "mannequins, models, show-girls, and prostitutes . . . are problematically uncertain realizations of the urban woman as model for emancipated identity" (144). Julia provides a tragic alternative to the educated, independent New Woman who confidently walks the streets.

In each of her protagonists' tragedies, Rhys denies the overly easy assumptions of modernity, that we may leave the past behind: her women are haunted by their individual pasts, just as they are pulled back by traditional stereotypes. "Every day is a new day; every day you are a new person. What have you to do with the day before?" Julia asks herself—shortly before returning to Mr. Mackenzie and his grudging support at the novel's end (157). Twice she sees the ghost of her youthful, well-dressed self: first in London, wearing "a long, very tight check skirt, a short dark-blue coat, and a bunch of violets bought from the man in Woburn Square"; and later in Paris, where an old menu reminds her of "a white crêpe de Chine dress, and red slippers" she used to wear (180). But to her former lovers her ghostlike reappearances are less appealing; she haunts Mackenzie, he feels, "as an ungenerous action does haunt one" (28). And when she visits Neil (the Lancelot Smith surrogate), Julia knows she must appear "an importunate ghost" (66). For the men her reappearance suggests, not the glamorously dressed woman of the past, but an expectation that she wants money—an expectation that Julia inevitably fulfills. In *After Leaving Mr Mackenzie*, the past is not dead enough for the men, while it is too much past for women.

Nevertheless it was through a return to the past that Rhys finally achieved her mature style. In *Voyage in the Dark* (1934) the writer effectively recalled her Gaiety-girl days and initial seduction, from two decades' vantage point.

This third, very autobiographical novel is not about Ford at all; yet it most effectively demonstrates the lessons he taught her. The shaped and cut ego displayed in *Voyage* is as jarring and as compelling as a stripped body. More impressionistic than ever, this fiction keeps us almost entirely within Anna's point of view; yet as she receives her unhappy sentimental education she learns to see others' perspectives. And the childlike Anna, like her creator, learns to objectify feminine grief through a broadened modern vision of dress and the inescapable self.

Youth dominates *Voyage*, which begins with birth imagery and ends with an abortion. (Rhys had wanted it to end with Anna's death, but her publisher persuaded her to create a supposedly more hopeful conclusion.) The birth motif corresponds to Anna's daydreams of her childhood: unlike Rhys's first two novels, *Voyage* is filled with memories of Dominica, and its protagonist, like Rhys herself, was born in the West Indies. In certain ways the narrative is consciously childish: "It's written almost entirely in words of one syllable," Rhys wrote to a friend. "Like a kitten mewing" (*Letters*, 24). The kitten image is appropriate, since the vulnerable Anna frequently is seen as too young for her predicament. Her lover, Walter Jeffries (a full portrayal of Lancelot Smith), questions her age when he first meets her (12). And after their affair begins, his love talk assumes her naïveté: "You rum child, you rum little devil" (48). To his cold-hearted cousin Julian, who will persuade him to break off the affair, she is "infantile Anna" (69). Walter, he remarks, "has been doing a bit of baby-snatching" (73).

Moreover Anna is first depicted with a childlike fixation, similar to Julia's, on dress: "When I thought about my clothes I was too sad to cry" (21). She longs for beautiful clothes and wears black as often as possible, since she has read that "Men delighted in that sable colour" (19). With the first money Walter sends her she hurries to Cohen's dress shop in Shaftesbury Avenue, where the proprietors dress her as if she "were a doll." Her outfit is very similar to the one Julia's younger ghost-self wears, dark blue with a long, tight skirt "so that when I moved in it I saw the shape of my thighs" (25). Whether Anna recognizes the style's sexuality is unclear. Her excited response again evokes birth. " '*This is a beginning*,' she thinks. '*Out of this warm room that smells of fur I'll go to all the lovely places I've ever dreamt of*'" (25; emphasis original). Anna depends upon clothing to create a new life—one that naturally involves dressing herself for men.

The novel, however, offers a dual perspective on modeling for men. By the narrative's midpoint, Walter has broken off the affair and in so doing inadvertently begins to break her clothing dependence. Far from Julia's "voluptuous" obsession with clothing, the disillusioned Anna exhibits an independence from dress concerns startling in the young chorus girl who earlier had "want[ed] pretty clothes like hell" (22). She learns both to analyze and to sympathize with other modern women on the street. She observes "a black velvet dress in a shop window, with the skirt slit up so that you could see the light stocking. A girl could look lovely in that, like a flower or doll." The familiar imagery first suggests Anna's sisterhood with Rhys's other dress-conscious women: black again; sexualized again; and once again aiming to resemble a beautiful inanimate object. But she carries her observation further, by acknowledging others' perspectives: "The clothes of most of the women who passed were like caricatures of the clothes in the shop-windows, but when they stopped to look you saw that their eyes were fixed on the future" (111). Equal parts dispassionate criticism and pity, Anna's observation is very mature indeed, as is her subsequent commentary. "Keep hope alive and you can do anything," she observes, acknowledging her own sense of despair. She recognizes that new clothes do not equal love, but they may create hope for a future.

For Anna personally, the novel's end offers little hope; rather the narrative ironically emphasizes the impossibility of escaping one's past. When she becomes pregnant (as did Rhys herself) by one of the unknown men she has picked up, she sells the fur coat her former lover gave her but still must write to him requesting help (144). Walter's intermediary Julian appears, assuring Anna that wanting the baby is "nonsense" and that they will provide the money for an abortion. Then she must try to "start fresh. . . . You'll forget it and it'll be just as though it had never happened" (147). Likewise the cynical doctor, called in to see her after the abortion is botched, laughs: "She'll be all right. . . . Ready to start all over again in no time, I've no doubt." And so the book ends with Anna lying there, hearing his words and thinking "about starting all over again, all over again . . ." (158). The repetition points up the hopeless cycle in which the young *demimondaine* is caught. Although Rhys changed the ending so that Anna does not die, the doctor's words serve as epitaph for her life, and for the lives of all of Rhys's women.

"I can abstract myself from my body," Jean Rhys once remarked to a shocked Frenchman in Paris (*Smile*, 95). If so, it is because she felt she must learn to strip off her self as one would strip clothes from one's body—and her characters struggle to do the same. And if indeed "clothes are separated from all other objects by being inseparable from the self" (Hollander, *Seeing*, 451), Rhys nevertheless depicts women's strategies for comprehending and managing that inseparability. Certainly the writer used her often retrograde dependence upon men and clothes in the service of a pared modernist style, and vice versa: if clothing is a metonymy for the tragic dependence of women "modeling for men," the impressionism modeled by men offered a way for Jean Rhys to "write back."

NOTES

1. Critics have varied in the extremity of these identifications; early Rhys scholars tended to speak of "the Rhys woman," as if her protagonists Anna, Julia, Marya, Sasha, and even Antoinette of *Wide Sargasso Sea* were manifestations of the same person; and Lillian Pizzichini's recent biography, *The Blue Hour*, often simply describes incidents from the novels as if they happened to Rhys herself. Clearly this is not always the case—yet she inarguably did use many scenes, characters, and even significant bits of dialogue from her own experience.

2. For more on modern *flânerie*, see Janet Wolff, "The Invisible Flâneuse: Women and the Literature of Modernity," *Theory, Culture and Society* 2, no. 3 (November 1985): 37–46; Walter Benjamin, *The Arcades Project*.

Bibliography

Achebe, Chinua. "An Image of Africa: Racism in Conrad's *Heart of Darkness*." Reprinted in *Heart of Darkness*, edited by Robert Kimbrouch, 251–62. 3rd edition. New York: W. W. Norton, 1988.

Adam, Alexander. *Roman Antiquities: An Account of the Manners and Customs of the Romans*. Philadelphia: Mathew Carey, 1807.

Adburgham, Alison. "The Early Years." In *The House of Liberty: Masters of Style and Decoration*, edited by Stephen Calloway, 18–45. London: Thames and Hudson, 1992.

Adorno, Theodor, and Walter Benjamin. *The Complete Correspondence 1928–1940*, edited by Henri Lodnitz and translated by Nicholas Walker. Cambridge, MA: Harvard University Press, 1999.

The Age We Live In: A Fragment. Dedicated to Every Young Lady of Fashion. London: Lackington, Allen, and Co., 1813. books.google.com/books. August 13, 2008.

Allaback, Steven. "Oak Hall in American Literature." *American Literature* 46, no. 4 (1975): 545 49.

Angier, Carole. *Jean Rhys: Life and Work*. Boston: Little, Brown, 1990.

Anonymous. *The Sins of the Cities of the Plain, or the Recollections of a Mary-Ann*. London: Privately printed, 1881.

Aria, Mrs. [Eliza]. *My Sentimental Self*. London: Chapman and Hall, 1922.

Ashelford, Jane. *Art of Dress: Clothes and Society 1500–1914*. London: The National Trust, 2011.

Audax, Frederick. *A Hint from Modesty to the Ladies of England on the Fashion of Low-Dressing*. London, 1855.

Austen, Jane. *Jane Austen's Letters*, edited by Deirdre Le Faye. 3rd ed. Oxford: Oxford University Press, 1995.

——. *Juvenilia*, edited by Peter Sabor. New York: Cambridge University Press, 2006.

——. *Northanger Abbey*, edited by Barbara M. Benedict and Deirdre Le Faye. New York: Cambridge University Press, 2006.

——. *Sense and Sensibility*, edited by Edward Copeland. New York: Cambridge University Press, 2006.

Baines, Edward. *History of the Cotton Manufacture in Great Britain*. London: H. Fisher, R. Fisher, and P. Jackson, 1835.

Baldwin, Davarian L. "From the Washtub to the World: Madame C. J. Walker and the 'Re-creation' of Race Womanhood, 1900–1935." In *The Modern Girl Around the World: Consumption, Modernity, and Globalization* edited by Tani Barlow et al., 55–76. Durham, NC: Duke University Press, 2008.

Banner, Lois. *American Beauty.* Chicago: University of Chicago Press, 1983.

Banta, Martha. *Imaging American Women: Idea and Ideals in Cultural History.* New York: Columbia University Press, 1987.

Barthes, Roland. 1967. *The Fashion System,* translated by Matthew Ward and Richard Howard. New York: Hill and Wang, 1983.

Bartlett, Neil. *Who Was That Man? A Present for Mr. Oscar Wilde.* London: Serpent's Tail, 1988.

Batchelor, David. *Chromophobia.* London: Reaktion Books, 2000.

Bederman, Gail. *Manliness and Civilization: A Cultural History of Gender and Race in the United States, 1880–1917.* Chicago: University of Chicago Press, 1995.

Beetham, Margaret. *A Magazine of Her Own?: Domesticity and Desire in the Woman's Magazine, 1800–1914.* London: Routledge, 1996.

Bender, Todd K. "Jean Rhys and the Genius of Impressionism." *Studies in the Literary Imagination* 11, no. 2 (Fall 1978): 43–53.

Benjamin, Walter. *The Arcades Project,* translated by Howard Eiland and Kevin Mclaughlin. Cambridge, MA: Belknap Press of Harvard University Press, 1999.

———. *Illuminations,* edited by Hannah Arendt and translated by Harry Zohn. New York: Schocken Books, 1969.

———. *Selected Writings Volume 4, 1938–1940,* edited by Howard Eiland and Michael William Jennings. Cambridge, MA: Belknap Press of Harvard University Press, 2006.

Berrong, Richard M. "Modes of Literary Impressionism." *Genre* 39 (Summer 2006): 203–28.

Bhabha, Homi. *The Location of Culture.* London: Routledge, 1994.

Bilski, Emily D., and Emily Braun. *Jewish Women and Their Salons: The Power of Conversation.* New Haven, CT: Yale University Press, 2005.

Bone, Robert. *The New Negro Novel in America.* 1958. Revised edition. New Haven, CT: Yale University Press, 1965.

Booth, Michael R., and Joel H. Kaplan. *The Edwardian Theatre: Essays on Performance and the Stage.* Cambridge: Cambridge University Press, 1996.

Bourdieu, Pierre. *Outline of a Theory of Practice,* translated by Richard Nice. Cambridge: Cambridge University Press, 1977.

Bowen, Stella. *Drawn from Life: A Memoir.* London: Collins, 1941.

Brantlinger, Patrick. "Victorians and Africans: The Genealogy of the Myth of the Dark Continent." *Critical Inquiry* 12 (1985): 166–203.

Bremer, Sidney. "Exploring the Myth of Rural American and Urban Europe: 'My Kinsman, Major Molineux' and 'The Paradise of Bachelors and the Tartarus of Maids.'" *Studies in Short Fiction* 18 (1981): 49–57.

Breward, Christopher. "Aestheticism in the Marketplace: Fashion, Lifestyle and Popular Taste." In *The Cult of Beauty: The Aesthetic Movement, 1860–1900*, edited by Stephen Calloway and Lynn Federle Orr, 194–205. London: V&A Publishing, 2011.

———. *The Culture of Fashion.* Manchester: Manchester University Press, 1996.

———. *The Hidden Consumer: Masculinities, Fashion, and City Life 1860–1914.* Manchester: University of Manchester Press, 1999.

Brooke, Iris. *A History of English Costume.* London: Methuen and Co., 1937.

Brooks, Daphne A. *Bodies in Dissent: Spectacular Performances of Race and Freedom, 1850–1910.* Durham, NC: Duke University Press. 2006.

Brown, Bill. *The Material Unconscious: American Amusement, Stephen Crane, and the Economies of Play.* Cambridge, MA: Harvard University Press, 1996.

———. "Objects, Others, and Us (The Refabrication of Things)." *Critical Inquiry* 36, no. 2 (2010): 183–217.

———. "Thing Theory." *Critical Inquiry* 28, no.1 (2001): 1–22.

Brown, Gillian. *Domestic Individualism: Imagining Self in Nineteenth-Century America.* Berkeley: University of California Press, 1990.

Brown, Jayna. *Babylon Girls: Black Women Performers and the Shaping of the Modern.* Durham, NC: Duke University Press, 2008.

Bushman, Richard L. *The Refinement of America: Persons, Houses, Cities.* New York: Vintage, 1992.

Byatt, A. S. *The Children's Book.* London: Chatto and Windus, 2009.

Bynum, Caroline W. *Metamorphosis and Identity.* New York: Zone Books, 2001.

Byrde, Penelope. *Nineteenth Century Fashion.* London: B. T. Batsford, 1992.

Byron, George Gordon, Baron. *Don Juan.* Edited by T. G. Steffan and W. W. Pratt. New York: Penguin, 2005.

Calloway, Stephen, and Lynn Federle Orr, eds. *The Cult of Beauty: The Aesthetic Movement 1860–1900.* London: V&A Publishing, 2011.

Carby, Hazel. *Reconstructing Womanhood: The Emergence of the Afro-American Woman Novelist.* Oxford: Oxford University Press, 1989.

Carroll, Anne Elizabeth. *Word, Image, and the New Negro: Representation and Identity in the Harlem Renaissance.* Bloomington: Indiana University Press, 2005.

Caryll, Ivan, and Lionel Monckton. *Our Miss Gibbs: A Musical Play in Two Acts by "Cryptos"* (Adrian Ross and Percy Greenbank). London: Chappell and Co., 1909.

Castronovo, Russ. "Beauty Along the Color Line: Lynching, Aesthetics, and the *Crisis.*" *PMLA* 121.5 (October 2006): 1443–59.

Cendrars, Blaise. *Complete Poems,* translated by Ron Padgett. Berkeley: University of California Press, 1992.

Chroniqueuse. *Photographs of Paris Life: A Record of the Politics, Art, Fashion and Anecdote of Paris during the Past Eighteen Months.* London, 1861.

Cohen, William A. *Sex Scandal: The Private Parts of Victorian Fiction.* Durham, NC: Duke University Press, 1996.

Conrad, Joseph. *Heart of Darkness*, edited by Robert Kimbrouch. 3rd edition. New York: W. W. Norton, 1988.

———. *Joseph Conrad's Letters to R. B. Cunninghame Graham*, edited by C. T. Watts. Cambridge: Cambridge University, Press, 1969.

Constable, Catherine. "Making Up the Truth: On Lies, Lipstick, and Friedrich Nietzche." In *Fashion Cultures: Theories, Explorations, and Analysis*, edited by Stella Bruzzi and Pamela Church Gibson, 191–200. New York: Routledge, 2000.

Corrigan, Peter. "Chapter 3: More Than the Times of Our Lives: Dress and Temporality." In Peter Corrigan, *The Dressed Society: Clothing, the Body and Some Meanings of the World*, 47–71. London: Sage, 2008.

Crozier, Ivan. " 'All the Appearances Were Perfectly Natural': The Anus of the Sodomite in Nineteenth-Century Medical Discourse." In *Body Parts: Critical Explorations in Corporeality*, edited by Christopher Forth and Ivan Crozier, 65–84. Lanham, MD: Lexington Books, 2005.

Cunnington, Phillis. *Costumes in Pictures.* London: Studio Vista, 1964.

The Daily Telegraph. (London). "Men in Female Attire," May 23, 1870; "The Boulton and Park Prosecution," May 10, 11, 13, 1871.

Daly, Suzanne. *The Empire Inside: Indian Commodities in Victorian Domestic Novels.* Ann Arbor: University of Michigan Press, 2011.

Daves, Jessica. *Ready-Made Miracle: The American Story of Fashion for the Millions.* New York: G. P. Putnam's Sons, 1967.

Davies, Mel. "Corsets and Conception: Fashion and Demographic Trends in the Nineteenth Century." *Comparative Studies in Society and History* 24, no. 4 (October 1982): 611–41.

Davis, Angela Y. *Blues Legacies and Black Feminism: Gertrude "Ma" Rainey, Bessie Smith, and Billie Holiday.* New York: Vintage, 1998.

Davis, Simone Weil. *Living Up to the Ads: Gender Fiction of the 1920s.* Durham and London: Duke University Press, 2004.

Davis, Thadious M. "Introduction." In Jessie Fauset, *The Chinaberry Tree: A Novel of American Life*, xv–xxxiv. 1931. New York: GK Hall, 1995.

Dee, Phyllis Susan. "Female Sexuality and Triangular Desire in *Vanity Fair* and *The Mill on the Floss. Papers on Language and Literature* 35, no. 4 (Fall 1999): 391–416.

De Marly, Diana. *Worth: Father of Haute Couture.* New York: Holmes and Meier, 1980.

Detmold, Rita. "Frocks and Frills." *The Play Pictorial* 108 (1911): n.p.

Dickens, Charles. *American Notes for General Circulation.* London: Chapman and Hall, 1842.

Dixon, Ella Hepworth. *The Story of a Modern Woman.* 1894. Reprint. Edited by Steve Farmer. Peterborough, ON: Broadview, 2004.

Dobson, Kit. "'An Insuperable Repugnance to Hearing Vice Called by Its Proper Name': Englishness, Gender and the Performed Identities of Rebecca and Amelia in Thackeray's *Vanity Fair.*" *Victorian Review* 32, no. 2 (2006): 1–25.

Dorré, Gina Marlene. "Horses and Corsets: Black Beauty, Dress Reform, and the Fashioning of the Victorian Woman." *Victorian Literature and Culture* 30, no. 1 (2002).

Du Bois. W .E. B. "Editorial." *The Crisis: Record of the Darker Races.* November 1920. 10.

DuCille, Anne. *The Coupling Convention: Sex, Text, and Tradition in Black Women's Fiction.* New York: Oxford University Press, 1993.

Dyer, Gary R. "The 'Vanity Fair' of Nineteenth-Century England: Commerce, Women, and the East in the Ladies' Bazaar." *Nineteenth-Century Literature* 46, no. 2 (September 1991): 196–222.

Edwards, Brent Hayes. *The Practice of Diaspora: Literature, Translation, and the Rise of Black Internationalism.* Cambridge: Harvard University Press, 2003.

Egerton, George [Mary Chavelita Dunne]. "At the Heart of the Apple." In *Symphonies*, 160–218. London: John Lane: The Bodley Head, 1897.

———. "The Mandrake Venus." In *Fantasias*, 55–72. London and New York: John Lane: The Bodley Head, 1897.

Eisler, Benita, ed. *The Lowell Offering: Writings by New England Mill Women (1840–1845).* New York: W. W. Norton, 1998.

Ellis, Sarah Stickney. *The Women of England, Their Social Duties, and Domestic Habits.* London: Fisher, Son and Co., 1839. Victorian Women Writers Project. February 5, 1999. Indiana University. March 6, 2004. http://www.indiana.edu/~letrs/vwwp/ellis/womeneng.html.

Engen, Rodney. *Kate Greenaway: A Biography.* New York: Schocken Books, 1981.

The Englishwoman's Domestic Magazine. (London.) "The Fashions," January, February, March, April 1869; "New Year Paris Fashions," January 1870; "The March Fashions," March 1870; "The April Fashions," April 1870.

Enstad, Nan. *Ladies of Labor, Girls of Adventure: Working Women, Popular Culture, and Labor Politics at the Turn of the Twentieth Century.* New York: Columbia University Press, 1999.

Etherington-Smith, Meredith. *Patou.* New York: St, Martin's Press / Marek, 1983.

Evangelista, Stefano. "Vernon Lee and the Gender of Aestheticism." In *Vernon Lee: Decadence, Ethics, Aesthetics*, edited by Catherine Maxwell and Patricia Pulham, 91–111. Houndmills, UK: Palgrave Macmillan, 2006.

Evans, Caroline. "Multiple Movement, Model, Mode: The Mannequin Parade 1900–1929." In *Fashion and Modernity*, edited by Christopher Breward and Caroline Evans, 125–45. Oxford: Berg, 2005.

Ewing, Elizabeth. *Dress and Undress: A History of Women's Underwear.* London: Batsford, 1989.

Faludi, Susan. "American Electra: America's Ritual Matricide." *Harper's*, October 2010: 29–42.

Farley, Harriet Jane. "Editorial." *Lowell Offering* 3 (January 1843): 95–96.

Fauset, Jessie. *The Chinaberry Tree: A Novel of American Life*. 1931. New York: G. K. Hall, 1995.

——. "Emmy." *The Crisis: A Record of the Darker Races*. December 1912: 79–87; January 1913: 134–42.

——. *Plum Bun: A Novel Without a Moral*. 1929. Boston: Beacon Press, 1990.

——. "The Sleeper Wakes: A Novelette in Three Installments." *The Crisis: A Record of the Darker Races*. August 1920: 168–73; September 1920: 226–29; October 1920: 267–74.

Field, Michael [Katharine Bradley and Edith Cooper]. *Long Ago*. London: George Bell and Sons, 1889.

Fisher, Judith Law. "Siren and Artist: Contradiction in Thackeray's Aesthetic Ideal." *Nineteenth-Century Fiction* 39, no. 4 (March 1985): 392–419.

Flaubert, Gustave. *The Letters of Gustave Flaubert 1830–1857*. Selected, edited, and translated by Francis Steegmuller. Cambridge, MA: Harvard University Press, 1980.

Flügel, J. C. *The Psychology of Clothes*. London: The Hogarth Press, 1971.

Flynn, Katherine E. "Emmy Dunham Kelley-Hawkins 1863–1938." *Legacy: A Journal of American Women Writers*. Special issue: "Racial Identity, Indeterminancy, and Identification in the Nineteenth Century" 24, no. 2 (2007): 278–93.

Ford [Hueffer], Ford Madox. *Joseph Conrad: A Personal Remembrance*. Boston: Little, Brown, 1924.

——. "On Impressionism." *Poetry and Drama* 6 (June 1914): 167–75.

——. "On Impressionism: Second Article." *Poetry and Drama* 8 (December 1914): 323–34.

——. "Preface: Left Bank." In Jean Rhys, *The Left Bank and Other Stories*, 7–27. 1927. Freeport, NY: Books for Libraries Press, 1970.

Foreman, P. Gabrielle. "Reading/Photographs: Emma Dunham Kelley-Hawkins's *Four Girls at Cottage City, Victoria Earle Matthews,* and *The Woman's Era*." *Legacy: A Journal of American Women Writers*. Special issue: "Racial Identity, Indeterminancy, and Identification in the Nineteenth Century" 24, no. 2 (2007): 248–77.

Forgue, Sue. "The Mighty Muslin." *JASNA (Jane Austen Society of North America) News* 26, no. 3 (2010): 15.

Frawley, Maria. "Behind the Scenes of History: Harriet Martineau and 'The Lowell Offering.'" *Victorian Periodicals Review* 38 (2005): 141–57.

Freedgood, Elaine. "Fringe." *Victorian Literature and Culture* 30, no. 1 (2002).

Fuss, Diana. "Fashion and the Homospectatorial Look." *Critical Inquiry* 18, no. 4 (Summer 1992): 713–37.

Galperin, William. *The Historical Austen*. Philadelphia: University of Pennsylvania Press, 2003.

Galt, Rosalind. *Pretty: Film and the Decorative Image*. New York: Columbia University Press, 2011.

Gere, Charlotte. *Artistic Circles: Design and Decoration in the Aesthetic Movement*. London: V&A Publishing, 2010.

Gernsheim, Alison. *Victorian and Edwardian Fashion: A Photographic Survey*. New York: Dover, 1981.

Gilman, Charlotte Perkins. *The Dress of Women: A Critical Introduction to the Sociology of Clothing*, edited by Michael R. Hill and Mary Jo Deegan. 1915. Westport, CT.: Greenwood Press, 2002.

Gilman, Sander. "The Hottentot and the Prostitute: Toward an Iconography of Female Sexuality." In *Race-ing Art History: Critical Readings in Race and Art History*, edited by Kymberly N. Pinder, 119–38. New York: Routledge, 2002.

Goeser, Caroline. *Picturing the New Negro: Harlem Renaissance Print Culture and Modern Black Identity*. Lawrence: University of Kansas Press, 2007.

Goldsmith, Meredith. "Shopping to Pass, Passing to Shop: Self-Fashioning in the Fiction of Nella Larsen." In *Recovering the Black Female Body: Self-Representations by African American Women*, edited by Michael Bennett and Vanessa D. Dickerson. New Brunswick, NJ: Rutgers University Press, 2001. 97–120.

Goodyear, Frank H., III. *Zaida Ben-Yusuf: New York Portrait Photographer*. NY: Merrell, 2008.

Goudie, S. X. "Fabricating Ideology: Clothing, Culture, and Colonialism in Melville's *Typee*." *Criticism* 40, no. 2 (1998): 217–35.

Greenblatt, Stephen. *Marvelous Possessions: The Wonder of the New World*. Chicago: University of Chicago Press, 1991.

Greenlees, Janet. *Female Labour Power: Women Workers' Influence on Business Practices in the British and American Cotton Industries, 1780–1860*. Burlington, VT: Ashgate, 2007.

Gretchko, John. "The White Mountains, Thomas Cole, and 'Tartarus': The Sublime, the Subliminal, and the Sublimated." In *Savage Eye: Melville and the Visual Arts*, edited by Christopher Sten, 127–44. Kent, Ohio: Kent State University Press, 1991.

Halttunen, Karen. *Confidence Men and Painted Women: A Study of Middle-Class Culture in America, 1830–1870*. New Haven, CT: Yale University Press, 1982.

Hammond, Mary. "Thackeray's Waterloo: History and War in *Vanity Fair*." *Literature and History* 11, no. 2 (2002): 19–38.

Harker, Jaime. *America the Middlebrow: Women's Novels, Progressivism, and Middle-Brow Culture*. Amherst: University of Massachusetts Press, 2009.

Harrison-Kahan, Lori. "No Slaves to Fashion: Designing Women in the Fiction of Jessie Fauset and Anzia Yezierska." In *Styling Texts: Dress and Fashion in Literature*, edited by Cynthia Kuhn and Cindy Carlson, 311–32. Amherst, MA: Cambria Press, 2007.

Haweis, Mary Eliza. *The Art of Beauty.* 1878. Reprinted in Mary Eliza Haweis, *The Art of Beauty and The Art of Dress.* New York: Garland, 1978.

———. *The Art of Beauty.* 1878. Reprint. N.P.: Elibron Classics/Adamant Media, 2004.

———. *The Art of Decoration.* London: Chatto and Windus, 1881.

Hawthorne, Nathaniel. *The Centenary Edition of the Works of Nathaniel Hawthorne.* Vols. I–III and VIII–XI. Columbus: Ohio State University Press, 1962–1974.

Haynes, Patrice. "'To rescue means to love things': Adorno and the re-enchantment of bodies." *Critical Quarterly* 47, no. 3 (2005): 64–78. onlinelibrarywiley.com. December 3, 2012.

Heydt-Stevenson, Jill. *Austen's Unbecoming Conjunctions: Subversive Laughter, Embodied History.* New York: Palgrave Macmillan, 2008.

Hollander, Anne. *Seeing through Clothes.* Berkeley: University of California Press, 1975, 1993.

———. *Seeing through Clothes.* NY: Viking, 1978.

———. "Women and Fashion," in *Women, the Arts, and the 1920s in Paris and New York*, edited by Kenneth W. Wheeler and Virginia Lee Lussier, 109–25. New Brunswick, NJ: Transaction, 1982.

Holloway, Karla F. C. "The Body Politic." In Karla F. C. Holloway, *Codes of Conduct: Race, Ethics, and the Color of Our Character*, 16–71. New Brunswick, NJ: Rutgers University Press, 1995.

Hughes, Clair. "Talk about Muslin: Jane Austen's Northanger Abbey." *Textile: The Journal of Cloth and Culture* 4, no. 2 (2006): 184–97.

Hughes, Langston. *The Big Sea.* Reprinted in *The Langston Hughes Reader.* New York: George Brazilier, 1958.

———. "The Negro Artist and the Racial Mountain." In Venetria and Honey, *Double-Take: A Revisionist Harlem Renaissance Anthology*, 40–44.

Hughes, Linda K. *Graham R.: Rosamund Marriott Watson, Woman of Letters.* Athens: Ohio University Press, 2005.

Hunt, Alan. *Governance of the Consuming Passions: A History of Sumptuary Law.* New York: St. Martin's Press, 1996.

Illustrated Police News (London). "Capture of Men Dressed Up As Women," May 7, May 14, 1870; "The Men in Female Attire." May 28, 1870.

Inikori, Joseph. *Africans and the Industrial Revolution in England: A Study in International Trade and Economic Development.* New York: Cambridge University Press, 2002.

Irigaray, Luce. *This Sex Which Is Not One*, translated by Catherine Porter and Carolyn Burke. Ithaca; NY: Cornell University Press, 1985.

Jadwin, Lisa. "The Seductiveness of Female Duplicity in *Vanity Fair.*" *SEL: Studies in English Literature* 32, no. 4 (Autumn 1992): 663–87.

Jenkins, Richard. *Pierre Bourdieu.* London: Routledge, 2002.

Johnson, Barbara E. "Euphemism, Understatement and the Passive Voice: A Genealogy of Afro-American Poetry." In *Reading Black, Reading Feminist: A Critical Anthology*, edited by Henry Louis Gates Jr., 204–11. New York: Penguin, 1990.

Johnson, McDougald Elise. "The Task of Negro Womanhood." 1925. Reprinted in Venetria and Honey, *Double-Take: A Revisionist Harlem Renaissance Anthology*, 103–12.

Joslin, Katherine. *Edith Wharton and the Making of Fashion.* Becoming Modern Series; Reading Dress Subseries. Durham: University of New Hampshire Press, 2009; Hanover: University Press of New England, 2011 (paperback).

Kaplan, Joel H., and Sheila Stowell. *Theatre and Fashion: Oscar Wilde to the Suffragettes.* Cambridge: Cambridge University Press, 1994.

Kasson, John F. *Civilizing the Machine: Technology and Republican Values in America, 1776–1900.* New York: Hill and Wang, 1976.

Knight, Charles. "Introduction." In *Mind Amongst the Spindles*, edited by Charles Knight, v–xiv. Boston: Jordan, Swift, and Wiley, 1845.

Koda, Harold. *Extreme Beauty: The Body Transformed.* New York: Metropolitan Museum of Art, 2001.

Kronegger, Maria Elisabeth. *Literary Impressionism.* New Haven, CT: College and University Press, 1973.

Larsen, Nella. *Quicksand* (1928) and *Passing* (1929), edited by Deborah McDowell. New Brunswick, NJ: Rutgers University Press, 1986.

Laver, James, and Amy De la Haye. *Costume and Fashion.* London: Thames and Hudson, 1982.

"La Mode." August 1869; "Guys in Disguise." November 1869.

LeFavour, Cree. "Acting 'Natural': *Vanity Fair* and the Unmasking of Anglo-American Sentiment." In *Sullen Fires Across the Atlantic: Essays in Transatlantic Romanticism*, edited by Lance Newman, Joel Pace, and Chris Koenig-Woodyard. Romantic Circles Praxis Series. 2006. www.rc.umd.edu/praxis/sullenfires. November 5, 2008.

Le Follet, Journal du Grande Monde, Fashion, Polite Literature, Beaux Arts, &c. (London/Paris).

Lemire, Beverly. *Cotton.* Textiles that Changed the World Series. New York: Berg, 2011.

———. "Domesticating the Exotic: Floral Culture and the East India Calico Trade with England, c. 1600–1800." *Textile: The Journal of Cloth and Culture* 1, no. 1 (2003): 65–85.

———. *Dress, Culture, and Commerce: The English Clothing Trade before the Factory, 1660–1800.* New York: Palgrave, 1997.

———. "Fashioning Global Trade: Indian Textiles, Gender Meanings and European Consumers, 1500–1800." In *The Spinning World: A Global History of Cotton Textiles,*

1300–1850, edited by Giorgio Riello and Prasannan Parthasarathi, 371–81. Oxford: Oxford University Press, 2009.

———. *Fashion's Favourite: The Cotton Trade and the Consumer in Britain, 1660–1800*. Oxford: Oxford University Press, 1991.

Lemire, Beverly, and Giorgio Riello. "East and West: Textiles and Fashion in Early Modern Europe." *Journal of Social History*. 41, no. 4 (2008): 887–909. *Project Muse*. muse.jhu.edu. July 18, 2012.

Licht, Walter. *Industrializing America: The Nineteenth Century*. Baltimore: Johns Hopkins University Press, 1995.

Linton, Eliza Lynn. *The Girl of the Period and Other Social Essays*. London: Richard Bentley and Son, 1883.

———. *Modern Women and What Is Said of Them*. Reprint of series of articles in the *Saturday Review*. New York: J. S. Redfield, 1868.

Littlejohn, David. *Black on White: A Critical Survey of Writing by American Negroes*. New York: Grossman, 1966.

Litvak, Joseph. *Strange Gourmets: Sophistication, Theory, and the Novel*. Durham, NC: Duke University Press, 1997.

Lonitz, H. *The Complete Correspondence 1928–1940: Theodor W. Adorno and Walter Benjamin*. Cambridge, MA: Harvard University Press, 1999.

Loos, Adolf. "Ornament and Crime." 1908. In *Programs and Manifestos on 20th-Century Architecture*, edited by Ulrich Conrads and translated by Michael Bullock, 19–25. Cambridge, MA: MIT Press, 1971.

Lurie, Alison. *The Language of Clothes*. 1981. Reprint. New York: Henry Holt, 2000.

Mackie, Dorothea Sophia. *A Picture of the Changes of Fashion*. London. 1818. books.google.com/books. August 8, 2010.

Macqueen-Pope, W. *Gaiety: Theatre of Enchantment*. London: W. H. Allen, 1949.

Manchester Times. "The Ladies' Column," June 27, 1868.

Mandel, Miriam B. "Significant Patterns of Color and Animal Imagery in Conrad's *Heart of Darkness*." *Neophilologus* 73 (1989): 305–19.

Marcus, Sharon. *Between Women: Friendship, Desire, and Marriage in Victorian England*. Princeton, NJ: Princeton University Press, 2007.

———. "Reflections on Victorian Fashion Plates." *Differences* 14, no. 3 (Fall 2003): 4–33.

Marks, Patricia. "'*Mon Pauvre Prisonnier*': Becky Sharp and the Triumph of Napoleon." *Studies in the Novel* 28, no. 1 (Spring 1996): 76–92.

Martineau, Harriet. "Introduction." In *Mind Amongst the Spindles*, edited by Charles Knight, v–xxii. Boston: Jordan, Swift, and Wiley, 1845.

McDowell, Deborah E. "Introduction: Regulating Midwives." In Jessie Fauset, *Plum Bun: A Novel Without a Moral*, ix–xxxiii. Boston: Beacon Press, 1990.

———"The Neglected Dimension of Jesse Redmon Fauset." In *Conjuring: Black Women,*

Fiction, and Literary Tradition, edited by Marjorie Pryse and Hortense J. Spillers, 86–104. Bloomington: Indiana University Press, 1985.

———. "New Directions in Black Feminist Criticism." In *New Feminist Criticism: Essays on Women, Literature, and Theory*, edited by Elaine Showalter, 186–99. New York: Pantheon, 1985.

Melville, Herman. "The Paradise of Bachelors and the Tartarus of Maids." 1855. In *Billy Budd, Sailor, and Selected Tales*, edited by Robert Milder, 74–96. Oxford: Oxford University Press, 2009.

Meredith, George. *Diana of the Crossways*. 1897. Doylestown, PA: Wildside Press, 2002.

Meyer, Moe. "Under the Sign of Wilde: An Archeology of Posing." In *The Politics and Poetics of Camp*, edited by Moe Meyer, 1–22. New York: Routledge, 1994.

Midnight in Paris. Film. Woody Allen, dir. Sony, 2011.

Milder, Robert. "Introduction." In *Billy Budd, Sailor, and Selected Tales*, vii–xxxix. Oxford: Oxford University Press, 2009.

Miles, Robert. "*The Blithedale Romance*, Rousseau, and the Feminine Art of Dress." *Texas Studies in Literature and Language* 31, no. 2 (1989): 215–36.

Miller, Christopher R. "Jane Austen's Aesthetics and Ethics of Surprise." *Narrative* 13, no. 3 (2005): 238–60. *Project Muse*. muse.jhu.edu. June 30, 2011.

A Mirror of the Graces, Or, The English Lady's Costume. London: Printed for B. Crosby and Co. 1811. books.google.com/books. August 8, 2010.

Mitchell, W. J. T. "Romanticism and the Life of Things: Fossils, Totems, and Images." In *Things*, edited by Bill Brown, 227–44. Chicago: University of Chicago Press, 2004.

Moon, Michael. *A Small Boy and Others: Imitation and Initiation in American Culture from Henry James to Andy Warhol*. Durham, NC: Duke University Press, 1998.

Moyle, Franny. *Constance: The Tragic and Scandalous Life of Mrs. Oscar Wilde*. London: John Murray, 2011.

Mukerji, Chandra. *From Graven Images: Patterns of Modern Materialism*. New York: Columbia University Press, 1983.

Nadell, Martha Jane. *Enter the New Negroes: Images of Race in American Culture*. Cambridge, MA: Harvard University Press, 2004.

Newman, Lance, Chris Koenig-Woodyard, and Joel Pace, eds. *Sullen Fires Across the Atlantic: Essays in Transatlantic Romanticism*. Romantic Circles Praxis Series. 2006. www.rc.umd.edu/praxis/sullenfires. November 5, 2008.

Nigro, Jeffrey A. "Estimating Lace and Muslin: Dress and Fashion in Jane Austen and Her World." *Persuasions: Journal of the Jane Austen Society of North America* 23 (2001): 50–62.

Nixon, Nicola. "Men and Coats; or, The Politics of the Dandiacal Body in Melville's 'Benito Cereno.'" *PMLA* 114 (1999): 359–72.

O'Farrell, Mary Ann. *Telling Complexions: The Nineteenth-Century English Novel and the Blush.* Durham, NC: Duke University Press, 1997.

Pall Mall Gazette. (London). "Fashion," April 18, 1868; "La Mode—Bonnets and Mantles," December 17, 1868; "La Mode—Robes," December 23, 1868; "La Mode—Spring Bonnets and Mantles," April 28, 1869; "Law and Police," April 29, 1870.

Parsons, Deborah L. *Streetwalking the Metropolis: Women, the City, and Modernity.* Oxford: Oxford University Press, 2000.

Patterson, Martha H. *The American New Woman Revisited: A Reader, 1894–1930.* New Brunswick: Rutgers University Press, 2008.

Patton, Venetria K., and Maureen Honey. "Introduction." In *Double-Take: A Revisionist Harlem Renaissance Anthology,* edited by Venetria K. Patton and Maureen Honey, xix–xxxix. New Brunswick, NJ: Rutgers University Press, 2001.

Peiss, Kathy. *Hope in a Jar: The Making of America's Beauty Culture.* New York: Metropolitan Books, 1998.

Penny Illustrated Paper. (London). "The Female Impersonators," May 20, 1871; *Punch: Or the London Charivari;* "Fal-Lals for February," February 12, 1870; "Ladies and Their Long Tails," July 29, 1865.

Peril, Lynn. *Pink Think: Becoming a Woman in Many Uneasy Lessons.* London: W. W. Norton, 2000.

Peters, John G. *Conrad and Impressionism.* Cambridge: Cambridge University Press, 2001.

Peterson, Carla L. "Foreword: Eccentric Bodies." In *Recovering the Black Female Body: Self-Representations by African-American Women,* edited by Michael Bennett and Vanessa Dickerson, ix–xvi. New Brunswick, NJ: Rutgers University Press, 2001.

———."New Negro Modernity: Worldliness and Interiority in the Novels of Emma Dunham Kelley-Hawkins." in *Women's Experience of Modernity, 1875–1945,* edited by Ann L. Ardis and Leslie W. Lewis, 111–29. Baltimore: John Hopkins University Press, 2003.

Pizzichini, Lillian. *The Blue Hour: A Life of Jean Rhys.* New York: W. W. Norton, 2009.

Post-Lauria, Shelia. *Correspondent Coloring: Melville in the Marketplace.* Amherst: University of Massachusetts Press, 1996.

Psomiades, Kathy Alexis. *Beauty's Body: Femininity and Representation in British Aestheticism.* Stanford, CA: Stanford University Press, 1997.

Ranta, Judith. "Harriot F. Curtis: Worker, Author, Editor." *American Transcendental Quarterly* 22 (2008): 327–46.

Rappaport, Erika Diane. *Shopping for Pleasure: Women in the Making of London's West End.* Princeton, NJ: Princeton University Press, 2000.

Reid-Walsh, Jackie. "'Do You Understand Muslins, Sir?': The Circulation of Ball Dresses in *Evelina* and *Northanger Abbey*." *Lumen: Proceedings of the Canadian Society for Eighteenth-Century Studies* 10 (2000).

Reynolds's Newspaper. (London). "Apprehension of 'Gentlemen' in Female Attire," May

I, 1870; "The Men in Petticoats—Horrible and Revolting Disclosures," May 22, 1870; "The Hermaphrodite Clique," June 5, 1870; "The Trial of Boulton and Park—Extraordinary Disclosures About the Men in Petticoats," May 14, 1871.

Rhys, Jean. *After Leaving Mr Mackenzie.* 1931. New York: Random House, 1974.

———. *Good Morning, Midnight.* 1938. New York: W. W. Norton, 2000.

———. *The Left Bank and Other Stories.* 1927. Freeport, NY: Books for Libraries Press, 1970.

———. *The Letters of Jean Rhys*, edited by Francis Wyndham and Diana Melly. New York: Viking, 1984.

———. *Quartet.* 1928. New York: W. W. Norton, 1997.

———. *Smile Please: An Unfinished Autobiography.* New York: Harper and Row, 1979.

———. *Voyage in the Dark.* 1934. London: Penguin, 2000.

Ribeiro, Aileen. *The Art of Dress: Fashion in England and France 1750 to 1820.* New Haven, CT: Yale University Press, 1995.

Rinehart, Nana. "'The Girl of the Period' Controversy." *Victorian Periodicals Review* 13 (1980), 3–9.

Rogers, Henry N, III. "Of Course You Can Trust Me!: Jane Austen's Narrator in *Northanger Abbey*." *Persuasions On-line* 20 (2007), no. 1: 16. http://www.jasna.org/persuasions/on-line/vol20no1/rogers.html. November 19, 2012.

Rooks, Nowlie M. *Ladies' Pages: African American Women's Magazines and the Culture That Made Them.* New Brunswick, NJ: Rutgers University Press, 2004.

Rosenman, Ellen Bayuk. "Fear of Fashion; Or, How the Coquette Got Her Bad Name." *ANQ* 15, no. 3 (Summer 2002): 12–21.

Roses, Lorraine Elena, and Ruth Elizabeth Randolph, eds. *Harlem's Glory: Black Women Writing, 1900–1950.* Cambridge, MA: Harvard University Press, 1996.

Rubens, Paul. "No. 11 Song—Delia and Chorus—A Tiny Touch." In *The Sunshine Girl*, edited by Colin M. Johnson. *Victorian and Edwardian Musical Shows.* http://www.halhkmusic.com. n.p. n.d. October 1, 2011.

Said, Edward. *Culture and Imperialism.* New York: Knopf, 1993.

Santamarina, Xiomara. *Belabored Professions: Narratives of African American Working Womanhood.* Chapel Hill: University of North Carolina Press, 2005.

Schaffer, Talia. *The Forgotten Female Aesthetes: Literary Culture in Late-Victorian England.* Charlottesville, VA: University Press of Virginia, 2000.

Schaffer, Talia, and Kathy Alexis Psomiades. "Introduction." In *Women and British Aestheticism*, edited by Talia Schaffer and Kathy Alexis Psomiades, 1–22. Charlottesville: University Press of Virginia, 1999.

Schultz, Elizabeth, and Haskell Springer, eds. *Melville and Women.* Kent, Ohio: Kent State University Press, 2006.

Scott, Nancy F. *The Grounding of Modern Feminism.* New Haven, CT: Yale University Press, 1989.

Scott, Sir Walter. *Waverley: or 'Tis Sixty Years Since*, edited by Claire Lamont. Oxford World's Classics. Oxford: Oxford University Press, 2009.

Sheehan, Elizabeth M. "The Face of Fashion: Race and Fantasy in James VanDerZee's Photography and Jessie Fauset's Fiction." In *Cultures of Femininity in Modern Fashion*, edited by Ilya Parkins and Elizabeth M. Sheehan, 180–202. Lebanon: University of New Hampshire Press, 2011.

Sheets, Robin Ann. "Art and Artistry in *Vanity Fair*." *ELH* 42, no. 3 (Fall 1975): 420–32.

Sherrard-Johnson, Cherene. *Portraits of the New Negro Woman: Visual and Literary Culture in the Harlem Renaissance*. New Brunswick, NJ: Rutgers University Press, 2007.

Sinfield, Alan. *The Wilde Century: Effeminacy, Oscar Wilde and the Queer Moment*. New York: Columbia University Press, 1994.

Smith, Johanna M. "'Too Beautiful Altogether': Patriarchal Ideology in *Heart of Darkness*." In *A Case Study in Contemporary Criticism*, edited by Ross C. Murfin, 179–95. New York: St. Martin's Press, 1996.

Smith, Shawn Michelle. "Second-Sight: Du Bois and the Black Masculine Gaze." In *Next to the Color Line: Gender, Sexuality, and W. E. B. Du Bois*, edited by Susan Gilman and Alys Eve Weinbaum, 350–77. Minneapolis: University of Minnesota Press, 2007.

Smith-Rosenberg, Carroll. "The New Woman as Adrogyne: Social Disorder and the Gender Crisis, 1870–1936," In *Disorderly Conduct: Visions of Gender in Victorian America*, 245–96. New York: Oxford University Press, 1986.

Solomon-Godeau, Abigail. "The Other Side of Venus: The Visual Economy of Sexual Display." In *The Sex of Things: Gender and Consumption in Historical Perspective*, edited by Victoria de Grazia, 113–50. Berkeley: University of California Press, 1996.

Spanos, William. *Herman Melville and the American Calling: The Fiction after Moby-Dick, 1851–1857*. Albany: State University of New York Press, 2008.

Spenser, Edmund. *Spencer's Faerie Queen*. Oxford: Clarendon Press, 1961.

Spillers, Hortense. J. "Mama's Baby, Papa's Maybe: An American Grammar Book." 1987. In Hortense J. Spillers, *Black, White, and in Color: Essays on American Literature and Culture*, 203–29. Chicago: University of Chicago Press, 2003.

———. "'An Order of Constancy': Notes on Brooks and the Feminine." 1985. In Hortense J. Spillers, *Black, White, and in Color: Essays on American Literature and Culture*, 244–71. Chicago: University of Chicago Press, 2003.

Spivak, Gayatri Chakravorty. "Imperialism and Sexual Difference." In *The Current in Criticism: Essays on the Present and Future of Literary Theory*, edited by Clayton Koelb and Virgil Lokke, 319–38. West Lafayette, IN: Purdue University Press, 1988.

Stark, Bruce R. "Kurtz's Intended: The Heart of *Heart of Darkness*." *Texas Studies in Language and Literature* 16 (1974): 535–55.

Steele, Valerie. *The Corset: A Cultural History*. New Haven, CT: Yale University Press, 2004.

———. *Fashion and Eroticism: Ideals of Feminine Beauty from the Victorian Era to the Jazz Age.* New York: Oxford University Press, 1985.

———. *Paris Fashion: A Cultural History.* New York: Berg, 1998.

Stuart, Jessie. *The American Fashion Industry.* Boston: Simmons College, 1951.

Sturge Moore, T., and D. C. Sturge Moore, eds. *Works and Days: From the Journal of Michael Field.* London: John Murray, 1935.

Summers, Leigh. *Bound to Please: A History of the Victorian Corset.* Oxford: Berg, 2001.

Sylvander, Carolyn. *Jessie Redmon Fauset, Black American Author.* Troy, NY: Whitson, 1981.

Syrett, Netta. *The Sheltering Tree.* London: Geoffrey Bles, 1939.

Taylor, Lou. "The Wardrobe of Mrs. Leonard Messel, 1895–1920." In *The Englishness of English Dress*, edited by Christopher Breward, Becky Conekin, and Caroline Cox, 113–32. Oxford: Berg, 2002.

Taylor, Lou. *Establishing Dress History.* Manchester: Manchester University Press, 2004.

Thackeray, William Makepeace. *Vanity Fair.* 1848. Edited by J. I. M. Stewart. London: Penguin, 1985.

———. *Vanity Fair: A Norton Critical Edition with Illustrations.* 1848. Edited by Peter L. Shillingsburg. New York: W. W. Norton, 1994.

Thaggert, Miriam. *Images of Black Modernism: Verbal and Visual Strategies of the Harlem Renaissance.* Amherst: University of Massachusetts Press, 2010.

Thomas, Julia. *Pictorial Victorians: The Inscription of Value in Word and Image.* Athens: Ohio University Press, 2004.

Thoreau, Henry David. *Walden.* 1842. In *The Portable Thoreau*, edited by Carl Bode. New York: Penguin, 1947.

Thurman, Wallace. "Negro Artists and the Negro." 1927. Reprinted in *The Collected Writings of Wallace Thurman: A Harlem Renaissance Reader*, edited by Amritjit Singh and Daniel M. Scott III, 195–200. New Brunswick, NJ: Rutgers University Press, 2003.

The Times. (London). "The Young Men in Women's Clothes," May 16, 1870; "The Men in Women's Clothes," May 21, 30, 1870; "[For a whole month . . .]," May 31, 1870; "Court of Queen's Bench: The Queen v. Boulton and Others," May 10, 11, 1871.

The Trial of Boulton and Park, with Hurt and Fiske: A Complete and Accurate Report of the Proceedings Extending Over Six Days, from Tuesday, May 9th, to Monday, May 15th, 1871. London: George Vickers, 1871.

Troy, Nancy J. *Couture Culture: A Study in Modern Art and Fashion.* Cambridge, MA: MIT Press, 2003.

Upchurch, Charles. "Forgetting the Unthinkable: Cross-Dressers and British Society in the Case of the Queen vs. Boulton and Others." *Gender & History* 12, no. 1 (2000).

Veblen, Thorstein. *The Theory of the Leisure Class.* 1899. Reprint. New York: Penguin, 1967.

Walker, Caroline. *Metamorphosis and Identity.* New York: Zone Books, 2001.

Wardrop, Daneen. *Emily Dickinson and the Labor of Clothing.* Becoming Modern Series. Durham; Reading Dress Subseries: Hanover: University of New Hampshire Press, 2009.

Ware, James Redding. *Passing English of the Victorian Era: A Heterodox Dictionary of English, Slang, and Phrase.* London: Routledge, 1909.

Watt, Ian. *Conrad in the Nineteenth Century.* Berkeley: University of California Press, 1979.

Waugh, Norah. *The Cut of Men's Clothes: 1600–1900.* London: Faber and Faber, 1964.

Weeks, Jeffrey. "Inverts, Perverts, and Mary-Annes: Male Prostitution and the Regulation of Homosexuality in England in the Nineteenth and Early Twentieth Centuries." *Journal of Homosexuality* 6, nos.1 and 2 (1980–1981), 113–34.

Weinbaum, Alys. "Racial Masquerade: Consumption and Contestation of American Modernity." In *The Modern Girl Around the World: Consumption, Modernity, and Globalization,* edited by Alys Eve Weinbaum, Lynn M. Thomas, Priti Ramamurthy, Uta G. Poiger, Madeleine Yue Dong, and Tani E. Barlow, 120–46. Durham, NC: Duke University Press, 2008. 120–146.

Weinbaum, Alys Eve, Lynn M. Thomas, Priti Ramamurthy, Uta G. Poiger, Madeleine Yue Dong, and Tani E. Barlow, eds. *The Modern Girl Around the World: Consumption, Modernity, and Globalization.* Durham, NC: Duke University Press, 2008.

———. *Wayward Reproductions: Genealogies of Race and Nation in Transatlantic Modern Thought.* Durham, NC: Duke University Press, 2004.

Weyler, Karen. "Melville's 'The Paradise of Bachelors and the Tartarus of Maids': A Dialogue about Experience, Understanding, and Truth." *Studies in Short Fiction* 31 (1994): 461–69.

White King, Red Rubber, Black Death. Documentary. Peter Bate, dir. BBC in association with ZDF et al., 2006.

White, Shane, and Graham White. *Stylin': African American Expressive Culture from Its Beginnings to the Zoot Suit.* Ithaca, NY: Cornell University Press, 1998.

Whitman, Walt. *Leaves of Grass.* 1855/1892. Oxford: Oxford University Press, 1990.

Wilford, "Toward a Morality of Materiality: Adorno and the Primacy of the Object." *Space and Culture* 11, no. 4 (2008): 409–12. *Sage Journals Online.* sac/sagepub.com. September 9, 2011.

Williams, Raymond. *Keywords: A Vocabulary of Culture and Society.* London: Fontana, 1976.

Willis, Deborah. "The Sociologist's Eye: W. E. B. Du Bois and the Paris Exposition." In *A Small Nation of People: W. E. B. Du Bois and African American Portraits of Progress,* 51–78. Library of Congress. New York: HarperCollins, 2002.

Wilson, Elizabeth. *Adorned in Dreams: Fashion and Modernity.* London: Virago Press, 1985

Wineapple, Brenda. *Hawthorne: A Life.* New York: Knopf, 2003.

Winter, Aaron. "Seeds of Discontent: The Expanding Satiric Range of Melville's Transatlantic Diptychs." *Leviathan: A Journal of Melville Studies* 8 (2006): 17–35.

Wolff, Janet. "The Invisible Flâneuse: Women and the Literature of Modernity," *Theory, Culture and Society* 2 (3) (November 1985): 37–46.

Wollen, Peter. "The Concept of Fashion in the Arcades Project." *boundary 2* 30, no. 1 (2003): 131–42. *JSTOR.* www.jstor.org. November 29, 2012.

Wollstonecraft, Mary. *A Vindication of the Rights of Woman.* 1792. Edited by Deidra Shauna Lynch. 3rd Norton Critical Edition. New York: W. W. Norton, 2009.

Woolf, Virginia. *A Room of One's Own.* New York: Mariner Books, 2005.

Wordsworth, William. *The Prelude: 1799, 1805, 1850,* edited by M. H. Abrams, Stephen Gill, and Jonathan Wordsworth. Ithaca, NY: Cornell University Press, 1979.

Wylie, Judith. "'Do You Understand Muslins, Sir?': Fashioning Gender in *Northanger Abbey.*" In *Styling Texts: Dress and Fashion in Literature,* edited by Cynthia Kuhn, Cindy Carlson, and Suzanne Ferriss, 129–48. Amherst, NY: Cambria Press, 2007.

Yafa, Stephen. *Cotton: The Biography of a Revolutionary Fiber.* New York: Viking, 2005.

Yarwood, Doreen. *English Costume: From the Second Century B.C. to 1967.* London: B. T. Batsford, 1967.

Young, Lola. "How Do We Look? Unfixing the Singular Black (Female) Subject." In *Without Guarantees: In Honour of Stuart Hall,* edited by Paul Gilroy, Lawrence Grossberg, and Angela McRobbie, 416–30. London: Verso, 2000.

Yount, Janet Aikins. "Jane Austen Scholarship: The Richness of the Present Age." *Eighteenth-Century Life* 34, no. 1 (2010): 73–113. *Project Muse.* muse.jhu.edu. November 29, 2012.

Zakim, Michael. *Ready-made Democracy: A History of Men's Dress in the American Republic, 1760–1860.* Chicago: University of Chicago Press, 2003.

Žižek, Slavoj. *Tarrying with the Negative: Kant, Hegel, and the Critique of Ideology.* Durham, NC: Duke University Press, 1993.

Zlotnick, Susan. "Domesticating Imperialism: Curry and Cookbooks in Victorian England." *Frontiers* 16, nos. 2–3 (1996): 51–68.

Contributors

BABAK ELAHI is professor of English and associate dean in the College of Liberal Arts at Rochester Institute of Technology. He is the author of *The Fabric of American Literary Realism* (McFarland 2009). His scholarly articles on American literature, the Iranian diaspora, and Iranian literature have appeared in *College Literature*; *Iranian Studies*; *Cultural Studies*; *Comparative Studies of South Asia, Africa and the Middle East*; *Symploke*; *Middle Eastern Literatures*; and *Multi-Ethnic Literatures of the United States*.

LAURA GEORGE is professor of English at Eastern Michigan University. She has published articles on Wordsworth, Byron, Coleridge, and British Dandyism. "Austen's Muslin" is part of a larger project on fashion and figuration.

HOPE HOWELL HODGKINS earned her PhD from the University of Chicago and taught literature at the University of North Carolina at Greensboro for a dozen years. She has published essays on writers ranging from James Joyce to Muriel Spark and on topics including high-modern poetics, religious rhetorics, children's literature, postwar dress, and early-American literacies. She is completing "Style and the Single Girl," a study of modern British women writers' use of dress style.

ABIGAIL JOSEPH recently completed her PhD in English and comparative literature at Columbia University. Her book manuscript project traces the relationships between material culture and male homosexuality in Victorian England. She teaches in the Expository Writing Program at New York University.

KATHERINE JOSLIN is the author of *Edith Wharton and the Making of Fashion* (2009), winner of an American Library Association *Choice* Award as an Outstanding Academic Title. Her other books include *Jane Addams, A Writer's Life* (2004); *Edith Wharton* in the Women Writers Series (1991); and the co-edited *Wretched Exotic: Essays on Edith Wharton in Europe* (1993). She teaches American literature and culture at Western Michigan University, where she is the founding director of the University Center for the Humanities and has received the Distinguished Faculty Scholar Award and the Excellence in Teaching Award.

KIMBERLY LAMM has published essays on a range of topics, from African-American literature and visual culture to contemporary poetry's relationship to feminist theory. Her current book project, "Inadequacies and Interruptions: Language and Feminist Reading Practices in Contemporary Art," explores how contemporary artists incorporate language into their visual productions to create feminist and antiracist readings of spectacle culture. She is assistant professor of Women's Studies at Duke University.

Contributors

Amy L. Montz is an assistant professor of English at the University of Southern Indiana. She teaches courses in eighteenth- through twenty-first-century British literature, young adult literature, feminism, fashion history, and fashion theory. Her current book project, "Dressing for England: Fashion and Nationalism in Victorian Novels," shows how fashion becomes a symbol of national allegiance, power, or resistance.

Pouneh Saeedi teaches cultural studies at the University of Toronto. She has published articles on T. S. Eliot, Hermann Hesse, and Joseph Conrad, as well as Vergil's *Aeneid*. Her forthcoming article, "Women as Epic Sight/Sites and Traces in *Heart of Darkness*" (*Women's Studies*), unravels the gendered dichotomies in Conrad's novella.

Amber Shaw is an assistant professor of nineteenth-century American literature in the Department of English at Coe College. She is interested in the intersections of nineteenth-century transatlanticism, material culture, and gender studies. Her manuscript, "The Fabric of the Nation," considers textiles, nation, and identity in the nineteenth century.

Margaret D. Stetz is the Mae and Robert Carter Professor of Women's Studies and Professor of Humanities at the University of Delaware. She is author of *Facing the Late Victorians* (2007); *Gender and the London Theatre, 1880–1920* (2004); and *British Women's Comic Fiction, 1890–1990* (2001), among other books, and she has been curator or co-curator of ten exhibitions on late-Victorian print culture at venues ranging from Harvard University's Houghton Library to the Henry B. Plant Museum in Tampa, as well as co-editor of the volumes *Michael Field and Their World* (2007) and *Legacies of the Comfort Women of WWII* (2001).

Daneen Wardrop is the author of four books: *Emily Dickinson and the Labor of Clothing* (2009); *The Odds of Being* (2008); *Word, Birth, and Culture* (2002); and *Emily Dickinson's Gothic* (1996). She is the recipient of a National Endowment for the Arts Fellowship in Poetry and the Robert Winner Award from the Poetry Society of America. A professor at Western Michigan University, she teaches American literature and has been named the 2013 Distinguished Faculty Scholar.

Index

Page numbers in *italics* indicate figures.